John Banville and His Precursors

John Banville and His Precursors

Edited by
Pietra Palazzolo, Michael Springer and Stephen Butler

BLOOMSBURY ACADEMIC
LONDON • NEW YORK • OXFORD • NEW DELHI • SYDNEY

BLOOMSBURY ACADEMIC
Bloomsbury Publishing Plc
50 Bedford Square, London, WC1B 3DP, UK
1385 Broadway, New York, NY 10018, USA
29 Earlsfort Terrace, Dublin 2, Ireland

BLOOMSBURY, BLOOMSBURY ACADEMIC and the Diana logo are trademarks
of Bloomsbury Publishing Plc

First published in Great Britain 2019
Paperback edition published 2021

Copyright © Pietra Palazzolo, Michael Springer, and Stephen Butler, 2019

Pietra Palazzolo, Michael Springer, and
Stephen Butler have asserted their right under the Copyright, Designs and Patents Act,
1988, to be identified as Author of this work.

For legal purposes the Acknowledgements on p.xiv constitute
an extension of this copyright page.

Cover design: Eleanor Rose
Cover image © Getty Images

All rights reserved. No part of this publication may be reproduced or transmitted in any
form or by any means, electronic or mechanical, including photocopying, recording, or
any information storage or retrieval system, without prior permission in writing from
the publishers.

Bloomsbury Publishing Plc does not have any control over, or responsibility for, any
third-party websites referred to or in this book. All internet addresses given in this
book were correct at the time of going to press. The author and publisher regret any
inconvenience caused if addresses have changed or sites have ceased to exist, but
can accept no responsibility for any such changes.

A catalogue record for this book is available from the British Library.

Library of Congress Cataloging-in-Publication Data
Names: Palazzolo, Pietra, editor. | Springer, Michael, 1981- editor. |
Butler, Stephen (Stephen Joseph), 1978- editor.
Title: John Banville and his precursors / edited by Pietra Palazzolo,
Michael Springer, and Stephen Butler.
Description: London, UK; New York, NY: Bloomsbury Academic, 2019. | Includes
bibliographical references and index.
Identifiers: LCCN 2018058723 | ISBN 9781350084520 (hb) | ISBN 9781350084537
(ePDF) | ISBN 9781350084544 (epub)
Subjects: LCSH: Banville, John–Criticism and interpretation.
Classification: LCC PR6052.A57 Z725 2019 | DDC 823/.914–dc23
LC record available at https://lccn.loc.gov/2018058723

ISBN: HB: 978-1-3500-8452-0
PB: 978-1-3502-1156-8
ePDF: 978-1-3500-8453-7
eBook: 978-1-3500-8454-4

Typeset by Deanta Global Publishing Services, Chennai, India

To find out more about our authors and books visit www.bloomsbury.com
and sign up for our newsletters.

Contents

Contributors	vii
Foreword	x
Acknowledgements	xiv
Introduction *Michael Springer*	1

Part one National and transnational currents

1	John Banville and the idea of the precursor: Some meditations *Derek Hand*	17
2	Unknown unity: Ireland and Europe in Beckett and Banville *Peter Boxall*	34

Part two Literary engagements

3	'The vain thing menaced by the touch of the real': John Banville as a precursor to Henry James *Darren Borg*	53
4	From Isabel Archer to Mrs Osmond: John Banville reinterprets Henry James *Elke D'hoker*	68
5	Afterlives of a supreme fiction: John Banville's dialogue with Wallace Stevens *Pietra Palazzolo*	87
6	Effacing the subject: Banville, Kleist and a world without people *Rebecca Downes*	110
7	The limits of simile: Rilke, Stevens and Banville's scepticism *Michael Springer*	127
8	John Banville and Hugo von Hofmannsthal: Language, mundane revelation and profane sacrality *Joakim Wrethed*	146

Part three Philosophical, theoretical and artistic forebears

9	A fool's errand: Blanchot, mourning and *The Sea* *Karen McCarthy*	165
10	Reading Banville with Lacan: Hysteric aesthetics in *The Book of Evidence* *Mehdi Ghassemi*	177

11	Existential precursors and contemporaries in Banville's Alex Cleave trilogy *Stephen Butler*	195
12	'An *earthly* glow': Heidegger and the uncanny in *Eclipse* and *The Sea* *Michael Springer*	214
13	John Banville's ekphrastic experiments *Neil Murphy*	234

Index 251

Contributors

Charles I. Armstrong is Professor of English literature at the University of Agder. A Visiting Fellow at Wolfson College, Cambridge, he is currently Vice-president of the International Yeats Society and President of the Nordic Association of English Studies. In addition to co-editing several essay collections, he has published the following monographs: *Romantic Organicism: From Idealist Origins to Ambivalent Afterlives* (2003), *Figures of Memory: Poetry, Space and the Past* (2009) and *Reframing Yeats: Genre, Allusion and History* (2013).

Darren Borg is Professor of English at Los Angeles Pierce College, where he has taught English literature since 2008, and a doctoral candidate in English at Claremont Graduate University. His work explores the connections between subjectivity, ideology and representation, largely in British and American fiction of the nineteenth and twentieth centuries.

Peter Boxall is Professor of English at the University of Sussex. His books include *Don DeLillo: The Possibility of Fiction* (2006), *Since Beckett* (2009), *Twenty-First Century Fiction* (2013) and *The Value of the Novel* (2015). He is co-editor of volume 7 of *The Oxford History of the Novel*, editor of *1001 Books* and editor of *Textual Practice*. He is currently working on a monograph entitled *The Prosthetic Imagination: A History of the Novel as Artificial Life*.

Stephen Butler teaches contemporary British and world fiction at Ulster University, where he is a full-time lecturer in the School of English and History. His PhD studied the use of scientific theories and paradigms in experimental late-twentieth and twenty-first-century fiction. He has published various articles on both John Banville and his crime fiction alter ego Benjamin Black in various international settings, and is currently at work on a monograph on Banville tentatively titled *The Philosopher's Dogsbody – Philosophical Motifs in John Banville's Novels*. He is also the co-editor of *Crime Fiction: A Critical Casebook* (2018).

Elke D'hoker is Senior Lecturer of English literature at the University of Leuven, where she is co-director of the Leuven Centre for Irish Studies and of the modern literature research group, MDRN. She has published widely in modern and contemporary British and Irish fiction, with emphasis on the short story, women's writing and narrative theory. Her monographs include *Irish Women Writers and the Modern Short Story* (2016) and a critical study on John Banville (2004), and she edited and co-edited *Unreliable Narration* (2008), *Irish Women Writers* (2011), *Mary Lavin* (2013) and *The Irish Short Story* (2015).

Rebecca Downes works as an editor and independent scholar. She completed her PhD *Becoming Mortal: A Study of Death in Late Works by John Banville, Philip Roth and J. M. Coetzee* in 2017 at the National University of Ireland, Galway, where she was an Irish Research Council awardee. She has published on death in contemporary fiction and on the works of John Banville and Philip Roth.

Mehdi Ghassemi is Adjunct Lecturer in English at the University of Lille where he previously completed a doctoral thesis on John Banville's fiction. His research explores the intersection between Nietzsche and Lacan's elaborations of subjectivity and style especially in Banville's later novels. His publications include '(Im)possibility of Representation in John Banville's *Shroud*' (2013), 'Authorial and Perceptual Crises in Banville's *Shroud*' (2015) and 'Uncanny Corporeality in John Banville's *Eclipse*' (2016). He has also co-edited *La Représentation du Corps dans La Littérature* (2016). His forthcoming publications examine Gothic tropes and ekphrasis in *Mefisto*, *The Sea* and *Ancient Light*.

Derek Hand is Senior Lecturer and Head of the School of English in Dublin City University. His book *John Banville: Exploring Fictions* was published in 2002. He edited a special edition of the *Irish University Review* on John Banville in 2006. He was awarded an IRCHSS Government of Ireland Research Fellowship for 2008–2009. His *A History of the Irish Novel: 1665 to the Present* was published in 2011 and is now available in paperback.

Karen McCarthy is Lecturer of English literature at the Department of Childhood Education at the University of Johannesburg. Her research interest is in exploring the interaction between ethics and narrative fiction, particularly in representations of friendship and death. More recently, she has also begun to explore representations of children in literature. She has published on the limits of narrative representation, and her most recent publications are 'Untangling Nemesis and Echo from John Banville's Narcissistic *Shroud*' (2017) and 'Secrets and Grace in Sebastian Barry's *The Secret Scripture*' (2018).

Neil Murphy is Professor of English at NTU, Singapore. He is the author of *Irish Fiction and Postmodern Doubt* (2004) and editor of *Aidan Higgins: The Fragility of Form* (2010). He has co-edited (with Keith Hopper) a special Flann O'Brien centenary issue of the *Review of Contemporary Fiction* (2011) and *The Short Fiction of Flann O'Brien* (2013); and a four-book series of and on Dermot Healy's work, including *Fighting with Shadows* (2015), the collected short stories (2015) and plays (2016), and *Writing the Sky: Observations and Essays on Dermot Healy* (2016). His latest monograph is *John Banville* (2018).

Pietra Palazzolo is Associate Lecturer at The Open University and Visiting Fellow at Essex University where she serves on the Executive Committee of the Centre for Myth Studies. She teaches modern and contemporary literature, and critical theory. Her PhD examined John Banville's encounter with the work of Stevens and Beckett. She has co-edited *Translating Myth* (2016) and published a number of book chapters and articles on the fiction of John Banville, Jackie Kay and Caryl Phillips. Her current research is on performativity in contemporary fiction and poetry and on redefinitions of the concept of home and belonging in diasporic writing.

Michael Springer works as a writer and editor, and carries out research in an independent capacity. His PhD, completed at the University of York, considers Beckett's significance for later fiction (Paul Auster, John Banville and J. M. Coetzee). Central to his research interests has always been a focus on literary responses to philosophical challenges, including scepticism, the philosophy of emotions and ethics. He has published on Beckett and philosophy, and literary mediations of ecological responsibilities.

Joakim Wrethed is Senior Lecturer in the English Department at Stockholm University. His background is within continental philosophy, specifically within phenomenology and the philosophy of language. Much of his published work (including his dissertation) focuses on John Banville's prose fiction. He has contributed chapters on Banville to the collections *Recovering Memory: Irish Representations of Past and Present* (2007), *Beyond Ireland: Encounters Across Cultures* (2011) (which he also co-edited) and *The Crossings of Art in Ireland (2014), and in Nordic Irish Studies Journal*. He has also published research on Margaret Atwood, Don DeLillo and Tom McCarthy.

Foreword

What is the source of the singular fascination exerted by John Banville's fiction? From whence does its strange, seductive power stem? One might hazard that it is a matter of style – of an attraction caused by signature-like effects of his language. There is, as most commentators have noted, much to be cherished about Banville's wonderfully accomplished way with words. And yet something more is surely at play. For one thing, a noticeable tendency towards self-consciousness, frequently tipping over into self-irony, tends to be part and parcel of the verbal mastery of his narrators. Figures such as Alexander Cleave, Freddie Montgomery, Max Morden, Oliver Orme and the rest of Banville's motley menagerie are all masters of the well-turned phrase – yet cannot quite refrain from chuckling over their own verbal virtuosity and all the foibles that go with it. There is also a sense of borrowed lustre, with the allusions, nods and winks to other writings often on the verge of getting out of control.

At the end of *The Blue Guitar*, Oliver Orme recounts a childhood memory that would appear to present a redemptive close to a novel which, up to that point, mainly has circled around his failures and inability to commit to love. He recounts being bed-ridden with a fever, and his father's solicitous wiping away of his sweat just before sleep. The ecstatic finale celebrates an utter, solitary freedom unleashed by the father's touch:

> How odd his hand felt, too, not like the hand of anyone known to me, not like a hand at all, in fact, but like something reaching through to me from another world, and my head would seem to weigh nothing – all of me, indeed, would seem to be weightless, and for a moment I would float free, from the bed, from the room, from self itself, and be as a straw, a leaf, a feather, adrift and at peace on the soft, sustaining darkness. (Banville 2015: 250)

It can be hard to identify the ultimate direction of this movement into 'soft, sustaining darkness'. One might see this as a dream of nothingness: an embrace of mutability and ultimate extinction. Yet, at the same time, the reference to 'peace' would seem to suggest that the self here paradoxically and covertly survives its liberation 'from self itself', achieving a kind of illusory indestructability. The speaker's verbal virtuosity would suggest the same, as the narrative voice becomes inflected with a semblance of omnipotence that is not unrelated to the realistic novel's traditional stand-in for god, the omniscient narrator. There is arguably an inherent connection here, as elsewhere in Banville, between fiction and the nocturnal release of the realm of dreams. Yet at the same time the fictional prose is not a pure origin in itself, the words 'a straw, a leaf, a feather' for instance presenting a strong echo of Thomas Wolfe's evocative opening of *Look Homeward Angel*: 'A stone, a leaf, an unfound door; of a stone, a leaf, a door. And of all the forgotten faces. Naked and alone we came into exile' (Wolfe 2006: 3). If Banville reverses Wolfe's descent into finitude, trailing clouds of glory, he nonetheless echoes it, underlining that the world of fiction is itself a form of exile.

With exile comes self-division. Take for instance *Ghosts* – a novel obsessed with revenants and returns – where Freddie describes Felix as having a 'disjointed, improvised air, as if he had been put together in haste from disparate bits and pieces of other people' (Banville 1993: 12). This could with equal validity be said of Freddie himself, who later cites Diderot's *Rameau's Nephew*: 'The philosopher asks: *Can the style of an evil man have any unity?*' (Banville 1993: 54). The selves of Banville's narrators threaten to come unstuck, or to be revealed to be mere marionettes acting out obsessions over which they themselves have only limited control. Moreover, they frequently show evidence of guilt. Thus the entirety of *Ghosts'* precursor text, *The Book of Evidence*, is one long confessional. This comes to a head in another dream replete with implications for Banville's fiction. In an echo of the traumatic nightmares of the First World War soldiers that unleashed Freud's theory of the death drive in *Beyond the Pleasure Principle*, Freddie admits – soon after flagrantly committing the crime that will lead to his imprisonment – to have had a 'recurring dream' all of his adult life, where varying crimes, which he may or may not have committed, unleash an overpowering anxiety based on 'the simple, terrible fact having been found out' (Banville 1989: 123–4). What in Freud is a compulsion to repeat ultimately hinting towards the self-destructive impetus of the death drive is in Banville transformed to an imp of the perverse that propels the speaker to assume an ineluctable sense of guilt. Typically tricksters, con-men and thieves of different kinds and persuasions, Banville's narrators would seem to emblematize in their various ways T. S. Eliot's dictum that '[i]mmature poets imitate, mature poets steal'. Eminently fallible, Banville's narrators never speak directly from the source, as they instead weave and are woven by a web of language whose horizon stretches far out of sight.

The notion of the precursor is the source of a relentless, destabilizing pressure within Banville's texts. In *The Sea*, for instance, Max Morden's desire for a 'moment of earthly expression' whereby he 'shall be, in a word, *said*', remains an unfulfilled one (Banville 2005: 185). Instead of such an epiphany occurring, however, he finds himself cast into temporal relations that go beyond his own ego – forcing him to admit that 'we are defined and have our being through others' (Banville 2005: 217). The pressure of the precursor is hence not only an internal affair, to be analysed in terms of the psychology of his characters, but also comes from without. Just as Banville's characters and narrators are dependent upon others, Banville as an author is no island. This book unfolds in great breadth how Banville's writings respond in sophisticated ways to the imposing examples of important forerunners. Samuel Beckett, Elizabeth Bowen, Hugo von Hofmannsthal, Henry James, James Joyce, Heinrich von Kleist, Rainer Maria Rilke and Wallace Stevens are all demonstrated to be compelling presences in Banville's career, from the beginnings of *Long Lankin* (1970) to the surprising recent instalment of *Mrs Osmond* (2017). Further, dialogues are established with a diverse array of thinkers, including Maurice Blanchot, Sigmund Freud, Martin Heidegger and Jacques Lacan. Banville's persistent investment in the visual arts – which in his novels takes the form of a kind of sustained work of ongoing ekphrasis – is also addressed.

In his introduction, editor Michael Springer brings to the table an ineluctable participant in discussions about literary inheritance, namely Harold Bloom and his theory of the anxiety of influence. Following in the footsteps of feminists, Christopher Ricks's *Allusion to the Poets* and a long line of other scholars, Springer denies the ultimate validity of Bloom's model. Rather than debilitating competition, critics of Bloom claim, we should see literary influence as an enabling and open-ended process. The late-comer does not merely exist in the shadow of the preceding, illustrious greats. Despite his tendency to adopt a narrow, Oedipal conception of the relationship between the writer and his precursor, Bloom's model has however shown a surprising resilience, and ability to bounce back, over the years. Banville himself is a professed admirer of Bloom – 'Bloom is a bloom to be prized and widely propagated,' he enthuses in a book review (Banville 2011) – and there is indeed a characteristically Bloomian combination of overreaching erudition, intransigent bloody-mindedness and self-conscious hyperbole in most of the Irishman's narrators.

Banville is of course very far from being a passive or second-rate epigone to his illustrious forebears. Bloom's term for a process whereby a usurping writer presents himself as a precursor to his own antecedents, making the latter seem his own followers, is *apophrades*, or 'the return of the dead'. But is this a process of presumptuous usurpation or of genuine interaction and exchange? Certainly, the power of Banville's art is such that we revisit Beckett or Stevens or any number of his influences with a new gaze after reading his work. As argued in the chapters in this volume, the process involved also amounts more to a simple two-way traffic between literary creators. A precursor tends to come with accompanying baggage, involving a more encompassing imaginary that goes beyond a mere *agon* or dialogue of artistic personalities. The whole context surrounding the engagement between Banville and his precursors is influenced by the process itself, and is a multifaceted space implicating – as the chapters in this study eminently show – issues such as age, gender, nationality and the relationship between the sacred and the secular. Banville's interactions with those who went before him is a fascinating and complex process, and this book helps us understand and enjoy it more fully.

Charles I. Armstrong

References

Banville, J. (1989), *The Book of Evidence*, London: Minerva.
Banville, J. (1993), *Ghosts*, London: Picador.
Banville, J. (2005), *The Sea*, London: Picador.
Banville, J. (2011), 'John Banville on Harold Bloom', *The Guardian*, 2 December. Available online: https://www.theguardian.com/books/2011/dec/02/aouthor-author-john-banville (accessed 6 October 2018).
Banville, J. (2015), *The Blue Guitar*, London: Penguin.
Wolfe, T. (2006), *Look Homeward Angel*, New York: Scribner.

Acknowledgements

This volume emerged from a conference held at the University of York in November 2014. That event would not have been possible without the assistance of the university's Department of English and Related Literature, and the Humanities Research Centre. From the former, special thanks are due to Cathy Moore and Matt Campbell, for financial, moral and metaphysical support. From the latter, to Jason Edwards for the same. We hope that the ideals of dialogue and collaboration that animated the conference's beginnings are discernible here.

They have certainly been so, in abundance, in the generous contributions of time, effort, resources and good-will on the part of many who have played a role in the creation of this book. We thank Neil Murphy, Hugh Haughton, Lauren Addington, Charles Armstrong, Derek Attridge, Katherine Ebury, Bryan Radley and Declan Kiberd.

The support of the editorial team at Bloomsbury who took on this project has been a source of great encouragement and gratitude. Our thanks to David Avital, Clara Herberg and Lucy Brown for their role in bringing this volume to fruition.

Thanks are due to John Banville for his generosity in granting us permission to quote from his works; and to Bloomsbury for permission to reprint chapter 2 by Peter Boxall, previously published in *Since Beckett* (Continuum, 2009). We acknowledge permission from PanMacmillan to quote from *The Sea*, *Eclipse* and *Shroud*, and from Penguin to quote from *Mrs Osmond*. The third party-copyrighted material displayed in the pages of this book is used on the basis of fair dealing for the purposes of criticism, review and research only in accordance with international copyright laws, and is not intended to infringe upon the ownership rights of the original owners.

Finally, we thank the contributors for their engaging work and for meeting editorial requirements with commitment and light-heartedness.

Introduction

Michael Springer

Who talks through whom?

There is an intrinsic aspect to John Banville's work that makes the rationale for this volume all too clear. He is an author endlessly preoccupied with precursors in a number of fields, exploring their continuing significance and elaborating on their developments. The broken jar, the haunted house, the past that beats inside one 'like a second heart': his fiction is possessed by metaphors for the situation of ventriloquism. And the oeuvre itself instantiates and plays with the idea of the thrown voice in various ways too. There is the alter ego Benjamin Black, the latest in a long line of fictional pseudonyms that pepper Banville's prose; the deeply immersive first-person style characteristic of many of the novels; the theatrical and prose adaptations of Kleist, with the figure of Amphitryon; and, most recently, the extended act of literary ventriloquism that is *Mrs Osmond*. With the last example, it is difficult to conceive of more extreme an instance of a writer's relation to the past as an act of ventriloquism. Theorists and writers have made something like this central to their projects – and indeed existences – before: Keats's negative capability, Bakhtin's dialogism, Barthes's tissue of quotations. (If, of course, one sees the past as speaking through the present: it's possible to see it as the reverse.) Banville is fascinated by the way the voice can take up residence in another, and the effects of this.

    His engagements with precursors of importance to his work are filtered through this concept of the author. Frequently, Banville's discussions of forerunners bespeak an urgency and depth that evidences something much more searching than an 'academic' interest. To read him on Rilke, for example, whom he claims offers a solution to 'why we persist in our humanness', is to witness an attempt to get to the nub of a secret to existence: of a way of living that will prove redemptive, of the key to the ways in which language, used correctly, can save us. A consideration of Banville's engagements with his precursors is therefore often a means of exploring the processes of his own self-formation – ethically, aesthetically, philosophically – as well as the product of this process. He takes on various masks and roles, in true Yeatsian fashion, to illuminate the figure who lurks beneath the *façade*.

Just as a long succession of Banville's novels explore their characters' relationships to the past – or failure to achieve one – the author himself consistently returns to exemplary forebears, literary, philosophical and cultural. These autodidactic engagements with figures from the various traditions take many forms. There is a pantheon of modernists he returns to with great regularity, in both fictional and non-fictional contexts, often as a means of clarifying his own aims and hopes, his conceptions of his own art: Wallace Stevens, Beckett and Henry James in literature; Nietzsche and Heidegger in philosophy. Here the forebear is often the marker of the path taken, the route forged ahead along. There are theoretical precursors, who have laid down the foundations upon which his own explorations of self, memory and the whole mystifying business of being human proceed, or sometimes excavate. Freud numbers among these, as perhaps surprisingly do Copernicus and Kepler. Then there are cautionary tales, such as Heidegger (the man rather than the thinker – and the uncomfortable overlaps between the two) and de Man: Banville's apparent, and very Irish, fascination with con-men and charlatans feeds into his interest in peoples' capacity for blindness and self-deception even, or especially, in agents as committed to clear sight and understanding as these. And there is his exploration of his place in his nation and his world through his engagement with the Irish forebears he responds to and grapples with. The history of the pictorial tradition, and notable figures in it, also appear with great regularity in his writing, as do those from the theatre.

A recurrent characteristic of Banville's work is the delineation of connections between preceding intellectual and artistic models and contemporary cultural forms and norms, well evidenced by the thematic prominence of epistemological and ethical concerns and the relation of these to the fields of the aesthetic and the literary. The fact that this engagement is consistently foregrounded in his work, and frequently plays a primary focalizing role, means that a consideration of the author's relationship to such exemplary precursors is a particularly useful way of elucidating his project. Such instances also serve as indicators of how these intellectual legacies (e.g. modernist and existentialist) continue to inform various contemporary trends, and how such reception recasts or modifies prior understandings of the significance of these. In this sense, as Borges noted, Banville creates his own precursors – the present speaks through the past. His Heidegger is very much *his* Heidegger, for example, and Henry James's style will now frequently be seen through the prism of Banville's developments and adaptations of it. This is among the highest compliments that can be paid to an artist: that his work transforms how we see, what we can see. Borges intended this of Kafka when he observed how he created his own precursors, and the chapters in this volume establish something similar for Banville's writing.

'The ecstasy of influence'

But there are also developments extrinsic to the work that militate for a volume such as this. Notably, a number of contemporary writers foreground intertextuality and influence in their work in ways deeply resonant with Banville's own. The number of novels explicitly engaging with precursors seems an indication of this trend. Along with Banville's, there are Colm Toibin's and David Lodge's responses to and engagements with Henry James. Other prominent works that have adopted analogous strategies include Maya Lang's *The Sixteenth of June* (Joyce's *Ulysses*), Eimear McBride's *A Girl Is a Half-Formed Thing* (Joyce's *A Portrait of the Artist as a Young Man*), Tiphanie Yanique's *Land of Love and Drowning* (Marquez's *One Hundred Years of Solitude*), Joseph O'Neill's *The Dog* (Kafka's *The Trial*) and Galassi's *Muse* (Roth's *Ghost Writer*). J. M. Coetzee's fictional surrogate of the writer, the oracular Elizabeth Costello, claims,

> There are no bounds to the sympathetic imagination. If you want proof, consider the following. Some years ago I wrote a book called *The House on Eccles Street*. To write that book I had to think my way into the existence of Marion Bloom. … Marion Bloom never existed. Marion Bloom was a figment of James Joyce's imagination. If I can think my way into the existence of a being who has never existed, then I can think my way into the existence of a bat or a chimpanzee or an oyster, any being with whom I share the substrate of life. (Coetzee 2003: 112)

And from this view of the role of the sympathetic imagination, Costello develops a theory of ethical engagement with and responsibility for the other. Notwithstanding the eccentricities of Costello's views, the point gestures towards something central to these works. Out of the postmodern impasse where everything is pastiche, and nothing can be novel, they find a way to save imagination. And by parsing the imagination from pristine originality and allowing it to animate the past as well as the present, they similarly indicate a way beyond the ethical impasses entangled in the same construct. Instead of taking us further, the imagination takes us deeper. Instead of inventing the new, imagination reinvests the old with renewed significance. As a number of chapters in this volume argue, this is a central and striking aspect of Banville's writing, and one very close to the core of his understanding of the purpose and value of art.

This marks a vision of the question of inheritance significantly different to that of Harold Bloom's, which remains influential.[1] Bloom views the writer as a version of Alexander the Great, fretting that his predecessor's conquests will leave him no room for his own. In contrast, works of the kind mentioned above see infinity in a grain of sand, and the infinite recursions of postmodernism are embraced. Given that the very idea of the author is in large part a product of the printing press, it's hardly surprising that the advent of new information technologies should see important changes in this regard. Accordingly (or at least correspondingly), there is a greater willingness to adopt approaches to the question of literary inheritance other than the oedipal one.[2] Garber (2016) remarks this de-emphasizing of the Bloomian model; Bernard (2017) proposes the notion of 'confluences' as an alternative to it; and Ailwood and Harvey (2016) consider 'ecologies' of creativity and inspiration. This is of course not to deny the value of Freudian constructions of the matter. In Banville's case, there is the self-proclaimed oedipal relation with Joyce. It is simply not to preclude any other relation because of that. Allowing the discussion of progenitors and inheritors not to collapse into an exclusively oedipal frame makes possible an appreciation of continuities of the past in the present. It has also been instrumental in the overcoming of the generic elitism that has so frequently characterized literary studies. Demonstrations of the significance of science fiction, noir or other generic forms for 'literary' heavyweights such as Borges, Kafka or Beckett have enriched our appreciation of the phenomenon of literature as a whole – a trend Banville tips his hat to via his alter ego Benjamin Black.

An analogous shift is discernible in contemporary literary politics. Jonathan Lethem argues, in 'The Ecstasy of Influence' (2007), for an attitude to the work of art and the imagination that departs from that which sees it as a 'Napoleonic imposition of one's uniqueness upon the universe'. Instead of 'the violence and exasperation of another avant-garde, with its wearisome killing-the-father imperatives … might we be better off ratifying the ecstasy of influence – and deepening our willingness to understand the commonality and timelessness of the methods and motifs available to artists?' Lethem's point about avant-gardes is apposite. The relation of self-consciously autonomous art and literature to the political is a murkier one now than that the modernist model rejoiced in – or at least certain instances of the modernist model (surrealism and Breton, situationism). With Banville, this is certainly the case, for good or ill. The chapters in this volume do not take on this question foursquare, but they lay the groundwork for such a consideration. Lethem's idea of the role of the commons in the creation of the work of art, and vice versa, points to a way in which this might be clarified, and lent respectability. Certainly, the modernists Banville canonizes are those whose aesthetics relate obliquely to the political – and much the same could be said about the scientists, artists, philosophers and others his work engages with. But Lethem's ideas about the cultural and political valences of literature, and the ways these tie in to considerations of 'filiations, communities, and discourses', present significant similarities to Banville's own.

This shift is also exemplified in recent criticism and scholarship. The emergence of the field of Comparative Literature as an institutionalized field of study and teaching has played a significant role in this – itself helped by a shift from 'influence' to 'intertextuality', and from a concern with linear transmission to more ramified ecologies of persistence and reception. Some of this work to some extent bears out Borges's claim that 'every writer creates his own precursors': the critical canonization of Edgar Allen Poe, for notable example, is a function of the appraisal of the significance of his work for later writers such as Baudelaire and Borges himself. A wide range of influential studies take up the appraisal of reception and influence as their primary focus, from every time and place. Notable recent instances focusing on modern and contemporary figures include Boxall (2009), Hayes (2010), Monteiro (2015), Esplin (2016), Worthington (2011), Lernout and Van Mierlo (2004) and Cantalupo (2012).

This is of relevance for a writer as apparently, and often self-avowedly, apolitical as Banville. At a time when much of politics appears to be occurring upstream of politics proper, such examinations of the persistence and re-imagining of formal and aesthetic traditions allows for an exploration of things that shape culture. An explicit engagement with the history of cultural forms thus comes to appear itself a political act. One implication of this view is that the aesthetic object is necessarily performative. As the essays in this collection show, his persistent and searching interrogation of a range of literary, philosophical, and artistic forebears is a way of understanding the place of the work of literature in European culture and thought. The geographical qualifier is necessary: this is a Eurocentric tradition, and its exemplars European, and mostly male. The present volume's focus therefore, somewhat inescapably, reflects Banville's own.

Overview of chapters

The chapters in this volume bring the scholarship on Banville up to date with the most recent of his writing. Assembling an international concert of scholars, both established and emerging, they represent a cross-section of the foremost research being carried out on the author's work at present.

The book is arranged in three parts. In Part one, 'National and transnational currents', we return to a topic that animated much of the original reception of the fiction, in order to move it on: Banville's relation to Irish and European traditions. In the first chapter, 'John Banville and the idea of the precursor: Some meditations', Derek Hand considers the figure of the forebear in a range of Irish literary incarnations and Banville's own instantiation of this unique manifestation. Banville's texts' concern with the anxiety of inheritance and influence allow for a positioning and appreciation of how his work might be best understood within the Irish modernist and postcolonial dilemma about 'precursors' – that is, not only the need for them but also the need to break away from them and certainly to deny them authority and power. Hand explores this through the idea of self-invention and its centrality in modern Irish writing. Many Irish writers, like Banville, have proclaimed their uniqueness and originality, from Maria Edgeworth onward: the prevailing tone is one of pioneership, taking the Irish novel and Irish writing to places it has never been before. And concomitantly, of course, suggesting that there was nothing before them, no writer, no tradition, nothing before they began to write. The move is therefore towards an idea of making it new and making it up, of forging the uncreated conscience, rather than furthering what has already been achieved. Hand considers how these aspects of Irish literary modernism bear on the role of the past and tradition in Banville's writing.

In his chapter 'Unknown unity: Ireland and Europe in Beckett and Banville', Peter Boxall argues that, through its engaging with Beckett's work, and specifically Beckett's use of certain European literary traditions, Banville's fiction explores Ireland's current relation to Europe in conditions of increasing globalization. Boxall explores a relation of precursorship to the second degree: Banville's inheriting of Beckett's inheritance of Kleist. Where Beckett, in works such as *Ghost Trio* and *Nacht und Träume*, seeks to situate his work in the zone of indeterminacy Kleist identifies and explores (between, primarily, animate and inanimate, but extrapolated by Beckett into further dichotomies), Banville seeks to inhabit such an inhabiting of the interstitial. Boxall shows how *Eclipse* and *Shroud* mirror one another in this way, in certain respects remaining atomic, disconnected parts of a single drama, but in others hinting at how such relations give rise to moments of potential connection. Banville sees in Beckett's use of Kleist, Boxall argues, an exploration of Ireland's complicated relationship with Europe, and uses this Beckett–Kleist axis to stage aspects of this current instance of this relationship. Beckett's poetics of failure may be read as a utopian shading, by negation, of some possible post-national future, he argues; Banville's delineation of national connections under current federalist European arrangements emphasizes the continuing complexity of this question, against the grain of an optimistic globalization.[3] In light of this, Banville's 'manufactured tradition', as he describes it, comes to be seen as a strategic response to such factors.

Part two of the book, 'Literary engagements', focuses on Banville's encounters with specific literary precursors, the first two chapters both considering Henry James. In Chapter 3, 'The vain thing menaced by the touch of the real', Darren Borg reads 'John Banville as a precursor to Henry James', drawing on Borges's sense of 'every writer creat[ing] his own precursors'. The point of departure for Borg's analysis is Banville's observations regarding James's place in modernism, representing a thread distinct from the experimentalism of Joyce and Beckett, for example. This 'impressionistic' tradition initiated by James is characterized by an emphasis of the inaccessibility of the *Ding an Sich*, and, following from this, a preoccupation with the limits of the human imagination, and the implications of these limitations for our understanding of ourselves and others. Impressionistic modernism insists on the impossibility of clarity and certainty, and accordingly favours styles, techniques and perspectives that reflect this. In this chapter Borg details how Henry James and John Banville respectively demonstrate such choices, and how they differ, and how they coincide in such a project. Through his uncanny doubling of James, Borg argues, Banville achieves precisely the subjective alienation and self-splitting that the impressionist tradition centres so forcefully. In so doing, he brings this doubling in James to a greater prominence, thus making James the precursor he proves himself to be.

Elke D'hoker's chapter, 'From Isabel Archer to Mrs Osmond: John Banville reinterprets Henry James', considers Banville's engagement with Henry James primarily through *Mrs Osmond*. Her focus is on the ethical valences of James's work, and the way *Mrs Osmond* demonstrates Banville to be moving closer to a Jamesian view of ethics and the good life. Banville's earlier work evinces a deeply Nietzschean vision of human life and being, D'hoker argues: narcissism is more or less constitutive, relationships simply a function of this, and the scope for genuine ethical being strictly circumscribed. In *Mrs Osmond*, in contrast, he depicts a character capable of acting on the basis of deep consideration of the nature and force of intersubjective obligations, and demonstrating an ethical self-awareness and agency far exceeding that of any of his prior characters. D'hoker takes this to represent a novel development in the evolution of the writer's ethical sensibility – not least because it is the first of his novels with a female protagonist.

Pietra Palazzolo's chapter, 'Afterlives of a supreme fiction: John Banville's dialogue with Wallace Stevens', examines key Stevensian concepts in the fiction (imagination, supreme fiction, abstraction and transcendence). Banville's appreciation of Stevens's work is best reflected in his use of the imagination as inextricably intertwined with one's perceptions of things and the world's alterity, which also calls for a need to acknowledge the supreme fiction as a necessary imaginative act that constantly re-elaborates itself. Palazzolo's discussion shows how Banville's engagement with the concept of otherness is both thematic and structural, as explored in the Art trilogy – as well as in later works – with its focus on the ethical nature of one's relation with the world, but also in the 'radical openness' of his interlocking works (within and outside of the series). Palazzolo's study of the legacy of Stevens's concept of the supreme fiction reveals a unique dialogue between Banville's work and Stevens's idea of a poetry that is 'the poetry of life'. In focusing on an area that has received little attention, the chapter teases out a subtle understanding of 'inter-authorial' links, as well as the idea of precursorship that is central to the volume.

In her chapter 'Effacing the subject: Banville, Kleist and a world without people', Rebecca Downes examines the role that the mainly theatrical writer and important precursor Heinrich von Kleist plays in Banville's work – both prose and drama, with the focus on the former. She argues that, as was the case with Yeats, Banville's work follows the principle of *Maskenfreiheit* – examining the depths of the self through the medium of a mask. The mask considered here is Kleistian theatre and its utilizing of his theoretical conceit of the 'marionette theatre' that is such a focal point of the trilogy of novels *Eclipse*, *Shroud* and *Ancient Light* and how they all relate this concept to the character of Amphitryon. Amphitryon is a character who suffers from the same existential drama of personhood that afflicts the characters in the trilogy, be it Alex Cleave or his fictional mirror double, Axel Vander. The stylized nature of drama and the acting profession fits well with the various simulacra, repetitious tropes and doubles that populate Banville's work. The difference as discerned by Downes in these novels is that the thematic focus has shifted to two related areas. First, to time and death, an Orphic musing, with the aging narrators musing on their own mortality as well as others'. And second, the way the mortality of others begins to assume importance in how these characters interact with others in their lives morally and ethically. Life in all its messiness intrudes more into Banville's work after the new millennium as the stillness of both visual art and theatre is shown to be an inadequate response to the mysteries of life and death – both mysteries reflected in the other dimension that assumes significance in Banville's later work, the erotic.

Michael Springer traces Banville's engagement with the work of Rainer Maria Rilke in 'The limits of simile: Rilke, Stevens and Banville's scepticism'. He argues that this engagement wanes, from deep sympathy with the poet's stance to one much more dubious of it. Earlier in his career, Banville adopts a markedly Rilkean position. Reading *Doctor Copernicus* as a meditation on scepticism and possible responses to it, the novel is shown to adopt a position that parallels Rilke's very closely. Later fiction, however, demonstrates that the Rilkean response that is at this early stage advanced as an answer comes itself to seem a begging of the question, which leads to a perspective closer to that of Wallace Stevens. The chapter thus argues that, while Rilke's work remains of crucial importance to Banville throughout his career, Banville himself moves beyond it.

In his chapter on 'language, mundane revelation and profane sacrality', Joakim Wrethed traces the influence of Austrian *fin de siècle* author Hugo von Hofmannsthal on the fiction of John Banville. He mainly focuses on the authors' shared fictional contemplations of the gap between world and language (and other sign-systems). The common denominator between the two authors is the phenomenon of mundane revelation, which functions as an indicator of the desire to bypass the contaminating mediation of language. However, by means of a theory of language derived from generative anthropology, the investigation reveals the futility of such attempts, and shows that both Hofmannsthal and Banville utilize this paradox as a source of creative energy. Mundane revelation stages an imagined move back from a declarative language mode to a more primordial ostensive. But since that would eventually lead to the cancellation of signification altogether (art, imagination and the sacred) it constitutes a central paradox that instead reinforces the power of language and faith in the designatum. The relentless return to quotidian revelatory moments in Banville's fictional cognition accentuates its importance, and these instances may be seen as aesthetic breathing spaces that in turn constitute micro-constituents of a form of profane sacrality.

Part three of the volume turns to 'Philosophical, theoretical and artistic forebears'. In the first chapter, 'A fool's errand: Blanchot, mourning and *The Sea*',

Karen McCarthy explores the parallels between *The Sea* and Maurice Blanchot's use of the myth of Orpheus in the underworld as an allegory for the work of literature. In the essay 'The Gaze Orpheus', Blanchot argues that the, necessarily impossible, task of literature is to render in discursive expression that which exceeds discursive expression – to make darkness itself visible. Eurydice in Hades comes to stand for this darkness needing to be brought into the light, while remaining essentially itself; Orpheus's failure is the only possible outcome of the impossible endeavour. McCarthy demonstrates how, in *The Sea*, Banville figures a 'lyreless Orpheus' attempting to make an equivalent transfiguring journey. From this she elaborates the parallels between Blanchot's and Banville's ideas about the work of literature.

Mehdi Ghassemi's chapter, 'Reading Banville with Lacan: Hysteric aesthetics in *The Book of Evidence*', explores a common trope in Banville's work – mental illness. In the following chapter by Stephen Butler this is also examined when discussing the importance of Freud as a forebear, but in Ghassemi's chapter the theoretical precursor is argued to be Lacan rather than the Austrian. The chapter argues that Banville's characters are often related through a 'hysterical constellation of subjectivity'. The reason for the choice of Lacan over Freud in this discussion is that Ghassemi argues that in Banville's work, mental configurations such as hysteria and neurosis are exactly that, a psychic configuration rather than an illness or pathology. This psychic structure is the root cause for the various similarities between Banville's characters and their recurring search for authenticity, both of themselves and their endeavours. The chapter also argues that a Lacanian reading helps illuminate a feature of Banville's work that went relatively unnoticed until he started writing under the Benjamin Black pseudonym – his interest in criminals, spies and others with a problematic relationship with law and authority. For Ghassemi this can be explained by seeing Banville's work as engaging with the Law, understood in Lacanian terms, as expressive of the oppression of the Symbolic Order in people's everyday lives. For hysterics, reality is simply a man-made game with rules that they choose to flaunt, and Ghassemi convincingly shows that this is a perfect description of the majority of Banville's character/narrators.

As mentioned, in 'Existential precursors and contemporaries in Banville's Alex Cleave trilogy', Stephen Butler examines the influence of Freud in Banville's oeuvre, but as the title suggests it is more Freud the philosopher than the psychologist that is discussed. Freud's ideas are shown to have many parallels with fellow philosopher-psychologists; namely Kierkegaard, Heidegger and most importantly Nietzsche. The existential motifs common to these thinkers are explored – the questioning of rationality as a determinant for people's behaviours with the novel notion of the unconscious, the personal as well as the moral desire to interact with other people and how this is often reduced or debased to egotistic pleasures, the role of bad faith and inauthenticity as a fact of human personality. The chapter goes on to argue that Banville's engagement with contemporary moral philosophers such as Midgley, Gaita and John Gray emphasizes the ethical turn in Banville's postmillennial work that holds existential philosophy itself at fault for questionable behaviour in relation to sex and power. Many of Banville's male characters are erudite figures able to quote the names discussed in the chapter and yet have little to no moral compass. The philosophical precursors that both Banville and his narrators are fond of are shown to be culpable, if only through the implications of their ideas, in the morally dubious actions of Banville's characters.

In '"An *earthly* glow": Heidegger and the uncanny in *Eclipse* and *The Sea*', Michael Springer looks at the significance of the work of Martin Heidegger for Banville's writing. He locates this centrally in the idea of the uncanny. Banville refers to the idea of the uncanny frequently, in both fiction and non-fiction, and it is clear he considers it an important one for his art. Springer argues that the connections between Heidegger's and Banville's ideas of the uncanny illuminate the latter's fiction in two ways. First, they clarify what the instances of the uncanny in the novels mean, and thereby enhance understanding of the novels themselves. Second, given Banville's claims to the effect that the aim of art itself is the evocation of the uncanny, they allow for a deeper appreciation of what he conceives his art to be, and to be doing.

Neil Murphy's chapter 'John Banville's ekphrastic experiments' deals with the importance that the literary strategy of ekphrasis plays in Banville's novels. He argues that the novelist's work goes beyond the simple definition of being prose that discusses paintings – rather, the Irish author uses paintings in his novels to explore the very fact of representation itself. It is a strategy that itself is both creative and critical, according to Murphy, in that it is creative art that also examines its own principles and assumptions. Banville does this by pushing his prose novels as close to the aesthetic, formal and structural principles of the visual arts as he can – a strategy he has adopted with rigour and vigour from the Art trilogy of novels onward. In both *The Book of Evidence* and *Ghosts* the narrative is determined by amalgamating various paintings into an arguably coherent whole – a strategy that has also been adopted with less success in both *Athena* and the later *The Blue Guitar*. Murphy argues that Banville adopts this strategy as a means of embracing a key element of metafictional and postmodern prose narratives – the merging of the ontological levels of author, character and reader, not to mention precursors into a unified field theory that any of Banville's scientific characters would be envious of. The ekphrastic techniques adopted enable Banville to do away with the problems of sequentiality that plague prose fiction and get in the way of his being able to engage with Being in the manner discussed in the various other chapters in the volume.

Notes

1 The extent to which this reflects, and is embedded in, a wider shift is a fascinating question. Verhaege (2015) for example, touches on the ways in which psychoanalytic categories and constructs may need to be historicized.
2 This is not to claim that these are the first such to do so. As Charles Armstrong notes in the Foreword, alternative constructions have long been proposed. It is, however, to indicate the apparently continuing need to qualify the strictly oedipal take, given its continuing influence (as similarly noted by Armstrong).
3 Or as optimistic as this was in 2009, when the chapter was first published.

References

Ailwood, S. and Harvey, M. (2016), *Katherine Mansfield and Literary Influence*, Edinburgh: Edinburgh University Press.

Bernard, C. (2017), 'Introduction: Trying to Define Literature's Confluences', *Études britanniques contemporaines* 52. Available online: http://journals.openedition.org/ebc/3511 (25 January 2019).

Boxall, P. (2009), *Since Beckett: Contemporary Writing in the Wake of Modernism*, London: Continuum.

Cantalupo, B. (ed.) (2012), *Poe's Pervasive Influence*, Bethlehem, PA: Lehigh University Press.

Coetzee, J. M. (2003), *Elizabeth Costello: Fiction*, New York: Penguin Books.

Esplin, E. (2016), *Borges's Poe: The Influence and Reinvention of Edgar Allan Poe in Spanish America*, Athens, GA: University of Georgia Press.

Garber, M. (2016), 'Over the Influence', *Critical Inquiry* 42(4): 731–59.

Hayes, P. (2010), *J. M. Coetzee and the Novel: Writing and Politics after Beckett*, Oxford: Oxford University Press.

Lernout, G. and Van Mierlo, W. (eds) (2004), *The Reception of James Joyce in Europe*, London: Continuum.

Lethem, J. (2007), 'The Ecstasy of Influence: A Plagiarism', *Harpers*, February.

Monteiro, G. (2015), *The Presence of Pessoa: English, American, and Southern African Literary Responses*, Kentucky, VA: University Press of Kentucky.

Verhaege, P. (2015), 'Today's Madness Does Not Make Sense', in Gherovici, P. and Steinkoler, M. (eds), *Lacan on Madness: Madness, Yes You Can't*, 68–80. New York: Routledge.

Worthington, L. H. (2011), *Cormac McCarthy and the Ghost of Huck Finn*, Jefferson, NC: McFarland.

Part one

National and transnational currents

1

John Banville and the idea of the precursor: Some meditations

Derek Hand

We carry the dead with us only until we die too, and then it is we who are borne along for a little while, and then our bearers in their turn drop, and so on into the unimaginable generations.

(Banville 2005: 119)

John Banville's *The Sea* comes to an end with this observation from the narrator:

> The sky was hazed over and not a breeze stirred the surface of the sea, at the margin of which the small waves were breaking in a listless line, over and over, like a hem being turned endlessly by a sleepy seamstress. There were few people on the beach, and those few were at a distance from me, and something in the dense, unmoving air made the sound of their voices seem to come from a greater distance still. I was standing up to my waist in water that was perfectly transparent, so that I could plainly see below me the ribbed sand of the seabed, and the tiny shells and bits of crab's broken claw, and my own feet, pallid and alien, like specimens displayed under glass. As I stood there, suddenly, no, not suddenly, but in a sort of driving heave, the whole sea surged, it was not a wave, but a smooth rolling swell that seemed to come up from the deeps, as if something vast down there had stirred itself, and I was lifted briefly and carried a little way toward the shore and then was set down on my feet as before, as if nothing had happened. And indeed nothing had happened, a momentous nothing, just another of the great world's shrugs of indifference. (Banville 2005: 263–4)

It is an image, it might be suggested, that is repeated again and again, with variation, throughout Banville's long writing career. The reader is offered in these moments an image of a character at once alone and isolated in the midst of throbbing life and nature. His high cold heroes, Copernicus and Kepler, so caught up in their mathematical and astronomical pursuits seem destined to move towards such intense reflective moments:

> What had possessed it to climb so high, what impossible blue vision of flight reflected in the glass? ... Pressed in a lavish embrace upon the pane, the creature gave up its frilled grey-green underparts to this gaze, while the head strained away from the glass, moving blindly from side to side, the horns weaving as if feeling out enormous forms of air. But what had held Johannes was its method of crawling. He would have expected some sort of awful convulsions, but instead there was a series of uniform smooth waves flowing endlessly upward along its length, like a visible heartbeat. The economy, the heedless beauty of it, baffled him. (Banville 1990: 99)

Then there is Gabriel Godkin in *Birchwood*, one of Banville's earliest renditions of the self-conscious narrator who creates his world and himself, not through scientific formulae, but through an act of writing:

> Such scenes as this I see, or imagine I see, no difference, through a glass sharply. The light is lucid, steady, and does not glance in spikes or starts from bright things, but shines in cool cubes, planes and violet lines and lines within planes, as light trapped in polished crystal will shine. Indeed, now that I think of it, I feel it is not a glass through which I see, but rather a gathering of perfect prisms. ... Outside my memories, this silence and harmony, this brilliance I find again in that second silent world which exists, independent, ordered by unknown laws, in the depths of mirrors. This is how I remember such scenes. If I provide something otherwise, be assured I am inventing. (Banville 1984: 21)

The unnamed historian in *The Newton Letter*, Alexander Cleave the actor and Freddie Montgomery the murderer are all presented to us with these privileged epiphanic moments of revelation. Coupled with this encapsulating image of simultaneous isolation and enclosure, being both a part of and apart from, is the attendant and consequent exposé: a recognition of something essential about the individual life being lived and life generally, at once simple, straightforward, communicable and yet strange, on the verge of comprehension and language, vaguely profound but deeply and immeasurably weighty. That fluctuation between poles, between extremes, between definites, is *the* feature of Banville's writing.

They are also disruptive moments when thought of, not in and of themselves in terms of character and plot within the boundaries of the novel itself but in terms of the narrative flow of the novel generally. In other words, moments such as these – littered as they are throughout Banville's fiction – stop and halt the flow of narrative, arrest and seize the reader's attention, as they do to the perceiving character, that might want to gallop ahead and find out what happens next. They slow the world and the reader's attention down, funnelling our perspective towards a single spot of time. Increasingly in his fiction a central part of the dilemma for his narrators is to try and link these moments of luminous significance into something like a coherent narrative, something that might read like a complete life story.

As Freddie Montgomery declares in *Athena*: 'Ah, this plethora of metaphors! I am like everything except myself' (Banville 1995: 90). There is a need, therefore, to attend closely to the images Banville employs and how he employs them. In relation to the notion of 'precursors', and particularly literary precursors, scenes such as these – which emphasize both isolation and a yearning for connection – can become a way into beginning to think about and articulate Banville's relationship, if any, to his literary forebears. These moments accentuate, as has been suggested, being both a part of and being apart from. In other words, for Banville perhaps it might be argued that this notion also underpins his relationship and attitude to a literary tradition: his novels are both a part of tradition and apart from it. This certainly can be said in relation to an Irish literary tradition. These scenes are also illuminating on a micro level when we consider the type of characters being afforded these revelations. No matter what the context has been – from medieval Europe on the cusp of modernity, to the rarefied air of espionage in mid-twentieth-century Britain or the Anglo-Irish Big House – all of Banville's protagonists endure the dilemma of existing too much in the mind: their lives are spent in opposition to the world outside their imagination. Science and pictorial art and the craft of acting and spying, like acts of writing, have been used as a means of making this struggle – for it is a struggle – manifest in the novels. All of his characters discover that the truths they hoped to attain, the order they hoped to impose upon the world, was always just beyond them, maddeningly outside their grasp. The divergence between the perfection of the life or of the work is like a yawning wound: a wound that none of Banville's characters have been able to finally heal, and yet the desire to bridge that gap is what energizes each of Banville's characters and each of his novels.

The approach I want to take, then, with these images of rupture and concurrent ache for wholeness as an overarching guide, is consider the idea of the 'precursor' in Banville's writing at the macro and micro levels, both within the novels and outside the novels. In doing so it will be possible to engage with the numerous writers that are 'precursors' to Banville's work, those writers who have influenced him in terms of style and theme and literary fixation. The issue of the nature of Irish writing's uneasy relationship to literary traditions can also be considered and how this relates to Banville's work. This contextual discussion will inform the subsequent textual analysis focusing on Banville's stories which are all about the anxiety of inheritance and influence at some basic level and how his work might be best understood within the Irish modernist configuration that critiques the very notion of 'precursors', the need for them at all and the need to break away from them and certainly deny them.

John Banville himself looks to many precursors for the solace and comfort that a literary tradition can provide. Any such list of names would include James Joyce, Samuel Beckett, Henry James, Heinrich von Kleist, Vladimir Nabokov, Rainer Maria Rilke and Franz Kafka. A cursory trawl through the ever-growing critical scholarship surrounding Banville demonstrates not just literary forebears but philosophical and psychological influences too: such as Sigmund Freud, Jacques Lacan, Jacques Derrida and Jean Baudrillard. It is not just the 'plethora of metaphors' (Banville 1995: 90) consequently which haunt his writing, but it is these philosophers and their ideas as well as literary, theoretical and cultural movements which appear to get in the way of characters' self-realization. The constant employment of intertextuality throughout the oeuvre is one obvious manifestation of this. John Banville, not unlike his literary creations can echo everything and everyone rather than express himself as himself.

From an Irish perspective two of the more prominent names to conjure with are James Joyce and Samuel Beckett, and Banville himself has said that he chooses Beckett as a literary antecedent (Schwall 1997: 17). And one can obviously see why. Beckett's withdrawal or retreat from the magnificent bric-a-brac world of Joyce's *Ulysses* into the singular consciousness perceiving the world would seem to chime with Banville's own concern with mapping that postmodern interiority. In other words, if Joyce can be thought of, as I would argue, as struggling towards interiority in his writing, a thing that had not been done overly successfully in the Irish novel to that point, then Banville shares with Beckett in having that interiority as the starting point of their fictional universe. They inhabit the fictional world hollowed out by Joyce and therefore the dilemmas faced by both writers and their characters are markedly different. Their world is a fallen one in which there is nothing left to do other than endlessly tell one's own story again and again and again. The reorientation is towards a single voice talking and telling. The consequences of this are, in their own peculiar way, nightmarish. Think of the historian in *The Newton Letter*. All his exertions, in both the literary and the historical spheres, come to nought: he is, finally, a nobody, denied a name because he has found no place in the world to be. Ottilie, at one point, says to him:

> You know ... sometimes I think you don't exist at all, that you're just a voice, name – no, not even that, just the voice, going on. Oh God. Oh no. (Banville 1983: 67)

In the midst of the numerous fictions he has created, the historian lacks any tangible connection to the real world, his entire being condensed to a voice.

Banville's heroes share with Beckett's characters an overwhelming acceptance of failure as the very starting point of all (post)modern endeavour and desire. Others have explored these Beckettian influences in more detail (D'hoker 2006: 68–80) but what is important is to acknowledge the Beckettian sense of 'disinheritance' that pervades Banville's writing: characters are isolated, powerless, alone with a fading memory of some former time of glory and well-being, a memory which in itself may be but a construction, a fiction.

The other obvious precursor in this line is Elizabeth Bowen. Her work possesses an atmosphere somewhat similar to that of Beckett but with infinitely more detail and plot. Banville himself has celebrated her literary style above all other aspects of her art (Banville 2015), talking of her 'allusive' and 'subtle' prose. Its attractiveness for Banville might be the way in which her writing not only talks of things but embodies a self-reflexive anxiousness about language itself and what it hopes to achieve. He wrote the screenplay for a 1999 movie adaptation of her 1929 Anglo-Irish Big House novel *The Last September*, managing to pay homage to his precursor but failing to truly capture precisely that admired allusiveness of the original within the demands of a medium that must make everything visible and plain to see (Parezanović 2017: 141–59). As an artist Bowen straddles both British and Irish writing traditions, with much of her work focusing on adolescence thereby registering a mood of brittle being in the modern world as the focus is oriented towards characters and plots on the cusp of profound change. Her work charts the borderlines of an old world of aristocratic privilege and position facing into a newer world of bourgeois desire. Bowen herself came from a world of privilege, the Anglo-Irish Big House, and lived through its demise in the political realm while helping it continue in the sphere of culture and literature. Hers is not a Yeatsian vision with the emphasis on threnody; rather she is willing to critique her own class and caste.

John Banville's version of the Big House in novels such as *Birchwood* and *The Newton Letter* owes much to Bowen's delineation of the structures and ceremonies of life lived there: the poise, the aloofness, the 'dressing for dinner' that have in their way become the stereotypes and clichéd shorthand for that 'old' world. He uses these images and tropes as a limiting stereotype in that they are the tired commonplaces that envelope this world and its language and entrap its characters as is evidenced in *Birchwood*; yet he also uses them as a means, particularly in his later fiction, to register a worldview, to articulate the loss of individual power and status in the contemporary postmodern world, and to give expression to that shift away from a celebration of the individual as the measure of all things to an image of the individual being buffeted by external forces. Lois in Bowen's *The Last September* and Jane in her 1955 novel *A World of Love* play with the endless possibilities of differing roles and identities: very much like Banville's characters, they appear happier being everyone and anyone else other than themselves. Identity is reduced to style in a Wildean sense. And yet for Bowen the real fear is the rise of the unattached, unknown self-made person who will herald the final end of the old world and tradition. Thus, Bowen gives to Banville a discourse of uncertainty about the modern world and the modern individual's position within that world. All of his characters embrace the potential of being made from nothing and yet they too mourn the losses and the absences of some sense of given identity.

What is central to Bowen's writing is her portrayal of characters' relationship to the very notion of 'home' as a stable, comforting site, a place of safety, return and nurturing. Hers is an uncertain sense of home with her protagonists uneasily living in the world of burnt out Big houses, hotels, and in a short story such as 'The Disinherited', the new middle-class housing estates of suburban 1930s Britain. It is a story that essentially draws a picture of the conflict between the old world and the new world, between those who are 'made' out of a class structure which is passing away and those who 'make' themselves. Of particular interest is how the mysterious Prothero, a shady character with a past, writes out night after night the story of how he murdered his lover Anita. The emphasis on an act of writing makes a concrete link to Banville's oeuvre and his many characters who self-consciously narrate or write the story of their lives. It is a narrative concerning the creation of a new identity: he is simultaneously both Prothero and not Prothero. He has, thus, created himself but, in turn, does not know who he is or what he wants to do with this self. Bowen's description of him as he writes is telling:

> The pen rushed the hand along under some terrific compulsion, as though something, not thought, vital, were being drained out of him through the point of the pen. Words sprang to their places with deadly complicity, knowing each

other too well. ... Once or twice when a clinker fell in the stove, or the outside staircase unaccountably creaked as though a foot were upon it, he looked up, the tyrannic pen staggered, he looked round the room with its immutable fixtures as though he were a ghost. (Bowen 1983: 392)

His efforts to make himself 'real' through writing fail. Prothero – a 'new' man representative of those who, without a past, will come into power in the twentieth century – has no story to tell but the story of how he became this 'new' man. He is condemned to repeat it over and over again and is, consequently, trapped within a narrative with no future or possibility for change. Nothingness yawns frighteningly before him and, consequently, before the reader.

But it is also Bowen's style that is of interest to Banville: her ability to present images of absences, to slow narrative to a standstill, to prolong the quiet and the silence, to arrest the reader's gaze for a moment from the flotsam and jetsam of modernity. Stasis and arrested development predominate in her work, certainly her Irish work. Bowen masterfully renders the quotidian world of things, of places and buildings and the bric-a-brac world of mundane objects. How the human realm interacts with this world is something that John Banville is also interested in exploring, how we imbue things with meaning and significance, how the world out there only serves to render our isolation all the more complete and felt.

Bowen's focus on betrayal (always a central theme in Irish writing), on the world of spying in *The Heat of the Day* (which Banville exploits in *The Untouchable*), on out-of-place characters on the cusp of adulthood, on faded glory offers a writer like Banville much to emulate and work with. She also managed to render the historical as personal. While Banville consciously eschews such grand historical themes, they are of course present in his work: how could they not be? And yet, what he really takes from Bowen is a mood: jaded, faded, powerlessness, self-conscious awkwardness on the part of characters and, importantly, narrators. While never fully offering a portrayal of an artist in her work, there is self-awareness and self-reflexivity in terms of the perceiving imagination and consciousness of her characters. It is also interesting to note that she wrote many 'ghost' stories and deployed gothic motifs throughout her fiction. Of note is that her ghosts are real in the short stories but only figments of the imagination in the world of her novels. Banville too flirts with ghostly tropes, with glimpses of movement just at the corner of the eye, echoes barely heard, and an overwhelming sense of other lives being lived in a shadowy alternative universe. It is an impression of 'disinheritance' that links Banville and Bowen, a whole range of images and concerns that he takes from her literary world as a starting point for his own acting as a kind of shorthand code for his reader's appreciation of his character's position from the outset.

A precursor for Elizabeth Bowen, and therefore John Banville, is novelist George Moore (1852–1933) who brought a European sensibility and aesthetic to bear upon Irish writing in the late nineteenth and early twentieth centuries. He raised the possibility of Irish writing and certainly the Irish novel being art as opposed to merely being a medium for a story. Two of his Irish novels are worthy of mention: *Drama in Muslin* (1886) and *The Lake* (1903). The former is a Big House novel set during the 1880s with the Land War as a backdrop. Many of the tropes and images of the Big House find powerful articulation here (Hand 2014a: 41–56). Crucially though, in terms of making a link to Banville, Moore self-consciously and indeed self-reflexively opens up a discussion about the nature of art, the novel, the artistic imagination through his heroine Alice Barton. Alice can only be an artist once she gets away from Ireland: the Irish scene at a moment of historical turmoil is impossible and on many levels: politically and artistically. With Alice's exile at the close of the novel George Moore offers the reader an image of pre-Joycean escape. *A Drama in Muslin* encapsulates perfectly the anxieties central to the Irish novel form in the nineteenth century and beyond, and indeed through Alice's desire to be a novelist it manages to dramatize them. Again, it is a case of the pull between being a part of and apart from, of desiring connection while acknowledging rupture. Moore recognizes that to embrace the predominant themes of individual advancement and bourgeois desire is to lose some essential connection with Irish concerns and the energies they might offer the artist. We can easily reread John Banville's comments on his precarious relationship to Irish writing in light of Moore's presentment of the problem here. He too looks to a cultural world beyond Ireland for formal and thematic succour.

But George Moore also offers a more positive and sustaining image of the artist and her/his relationship to an Irish locale in his novel *The Lake*, which is a story of a Catholic priest who by the close abandons his calling. The Catholic world of the small town priest, his adherence to doctrine and ideology, is presented as utterly devoid of feeling and mystery in juxtaposition to the delicate changes of the seasons traced by the lake and its shores. The difficulty is that it is precisely this natural world with all its potential beauty that Gogarty the priest must abandon when he chooses exile. As he leaves he wonders about the lake:

> 'I shall never see that lake again, but I shall never forget it,' and as he dozed in the train, in a corner of an empty carriage, the spectral light of the lake awoke

him, and when he arrived at Cork it seemed to him that he was being engulfed in the deep pool by the Joycetown shore. On the deck of the steamer he heard the lake's warble above the violence of the waves. 'There is a lake in every man's heart', he said, 'and he listens to its monotonous whisper year by year, more and more attentive till at last he ungirds.' (Moore 1980: 179)

What Moore brilliantly does here, in a purely modernist manner, is present an artistic sensibility as being democratically open to all. For here Gogarty realizes not only what will be lost but also recognizes how that loss will fuel his imagination in his new life lived away from this place. Thus, loss and disconnection yields an artistic and imaginative gain which, it might be said, is increasingly the dominant register in much of Banville's recent fiction which revolves round narrators mulling over all that is absent, indeed making that absence the starting point of the act of telling itself, making it the only story to be told.

Escape into art, then, becomes a central motif of Irish writing. That image of the artist and the celebration of the artistic imagination are returned to again and again in Irish fiction throughout the twentieth century: penetrating and aloof, chronicler and isolation, both a part of and apart from. The romantic figure of an exceptional and unique mind whose ability to see beauty is to be fêted as a powerful intervention into ordinary life. Obviously, Banville embraces that persona in his fiction: actors, scientists, historians: each and every one is a surrogate representation of the artistic mind at work, creating and manipulating their material.

Banville also learns from George Moore in that the artistic cost for Moore in ushering this European sensibility into the world of Irish letters was that his work would remain resolutely unloved and unread outside the Academy. His fate, ironically, within the sphere of Irish studies is to be forever the 'precursor' to James Joyce: his short stories *The Untilled Field* existing simply to point towards *Dubliners*; *Drama in Muslin* and *The Lake* are important because they bring forth earlier images of the artist and exile, exploited more forcefully in *Portrait of the Artist as a Young Man*. Moore's achievement consequently is to outline and chart various 'key themes' that would evolve in the work of future writers of the twentieth century (Nolan 2007: 136ff). As I have argued elsewhere, Moore's work serves the purpose of liberating others into art rather than fully liberating himself (Hand 2014b: 130). Certainly such a destiny is to be feared and avoided from Banville's position. I would argue that while very much like Moore in terms of interest and his acceptance of a European literary heritage, Banville has remained relevant in a way that Moore sadly did not.

Irish writers in their relationship to their readers have difficulties moving between the public and private spheres, between the world of aesthetics and art and the political world. Moore's move to memoir in *Hail and Farewell* suggests a way of bridging that gap: the story of the self is the only important story to be told and perhaps, indeed, the only story that it is possible to tell. Autobiography was one means by which Revivalists could come to know themselves, precisely as themselves (Hughes 2003: 28–45), but this is accentuated in the proliferation of personalized fiction as can be witnessed in the work of James Joyce in particular. The autobiographical impulse in Irish fiction makes manifest a shift from the oral world into the world of writing and literary art: as writers insert themselves into their own stories, their struggles to be artists re-enact that movement into modernity.

Yet Banville is wary of such a manoeuvre towards autobiography and, in contrast, embraces a fictional world of concealment rather than revelation, thus reversing the modernist desire to unveil what is hidden, to expose the real world as it is. He is like many contemporary Irish authors who guard their private lives rigorously in a way that earlier generations – W. B. Yeats, Brendan Behan and Edna O'Brien – did not. He refuses to be the voice of a generation, to be engaged with society, to be a public figure with a public role as Sean O'Faolain or Seamus Heaney did. His is a work about submerging the 'self' of the author. While in essays and newspaper articles he does dabble with autobiography (Banville 2013a, b), he has mostly steered well clear of it in his fictional work, though he obviously makes use of the Wexford and Rosslare of his youth and childhood for *The Sea* and *Ancient Light*. All writers from everywhere and from every era wrestle with their public persona. In Ireland, perhaps because of the persistence in the popular imagination of the figure of the Gaelic bard, there is a sense in which the writer is meant to inhabit the public space. One result being that aesthetics can often be overlooked as a writer is forced to engage with matters of the day, pronounce on society and politics. Banville, as noted, has studiously avoided that type of public engagement, preferring to present a portrait of the artist as purveyor and connoisseur of aesthetics, famously declaring on winning the Booker Prize – that most public and popular of literary awards – that thankfully at least a work of art had won (Jeffries 2012). Literary critics who wish therefore to engage with political or societal contexts in their reading of his writing are met with an oeuvre that deliberately seems to be above all of that, or certainly wants to be. The creation of the alter ego Benjamin Black might be best understood within that public sphere, taking the concerns of all of his novels with identity, doubles and masks, and making them playfully real. It also further muddies the waters of who the real Banville might be.

The fate of George Moore opens up a wider question about the nature of literary inheritance and tradition generally, about the nature of creativity and originality and its possibility in the light of all that has gone before. 'Precursor' suggests an idea of a 'herald', of someone who points forward to what is to come. Such an understanding opens up the interesting idea, despite the nature of their aesthetic, that Beckett and Joyce are merely points along a journey to an end that has yet not arrived. They are not an end in themselves, so they act as forerunners with their function being to announce the approach of another. In this instance that end point is John Banville. And, of course, Banville himself does not want to be a precursor to someone else in the way that Moore has been: that would be self-annihilation. Certainly, that is a way of reading George Moore: his work is now forgotten and unread and unloved and yet he must exist in order that James Joyce can come after him.

While it can be argued that John Banville's work is of the highest order, one can doubt that all of modernist and particularly Irish modernist writing is there solely to announce his arrival on the literary scene. Still, this question of influence and the anxieties that surround it are important. Since Maria Edgeworth proclaimed her uniqueness and originality in the preface to her novel *Castle Rackrent* (1801) many Irish writers, like Banville and James Joyce, have self-consciously followed suit with the prevailing tone of their declarations being one of literary pioneership as they take the Irish novel and Irish writing to places it has never been before. Of course, in suggesting that there was nothing before them, no writer, no tradition, the focus now shifts towards self-invention, of making it new and making it up, of forging the uncreated conscience, rather than furthering what has already been achieved.

James Joyce, perhaps in the most sustained manner, meditates on this notion of creativity and originality throughout *Ulysses*. Stephen Dedalus ponders how to be truly original and what might the consequences of such an achievement be. On Sandymount Strand he talks of his father, Simon, 'the man with my eyes' (Joyce 1992: 46) and later in the National Library he propounds on his theory of William Shakespeare: 'Himself his own father' (Joyce 1992: 267). Now, Dedalus's dilemma, as it was Joyce's, is precisely centred on the modernist conundrum of being 'new', of confronting the world in ways other than it had been up till then. Certainly that is how Joyce has often been read: turning his back on tradition as he fashions something truly original. And yet, I would argue that throughout *Ulysses* Joyce is attempting to find a more engaged and energizing relationship with tradition and with the past. Such clumsy phrasing and articulation as in the quotes above are part of that struggle: he wants to reimagine himself not as an 'end' point, a terminus, but as a writer open to the past as he looks towards the future.

While the implication is that the modern moment demands of the artist that she/he be self-invented, it appears that what Joyce actually enacts throughout *Ulysses* is not a radical break with tradition and the past, but rather the desire for a free dialogue between tradition and modernity, past and present. One result is history is made relevant in the present moment with living links being acknowledged rather than disconnection and difference. In other words, Joyce reverses the accepted polarities, and in doing so creates a truly radicalized space wherein all opposites can exist as dualities. The result is that the modern moment *can* be a place of heroic action and thought, that Ireland – even existing as it does on the margins – *can* be a place of energy, innovation and invention. And such a problem, and indeed solution, still exists in Irish writing. John Banville's *The Infinities*, for example, which mingles the realm of the Greek gods with humdrum Irish life, obviously enacts something similar to Joyce. The subtle gesturing towards an alternative historical universe in the novel playfully recognizes the ways in which such thinking aid in moving away from deterministic readings of the past, and particularly the Irish past. I have argued elsewhere that Irish novelists from the seventeenth century onward attempted to create a medium through which the Irish personality and Irish voice might emerge, as it were, speaking to itself (Hand 2014b: 1–13). The anxiety of influence hung heavily on Irish writers because of the colonial link to Britain and being on the margins of greater, more powerful cultures in Europe and beyond. Joyce's solution was to re-orientate the polarities that placed Ireland on the periphery that suggested that the Irish past and history generally needed to be transcended in order that the present and the future might be lived in. Banville too must confront, and does confront, this problem in his writing. From the chaotic incoherence of *Birchwood* which suffers from being so utterly aware of a single tradition in Irish writing, the Big House novel, that it sinks beneath its own self-consciousness, to *Doctor Copernicus* and *Kepler* which seemingly abandon Ireland as a site of fiction altogether. More recently his novels have become increasingly enclosed and centred on men who meditate on lives lived and choices made and their consequences. However, it can be argued that, amidst this diversity, all of his writing focuses to a greater or lesser degree on characters who must struggle to articulate themselves as themselves. These characters do so against the backdrop of the issue of the past and history precisely as a grand narrative that challenges the individual as an individual. In

Birchwood history itself, as a narrative that can be reassuringly objective, breaks down as reference is made to moments such as the Great Famine and the War of Independence occurring simultaneously. Ultimately Gabriel Godkin's narrative, for instance, is about the nature of writing itself, raising serious questions about the adequacy of language to confront the demands of the present moment in Ireland. This self-consciousness about narratives and their reliability – a built-in postmodernism suspicion of Enlightenment values – is a feature of much Irish writing in this period. Certainly, a novelist such as John Banville exploits the tropes of postmodernism thereby furnishing his work with layers of potential meaning with regard to narratives of the self and nation.

In his modernist manoeuvre of proclaiming his work as unique and unIrish Banville, like all writers, is attempting to fashion the critical narrative by which their work might be best understood. As Gerard Genette declares, each writer 'chooses his peers and thus his place in the pantheon' (Quoted in Harte 2014: 30). Certainly in the realm of Irish letters with W. B. Yeats, James Joyce, Sean O'Faolain and others this has been the case: they are all to a certain extent both creators and first literary critics of their own work. As critics ourselves we must be wary of such scheming. One element of this kind of posturing is that Banville, like every writer and every other generation, sees his own era as truly exceptional and revels – certainly in his early work – in the 'newness' and originality of his own moment – even if it is not that new at all: as George O'Brien, in a recent study of the contemporary Irish novel, says, 'The young perceive their own novelty' (O'Brien 2012: xi). Maybe, then, what is being articulated is a matter of generations and their difference, because in those early science novels it is the moment of creation that is being enacted again and again, over and over: making a fetish of the moment and the act – all other aspects of existence and human experience paling into insignificance. Such an impasse is that which is reached by most, if not all, of John Banville's characters. They are caught and stuck at that moment of their own creation. That was Stephan Dedalus's dilemma also. In that way Banville is very much like many Irish writers – though with a twist – who in the twentieth century focus on that moment of becoming in fiction and memoir: the story of the self and the self's coming into being is the only story to tell or that can be told. The quality of Banville's most recent output, as John Banville and not as Benjamin Black, has altered and possesses a different, more humane quality, in that a wider human world of interaction is imagined and engaged with. Finally, it would seem, Banville as creator is at ease with himself and his literary inheritance.

Yet, concerns still remain in his writing about the 'precursor', not just the persona of the 'precursor' who might disappear from sight like George Moore, but the very notion of the past and tradition itself that is bound up in the idea of predecessors and precursors. Banville undoubtedly fears the postmodern impossibility of saying anything new: for many of his characters language's and indeed literature's storehouse of images and tropes are a prison that cannot be escaped from. All the myriad references and intertextual layering of quotations in his work suggest as much: everything has been said already; all experience is known and follows predetermined trajectories. The nightmare is not of history, or of history repeating itself as farce or otherwise, but rather it is a nightmare of having all experience already experienced and the knowledge that all feeling and emotion is lessened in the modern moment as a consequence.

It is fair to say, then, after these ruminations on precursors and the past and self-invention that it is the modern individual, the human being in modernity, which is the primary subject of all of John Banville's fiction. Walter Benjamin suggested that the modern novel is the best form to mediate the individual and, indeed, to meditate on the individual:

> The novelist has isolated himself. The birthplace of the novel is the solitary individual, who is no longer able to express himself by giving examples of his most important concerns, is himself uncounselled, and cannot counsel others. (Benjamin 1985: 87)

For our reading of Banville's work the implication is clear: the individual is trapped within herself, unable to make meaningful links with those beyond the realm of the self. As stated earlier, Banville's concerns with the limits of language exemplify the modern person's aloneness and disconnection.

One particular aspect of Benjamin's diagnosis of modern man is worth considering in relation to Banville's work: that is the idea that the modern world strips 'experience' of its value, as Benjamin opines, 'He too has been cheated out of his experience' (Benjamin 1985: 180). This might explain the heavy air of world-weariness which permeates Banville's work, especially the recent novels: the sense that these characters have seen and felt it all before and nothing seems to be able to penetrate that hard skin. A reader might consider, for instance, how Banville's narrators have recourse to the word and the notion of the uncanny, of something having happened or having been experienced before usually rendered in the work as a sense of off-kilter déjà vu. Consequently, a fundamental element of his protagonists' difficulty is how reality never matches up to their preconception of it: there is always a hidden world of what ought to be happening off stage troubling what is actually happening in Banville's fictional world. This, too, might account for a curious feature of Banville's recent writing: the at times overwhelming 'wondering bafflement' in the face of life, of existence. It is as if to 'be' at all is stranger than anything that might happen. Thus, the reader is witness to characters who muse upon the smallest of details, the most seemingly insignificant of feelings and moments. In a modern world devoid of 'meaning', Banville wants, at least, to focus on moments where 'meaning' might once again be possible: to begin again to invest 'experience' with energy.

Thus, Banville's return to the locale of adolescence in *The Sea* and *Ancient Light* is an attempt to recapture some of the energies of the unknown and the not-yet-lived. And yet the interplay between the present and the past remains, as memory is offered now as the latest proxy trope that will allow for a meditation on creative art and the creative imagination. Still, this focus on memory is one more way to re-engage with the past on a personal level, to reopen it and examine it for the present moment. All these 'self-made' men: Max Morden and Alexander Cleave are unable to fully distance themselves from their pasts. Again, to return to Walter Benjamin and his famous musings on history and the past:

> It means to seize hold of a memory as it flashes up at a moment of danger. In every era the attempt must be made anew to wrest tradition away from a conformism that is about to overpower it. (Benjamin 1985: 255)

The 'moment of danger' or crisis is the quickening of Time itself – its maddening liquidity in Zygmunt Bauman's phrase (Bauman 2000): Banville's characters wish to slow things down and to halt, even momentarily, progress. This seems counter-intuitive to how Banville has been read by critics: they turn their backs on tradition and the timelessness of the narrow Irish scene in their desire to move into modernity itself. As has been argued though, his work can be read in the opposite way too. And so what remains is a profoundly uneasy relationship to the past and tradition that undoubtedly permeates the fiction. Perhaps, as with Walter Benjamin, it is a case of Banville not wanting to conform to the tradition but wanting to make it relevant in the present moment nonetheless. So, Banville oscillates between the desire to be self-made and the recognition as articulated in *Eclipse* that 'the self-made man has no solid ground to stand on' (Banville 2000: 37).

Returning to that opening quotation from *The Sea*, and in comparison with the other quotations it is, perhaps, the registering of stillness which is important. The waves are 'listless' and the air 'unmoving' and being slightly buffeted by the sea is negated: it was 'as if nothing had happened. And indeed nothing had happened, a momentous nothing, just another of the great world's shrugs of indifference' (Banville 2005: 263–4). The past and present mingle, and the imagination is alive to nuance and meaning and significance, both in the remembered moment of the past and in the presenting remembering moment. Nothing in the past is ever done, finished or without possible significance in the present. From *Mefisto* comes a phrase that, in its way, encapsulates this dynamic at the heart of John Banville's work and his thinking about the nature of the past, tradition and literary precursors:

> Cancel, yes, cancel, and begin again. (Banville 1987: 120)

References

Banville, J. (1983), *The Newton Letter: An Interlude*, London: Secker & Warburg.
Banville, J. (1984), *Birchwood*, London: Panther Books.
Banville, J. (1987), *Mefisto*, London: Paladin.
Banville, J. (1990), *Kepler*, London: Minerva.
Banville, J. (1995), *Athena*, London: Secker & Warburg.
Banville, J. (2000), *Eclipse*, London: Picador.
Banville, J. (2005), *The Sea*, London: Picador.
Banville, J. (2013a), 'A Father Tortured by Guilt after Neglecting His Children for Years', *Daily Mail*, 28 April. Available online: http://www.dailymail.co.uk/femail/article-2316298/Booker-prize-winning-novelist-John-Banville-admits-selfish-good-dad.html (accessed 24 August 2018).
Banville, J. (2013b), 'My Parents Were Born Old', *Daily Mail*, 4 January. Available online: http://www.dailymail.co.uk/femail/article-2257399/Booker-prize-winning-novelist-JOHN-BANVILLE-reflects-mysteries-ageing.html (accessed 24 August 2018).
Banville, J. (2015), 'In Praise of Elizabeth Bowen', *Irish Times*, 7 May. Available online: https://www.irishtimes.com/culture/books/in-praise-of-elizabeth-bowen-by-john-banville-1.2128995 (accessed 24 August 2018).
Bauman, Z. (2000), *Liquid Modernity*, Cambridge: Polity.
Benjamin, W. (1985), *Illuminations: Essays and Reflections*, edited with an Introduction by Hannah Arendt, New York: Schocken Books.
Bowen, E. (1983), *Collected Short Stories of Elizabeth Bowen*, with an Introduction by Angus Wilson, Harmondsworth: Penguin Books.
D'hoker, E. (2006), 'Self-Consciousness, Solipsism, and Storytelling: John Banville's Debt to Samuel Beckett', *Irish University Review*, 36(1): 68–80 Special Issue: John Banville, Spring-Summer.

Hand, D. (2014a), 'George Moore's *Drama in Muslin*: Art and the Middle Classes', in Heidi Hansson and James H. Murphy (eds), *George Moore and the Land War*, 41–56. Bern: Peter Lang.

Hand, D. (2014b), *A History of the Irish Novel*, Cambridge: Cambridge University Press.

Harte, L. (2014), *Reading the Contemporary Irish Novel 1987-2007*, London: Wiley Blackwell.

Hughes, E. (2003), '"The fact of me-ness": Autobiographical Writing in the Revival Period', in Margaret Kelleher (ed.), *Irish University Review*, 33(1): 28–45. Special Issue: New Perspectives on the Irish Literary Revival.

Jeffries, S. (2012), 'John Banville: A Life in Writing', *The Guardian*, 29 June. Available online: https://www.theguardian.com/culture/2012/jun/29/john-banvill-life-in-w riting (accessed 24 August 2018).

Joyce, J. (1992), *Ulysses*, with an Introduction and notes by Declan Kiberd, Harmondsworth: Penguin Books.

Moore, G. (1980), *The Lake*, with an Afterword by Richard Cave, Gerrards Cross: Colin Smythe.

Nolan, E. (2007), *Catholic Emancipations: Irish Fiction from Thomas Moore to James Joyce*, Syracuse, NY: Syracuse University Press.

O'Brien, G. (2012), *The Irish Novel: 1960-2010*, Cork: Cork University Press.

Parezanović, T. (2017), 'Discourse on Love in a Colonial Context: *The Last September* by Elizabeth Bowen and John Banville', *Lipar - Journal for Literature, Language, Art and Culture*, Issue No. 62/XVIII.

Schwall, H. (1997), 'An Interview with John Banville', *The European English Messenger* 6(1): 13–19.

2

Unknown unity: Ireland and Europe in Beckett and Banville[1]

Peter Boxall

In Banville's fiction, the tension between home and exile that is one of his most striking inheritances from Beckett manifests itself also in a difficult relationship between Ireland and Europe, and between Irish and European traditions.[2] Banville's is a haunted writing, which gives voice to a spectral Irish tradition of which Beckett might form a part, however partially (Boxall 2009). But, throughout Banville's oeuvre, this Irish lineage blends with his evocation of a European tradition. In *The Untouchable*, for example, a biographical portrait of Louis MacNeice is merged with a portrait of Anthony Blunt, producing a new European and Soviet context for MacNeice's 1930s Ireland. And in Banville's paired novels *Eclipse* and *Shroud*, Cleave's return to his unnamed Irish home in *Eclipse* is placed side by side with the Europe of *Shroud*, and with a return to the shadows of the Holocaust. While *Eclipse* tells the story of Cleave's mourning for his daughter – a story in which the daughter fails to appear – *Shroud* is a kind of parallel text, which tells the daughter's story, and in which Cleave is a haunting absence. Where Edgeworth's *Castle Rackrent* is a guiding text in *Eclipse*, modelling Cleave's house on an Anglo-Irish architecture, Paul de Man is the figure upon whom *Shroud* is hung. The central character of *Shroud*, Axel Vander – an academic whom Cass Cleave sets out to expose as the anti-Semitic author of pro-Nazi articles written during the Second World War – is loosely based on de Man, and positions Banville's novel in a European philosophical and theoretical tradition that goes back through de Man to Heidegger and Nietzsche. The investigation of spectral and uncertain identities, that is fed through the history of Anglo-Irish dispossession in *Eclipse*, is read back, in *Shroud*, to intellectual traditions that gave rise to and emerge from the Holocaust. Vander's anguished failure to find a means of articulating a stable identity is spliced into a reflection on the difficulty of producing a historical account of the Holocaust, when that event is so destructive of the very forces which produce historical narrative. In placing these two traditions side by side, Banville's novels suggest a kind of hybrid tradition, a peculiar conjunction of the Irish and the European, in which Beckett functions as a knot, or a bridge, belonging to both traditions at once.

Beckett's voice is allowed to resonate with a chorus of Irish voices in Banville's prose, but he is equally immersed in the European traditions upon which Banville draws (Boxall 2009). One of the major intertexts for *Eclipse*, for example, is Kleist's *Amphitryon*, which Banville loosely adapts to an Irish locale in his play *God's Gift*, published in the same year as *Eclipse*.[3] It is while performing as Amphitryon in Kleist's play, and as he prepares to deliver the clinching line 'Who if not I, then, is Amphitryon' (Banville 2000b: 89),[4] that Cleave experiences the crisis that leads him to abandon the stage, and sends him on his journey back to his mother's house. The moment of self-abandonment in Kleist – at which Amphitryon realizes that his identity has been usurped by a stranger – is the occasion for Cleave's evacuation of his lifelong role as actor. It is partly this central interest, in Kleist's play, in the possession of the self by others – Amphitryon's identity is stolen by Jupiter in order that the latter might seduce Amphitryon's wife – that makes it such a resonant intertext for Banville. Like *Eclipse*, it focuses on inhabitation and possession and, like *Eclipse*, the play is itself inhabited by other versions of itself: Kleist's play is a retelling, a usurpation, both of Molière's *Amphitryon*, and of the Greek myth upon which Molière, Kleist and Banville base their adaptations. This fascination with multiple identities makes Kleist a central figure not only in *Eclipse*, but also in *Shroud*: Cass Cleave, for example, is at work on a project which involves cataloguing the last moments of Kleist's life, and Axel Vander recalls attending a conference 'on Molière, Kleist and *Amphitryon*' (Banville 2002: 163). This Kleistian vein running through the two novels produces a European, Germanic flavour to the texts, which sits alongside the Edgeworthian cast of *Eclipse*. But while Kleist remains at odds with Edgeworth, exerting a kind of parallel influence, the Kleistian legacy is fed through and merges with the Beckettian legacy in Banville. If Kleist is a structuring presence in Banville, then it is also the case that he exerts a shaping influence in Beckett's work. Beckett's play *Ghost Trio*, for example, is inhabited by the spirit of Kleist. The figure stranded in his rectangular box in Beckett's play, straining to reach across its porous borders towards the spirits that might animate him – the spirit both of himself and of his loved ones – lives through a predicament investigated by Kleist not only in his plays, but also in his essays. Indeed, Beckett famously suggested to the director of the BBC version of *Ghost Trio*, Ronald Pickup, that it was to Kleist's essay 'Über das Marionettentheater' that he should refer, in order to visualize the figure's movements as he paces around his room (Knowlson 1996: 623–3). Kleist's essay on the marionette theatre – which incidentally is one of the texts that Cleave schools himself to read, in *Eclipse*, as part of his training to become an actor (Banville 2000b: 37) – turns around his perception that the puppet moves with a kind of grace, balance and harmony which eludes the human dancer or actor, because the puppet can move without the constrictions and flaws that are imposed on the body by consciousness of self. The body of the puppet, empty of the distorting presence of consciousness, achieves a 'more natural arrangement of the centres of gravity' than is possible for a living actor (Kleist 1955: 15). Kleist suggests that the natural movement of puppets allows us to see, by contrast, how unbalanced our own movements are, how imperfectly the soul is housed within the human body. It is this contrast between the flowing, graceful movements of the unconscious actor, and the awkward, unbalanced movements of the conscious actor, that Beckett asked Pickup to articulate in *Ghost Trio*. The figure in Beckett's play, as James Knowlson (1996: 633) suggests, is 'poised midway between two worlds', the human world and the inanimate world, separated by the imperceptibly open boundary marked by window and door. His movements as he attempts to negotiate between them, between remembering and forgetting, between clinging to and abandonment of self, are inhabited by Kleist, just as Amphitryon is inhabited by Jupiter. It is this close occupation of Beckett by Kleist that Banville inherits in *Eclipse*. The Kleistian frame that holds the novel in place, that animates Cleave's movements both as Amphitryon and as himself, is inhabited also by Beckett, as if Beckett, Kleist and Banville are coming together here, merging into a single, overpopulated body. The extent of this cohabitation is suggested, in fact, at a moment in *Eclipse* that I have already quoted above, in which Cleave reflects on his own possession by spectres. Puzzling over the meaning of his haunting at his mother's house, he asks,

> what am I to make of this little ghost trio to whose mundane doings I am the puzzled and less than willing witness?
>
> Trio? Why do I say trio. There is only the woman and the even more indistinct child – who is the third? Who, if not I? (55)

This is a multiply haunted moment in *Eclipse*. Beckett is present here, both in the title of his television play *Ghost Trio*, and in the title of his play *Not I*, which was broadcast alongside *Ghost Trio* as part of the Shades trilogy on BBC 2 on 17 April 1977. But even as *Ghost Trio* and *Not I* come together here, producing a spectral Beckettian undertone to Cleave's hauntings, Kleist can be felt under the surface also, joining with Beckett, and recalling the moment of Cleave's collapse on stage, the moment at which he became too conscious of himself to act. 'Who, if not I' calls not only to the denial of self-identity in Beckett's play, but to that moment in Kleist and in Molière at which Amphitryon demands, 'Who if not I, then, is Amphitryon'.

Beckett, then, inhabits both the European and the Irish cultures that Banville draws on in his 'manufacturing' of his own tradition. In Beckett's oeuvre, Banville finds a means of bringing Edgeworth and Kleist, a Germanic and an Irish tradition, into a cloven unity. In Beckett, these traditions offer themselves up to a kind of merging, even while they remain distinct from one another. His work, written both in French and in English, harbours the possibility of a unity between Ireland and continental Europe, a new kind of transcultural accommodation that would see beyond the national politics that have separated them; but at the same time, it performs the impossibility of finding such a unity, as Irish and European strands in his writing assert their opposition to each other, their historical, cultural and political specificity, even at the moment of their fusion. Banville's inheritance of Beckett's legacy builds on this simultaneous merging and separation of the Irish and the European, this search for an underlying unity that cannot quite come to the surface. Banville's poetics of eclipse, in which discrete things betray a hidden sameness, emerges partly from this legacy. If the ecliptical mechanics that I have described above turn around the relationship between Cleave and his daughter, then it is also the case that the same mechanics, the same difficult combination between proximity and distance, determines the relationship in Banville between Ireland and Europe. As I have argued, Banville's paired novels *Eclipse* and *Shroud* lie beside each other, occurring in a peculiarly simultaneous manner. The two novels belong to different landscapes and different traditions, but while they occupy such discrete national, political, cultural and philosophical arenas, they are written in such a way that it is possible, at all times, to read across from one to the other, to glimpse the shadows of one novel moving behind the thin partition that separates it from the other. The telepathic relationship between Cleave and his daughter, in which the distance that separates them is continually threatened with sudden extinction, opens a kind of back passage between *Shroud* and *Eclipse*, between Ireland and Europe, like that imperceptible passage between home and exile that is opened up in *Ghost Trio*. Just as the square in Cleave's Irish town reveals its capacity, at the moment of eclipse, to become a Mediterranean piazza, so, throughout both novels, there is an insistent interference across the boundary, an insistent possibility that the Irish might at any moment merge with the European, and vice versa.

The eclipse, in fact, that occurs and fails to occur in *Eclipse*, is one of the mechanisms by which this interference is effected. The title of the later novel first appears, in a kind of premonitory fashion, as the eclipse gathers in *Eclipse* – 'I remarked the peculiar light', Cleave says, 'insipid and shrouded' (179) – and the moment of eclipse that is somehow deferred in *Eclipse* is registered in *Shroud*, as if the occluded light of one novel shines through a thin curtain to illuminate the other. As the eclipse is struggling to take place in Ireland, a Turin square across which Axel Vander is wandering will start to darken, the 'sun being stealthily swallowed by a fat, barely moving cloud' (50). And later in the novel, Axel remembers the moment in his cloven, de Manian past, at which he stole his namesake's identity, and the eclipse emerges again, an 'enormous, grape blue cloud nudg[ing] its way up out of the low west, like a slow, sullen thickening of nameless possibilities' (227). Throughout both of these novels, the eclipse produces these 'nameless possibilities', in which an unnamable, hybrid space promises to emerge from the interstices. Vander, like Cleave, only partly occupies his space, finding part of himself always located elsewhere, on the other side of the boundary that separates the two novels, and that separates Ireland from Italy. Echoing Cleave's name, as if Cleave is an Irish alter ego to this European intellectual, he suggests that he 'is cloven in two' (13), that his 'true source and destination are always elsewhere' (69). In a near quotation from Beckett's play *All That Fall*, where the 'dark Miss Fitt' comments ruefully that 'the truth is that I am not there, Mrs Rooney, just not really there at all' (Beckett 2006: 182–3), Vander says that 'the fact is, I was never there, not really' (Banville 2002: 90). Even in his youth, when like Cleave he would 'prowl the back roads' (Banville 2000b: 33), when he would 'walk in the narrow secret streets' of the 'city where I was born' (Banville 2002: 90), Vander felt himself occupied by this other spectral presence, felt himself somehow displaced from himself, absent from the scene of his own becoming. Throughout both novels Axel and Alex – cloven, axial anagrams of each other – communicate in this way, finding their true source and destination, their Kleistian centre of gravity, thrown across the threshold that is produced and erased by the eclipse. And the figure that intervenes between them, that is closest to the imperceptible boundary marked by the eclipse, is Cass.

Cass, in her empathic hyper-sensitivity, offers a kind of window or door through which Axel and Alex, Ireland and Europe, might flow into each other. On the first, disturbing occasion that Cass and Axel have sex, this sense of a nameless possibility, of some kind of imperceptible, unnamable communication, starts to assert itself. The 'first time', Cass recalls in the third person, 'when he had come out of the bathroom at last and heaved himself on top of her, she had thought of one of those huge statues of dictators that were being pulled down all over Eastern Europe. Crash' (Banville 2002: 118). This is a peculiarly freighted moment, combining as it does a sense of the new Europe that is in the process of becoming, with the possibility of a merging between *Eclipse* and *Shroud*, a kind of nameless communication between them. There is an insistent preoccupation, in *Shroud*, with the shifting of the boundaries that divide nation states and direct the flow of capital in late-twentieth-century Europe – with the fate of those 'statelets wedged like boulders of basalt, though beginning rapidly to crumble now, between the straining continental plates of East and West' (Banville 2002: 43) – and the crashing down of European dictators at this moment in the novel resonates with this concern. It is as if the molestation of a young girl by an aged European intellectual, in a skewed version of Yeats's 'Leda and the Swan', is inaugurating here a new European regime, a new distribution of knowledge and power. But this moment also calls, if faintly, to *Eclipse*, and to Cass's father. The straining continental plates of East and West double, here, as a tectonic conjunction between *Eclipse* and *Shroud*. Cass's comparison of the rampant Vander with a falling statue blends uncannily with the same comparison attributed to Cleave in *Eclipse*. A newspaper covering the incident at which Cleave corpses during his performance in *Amphitryon* reports that watching Cleave dry on stage 'had been like witnessing a giant statue toppling off its pedestal and smashing into rubble on the stage' (Banville 2000b: 88). While this appearance of the father's shadow in the daughter's boudoir remains a fleeting visitation, however, on the second occasion that Vander and Cass have sex the paternal presence is much ruder. If the first sexual encounter was rather abrupt, the 'second time', Cass remembers, 'was different': 'He was all chest and churning elbows and quaking thighs, straining and heaving, until she thought she might split in two down the middle' (Banville 2002: 119). The repellent violence of Vander's assault opens a divide in Cass, through which the father might enter less obliquely. 'While Vander was busy goughing and grunting at her that second time', the narrative goes on, 'Daddy had opened the door of the room and walked in, speaking. He was barefoot, and was wearing an old pair of faded blue baggy trousers of the kind that he always wore when he was on holiday' (Banville 2002: 129). The door that separates *Shroud* from *Eclipse*, that remains imperceptibly ajar throughout, yawns wide here, as Cass suffers beneath Vander's foul onslaught. Where Cleave glimpses something of his home through the parent's window, past the erotically draped figure of Lily, his surrogate daughter, Cass sees here across a spectral threshold to a home that lies somewhere in the impossible interstices of the novel, in which she is once again in the comfort of the father's shade.

It is this 'unspeakable home', lying as a dormant possibility in the fold between Ireland and Europe, that is Beckett's final legacy to Banville. To travel in a Beckettian direction is to orient oneself to the unspoken possibility that this space harbours, a space which remains hidden in the back, which cannot show its face, but which nevertheless comes to a form of expression. Cleave himself thinks of this nameless possibility growing beneath the surface of the text, pushing up to occupy the furniture of both novels, as an 'unknown unity', a form of utopian possibility that Banville inherits from Beckett and that shimmers just beyond the borders of perception. Seeking yet again to understand the meaning of his haunting at his mother's house, Cleave reflects that 'some intricate system, elaborate yet mundane, an *unknown unity*, some little lost and desolated order, is trying to put itself into place here, to assemble itself within the ill-fitting frame of the house and its contents' (Banville 2000b: 47; emphasis added). In Banville's out-of-true novels, Beckett's legacy is a kind of unity between opposing states that cannot be accommodated within the 'ill-fitting frame' that Banville makes for it, but that nevertheless lies in wait under the surface of the novels, and in the impossible space between them. In Beckett's writing, as I have argued above, this possibility is fashioned from an impossible coming together of face and back. Beckett's late works both perform the failure to stitch face and back into a proper unity, to make them fit, and suggest a new kind of accommodation between them, a newly sutured body which might experience a negatively utopian unity, but which, in Ernst Bloch's terminology, cannot yet come to consciousness.[5] In Banville's writing, Beckett's remade but as yet unthinkable body reaches for a new kind of articulation. Some of the cultural pressures that exert themselves upon Beckett, that defer the utopian possibilities that his writing produces, have passed away at the beginning of the third millennium, or reshaped themselves. The straining between continental plates that doubles, disturbingly, as the bodily struggle between Vander and Cass in *Shroud*, has freed some pressures while producing others. The struggle to reimagine and rename Ireland that is one of the defining exertions in Beckett's writing has eased somewhat as Beckett is reimagined by Banville. The repositioning of nation states in relation to a newly federalized Europe, and in the context of globalized capital, has lifted some weight from the relation between Ireland and Europe that is so blocked in Beckett but that reaches for a greater fluency in Banville. But while Banville's inheritance of Beckett registers this easier exchange between Ireland and Europe, what this inheritance illuminates most starkly are the barriers that remain, the obstacles that stand in the way of thinking the forms of utopian unity and community that struggle for expression in Beckett. If Banville gives expression to an Irish Beckett placed in the context of globalized capital, then he reveals not only the possibility of a reconciliation with the difficulties of national belonging, but also the development of a new set of cultural forces which stand in the way of the 'unknown unity' that Banville inherits from Beckett.

In Banville, as in Beckett, one of the ways in which this continuing failure of the utopian imagination expresses itself is in the broken relation between the face and the back. Both *Eclipse* and *Shroud* are novels that are centrally preoccupied with faciality. The forms of communication and miscommunication that occur between Cass and her father, across the boundary between Ireland and Europe, are shaped by the image of Cass's face. It is the case, as I have said, that Cass fails to appear in *Eclipse*, remaining hidden behind the partition that separates Ireland from Italy, and *Eclipse* from *Shroud*. But her body does eventually make it across this boundary, at the close of the novel, returning from Turin to Cleave's unnamed Ireland in the cargo hold of an aeroplane. The cost of this transgression of the boundary, however, is not only Cass's life, but also her face. On the only occasion in the novel that Cleave is in the physical presence of his daughter, when he identifies her body in an Italian morgue, this defacement is poignantly revealed: 'The sheet was drawn back. *Stella Maris*. Her face was not there, the rocks and the sea had taken it. We identified her by a ring, and a little scar on her left ankle that Lydia remembered. But I would have known her, my Marina, even if all that was left of her was the bare, wave-washed bones' (Banville 2000b: 204). Eliot's poem 'Marina', his keening evocation of the daughter's face, at once immeasurably close and more distant than the stars, is a powerful presence at this moment in the novel. Taking possession of his daughter's body, here, does not bring Cleave any closer to her face, but rather reasserts its distance. To bring her home is to peel the back from the face, to bring to light that unthinkable plane that lies behind the face, featureless, unmade and uncanny. To bring her body home is to effect some kind of separation between face and back, and to recognize that they can only be rejoined, can only achieve their unknown unity, elsewhere, in an as yet unnameable, unspeakable place where the body that strives for expression in *Shroud* and *Eclipse* can find itself fully formed; where, as in Eliot, 'this form, this face, this life' is able to 'live in a world of time beyond me'. It is as if *Shroud* and *Eclipse* are separated by a partition which acts like a shroud, which speaks of a persistent presence only by separating face from body.

In his essay 'The Exhausted', Gilles Deleuze notes Beckett's recurrent interest in faciality, and in the figure of the shroud. 'In ... *but the clouds* ...', Deleuze writes, the female face has 'almost no head, a face without head suspended in the void'; and in *Nacht und Träume*, the dreamt face seems as if it were wrested from the cloth which mops away its sweat, like a face of Christ, and is floating in space (Deleuze 1998: 168).[6] Deleuze is no doubt thinking here of the well-known anecdote in which Beckett suggested to his cameraman Jim Lewis that the cloth which wipes the dreamt face in *Nacht und Träume* 'alluded to the veil that Veronica used to wipe the brow of Jesus on the Way of the Cross. The imprint of Christ's face remains on the cloth' (Knowlson 1996: 682). In *Nacht und Träume*, Deleuze is suggesting, the handkerchief which wipes the dreamt face brings Beckett's figure into a kind of paradoxical contact with the face of Christ. In 'wresting' the face from the shroud, from the veil, an act of defacement becomes also a moment of communication. A young Beckett, frustrated at the limits of language in expressing the inexpressible, thinks of his language as a 'veil that must be torn apart in order to get at the things (or the nothingness) behind it' (Beckett 1983: 171). By the time that Beckett writes *Nacht und Träume*, this violent attitude to the veil has to an extent passed away. For this later Beckett, the veil which hides, which occludes, is also the surface which offers a fleeting contact between things and nothingness, between presence and absence. The veil both defaces, and bears an inscription of what the director in Beckett's *Catastrophe* thinks of as a 'trace of face' (Beckett 2006: 459). The face of Christ, the face of the mother in *Company*, which, like the face of the daughter in Eliot's poem seems at once more and less distant 'than in reality it is' (Beckett 1992: 8), is brought to the point of a wordless communicability by the very shroud which covers it; the 'billowing shroud' (Beckett 2006: 394) that separates the voices in Beckett's play *That Time* while also offering the possibility of some fleeting union. In Banville's paired novels, the shroud works, similarly, as a simultaneously separating and connecting fabric. The unknown unity that lies under the surface both in Beckett and in Banville, that would allow a measure of peace to the seeker weary of 'wandering to find home' (Beckett 1973: 6), cannot yet express itself in the work of either writer, cannot show itself plain. Rather, the surface of the page, like the fabric of the shroud, or the 'little fabric' of which the whiteness is made in *Imagination Dead Imagine* (Beckett 1995: 182), can only image forth the possibility of unity from its performance of disunity, its separating of face from back, of figure from ground. The narrator of *The Unnamable* gives perhaps the most painful articulation of this aporia, in which connection can only be established through disjunction, and in which the expression of unity is a condition of its inexpressibility. The narrator thinks of himself, at one point in the novel, as a thin sheet which intervenes between separate states. 'Perhaps that's what I feel', he writes,

> an outside and an inside and me in the middle, perhaps that's what I am, the thing that divides the world in two, on the one side the outside, on the other the inside, that can be as thin as foil, I'm neither one side nor the other, I'm in the middle, I'm the partition, I've two surfaces and no thickness, perhaps that's what I feel, myself vibrating, I'm the tympanum, on the one hand the mind, on the other the world, I don't belong to either. (Beckett 1994: 386)

In imagining himself as a partition here, the narrator casts himself as a page, or as a shroud, a marked surface which brings opposed states together, but only at the cost of a terrible dismemberment. In order to imagine the world whole, it is necessary to cleave the world in two. To bring inside and outside together, to conjoin face with back, mind with world, is to find oneself ejected from the world, to find oneself composed of a surface with no thickness. This is the predicament that so tortures the narrator of *The Unnamable*, as it determines the expressive possibilities of Banville's fiction. *Eclipse* and *Shroud* are joined by a shroud, by a vibrating partition which brings Europe and Ireland together, which brings a daughter to her father, which sutures the face to the back. But for Banville, still, to summon this unity, to imagine this conjunction, is to find oneself divided, from others and from oneself. As Axel Vander has it in one of his de Manian essays – an essay that Kristina Kovacs suggests might have been written about the shroud of Turin – 'Real Presence' is a function of 'effacement' (Banville 2002: 156).[7]

If there is continuity between Beckett and Banville here, however, there is also difference. The forces which govern the speakability of unity between Ireland and Europe are different for Banville than they are for Beckett. Beckett's writing belongs partially and tangentially to a tradition of Irish writing, stretching from Edgeworth to Bowen and Yeats, that seeks to imagine a union between Ireland and Europe, that strives for a poetic reconciliation between spaces which remain materially irreconcilable. In engaging with this tradition, Beckett transforms the terms in which such unity might be imagined. His work suggests a new way of envisaging a cloven unity between Ireland and Europe, between face and back, which is won through and seamed with an expression of disunity. The utopian possibilities in Beckett's writing, the images of peace and unity which are threaded through his oeuvre, are more intimately related to disunity, to the dystopian failure of an expressive or political project, than in any preceding writer. The complete body, the body at home in its world that comes excruciatingly close to expression in Beckett's writing, is fashioned from torture, from dismemberment, from unhomeliness. This homeliness and this unhomeliness is Beckett's double-faced gift to those of us who come after him. But Banville's receipt of such a gift occurs at a time when the relation between Ireland and Europe is itself being reimagined and rewritten. Where Beckett's engagement with Ireland was with a post-war nation state engaged in a difficult, pseudo-colonial relationship with Britain, Banville's Ireland is a state in the process of incorporation into a new, arguably post-nationalist Europe. The lines of blocked communication between Ireland, England and continental Europe that run through Beckett's writing, and determine to an extent both its failures and its capacity to 'fail better' (Beckett 1992: 101), have as a result been redrawn. When Banville imagines a continuity between Ireland and Southern Europe, he is no longer imagining against the geopolitical grain, in quite the same way that Beckett does, as Ireland has reached a political accommodation with Europe that has allowed it, in a limited and difficult fashion, to reconceive its difficult relationship with the United Kingdom.

This sense of a new facility in the communication between Ireland and Europe expresses itself, in Banville's fiction, in terms of roads. As Alexander Cleave makes his way back to his childhood home, at the opening of *Eclipse*, he journeys not only backwards into the past, but also along a newly built road, a road which is part of Ireland's newly upgraded infrastructure, built on European and US inward investment.[8] As Cleave travels with his wife, 'bowling along through the country-side's slovenly and uncaring loveliness', the effect of this new infrastructure on the accessibility of the past becomes a direct focus. On the road the Cleaves overtake a circus – the circus in which Cleave will be re- and dis-united with his daughter, the circus in which he will experience and fail to experience the eclipse – and the caravanserai speaks of an obsolete form of travel, a form of travel that the Cleaves leave behind as they smoothly glide by. 'We passed by a circus', Cleave writes, 'going in our direction, one of the old-fashioned kind, rarely to be seen any more, with garishly painted horse-drawn caravans, driven by gipsy types with neckerchiefs and earrings' (Banville 2000b: 14). The sight of this antiquated equipage leads Cleave to a brooding reflection, to a nostalgia which becomes closely intermingled with the condition of his own journeying: 'I brooded on words. Sentimentality: unearned emotion. Nostalgia:

longing for what never was. I remarked aloud the smoothness of the road. "When I was young this journey took three hours, nearly." Lydia threw up her eyes and sighed. Yes, the past again' (Banville 2000b: 14–15). The smooth, newly surfaced road, here, offers easy access to the past while also threatening the past with erasure. The horse-drawn circus paraphernalia seems to belong to a past 'that never was', a past whose spectral persistence is reliant on the circuitousness of the back road. The Ireland to which Cleave belongs is one that is entering into a new relationship with modernity, one which is yielding up the secrets that have been hidden in the folds of the poorly maintained back roads. But at every stage of the novel there is a sense that the very structures, political as well as infrastructural, that allow for a new access to Ireland's past also work to delete it, as if national memory relies for its preservation on the uneven surface, on the roughness and obscurity of the way. As Michael Cronin (2002) has argued, in his Virilian analysis of the new speed of culture in 'Irish late modernity', 'the faster you go, the quicker you forget'.[9]

This fascination with the route back to the past is balanced in the novel against an equal interest in the way forward, the path towards Ireland's European future. While Cleave travels at the beginning of the novel towards the past along a newly built road, he travels at the novel's close by aeroplane towards the Italian village in which his daughter dies. And, again, the focus of the narrative is on the tension between ancient and modern forms of travel:

> On the endless journey out – in real time it took only from early morning until the middle of the afternoon – woe sat like lumpy satchels on our backs, weighing us down. I thought of a pair of mendicant pilgrims out of a Bible scene, bent under our burdens, making our toilsome way along a hot and dusty road leading off into an infinite perspective. … I sat slumped in the narrow aeroplane seat, numb of mind and heart, stewing in my crumpled clothes, my bilious frog's stare fixed on the stylised patchwork world passing slowly far below us. (Banville 2000b: 202)

This final journey is one that takes place in two time-frames at once. The journey is both endless and brief; it is both an impossibly slow tramp along an infinitely long, dusty road and a peculiarly weightless annihilation of distance. The long road that takes Cleave back to his daughter, that takes him back to his home, becomes a kind of fantasy here, as the temporality of air travel – called here 'real time', for all its counter-intuitive unreality – produces a new proximity, a kind of simultaneity, between Ireland and Europe. The 'passing of the stylized patchwork world' beneath the slowly speeding aeroplane suggests that the future does not belong to roads, that the globalization of capital has led to a reorganization of space in which different places become strangely contiguous, of a piece. The 'defaced daughter' (Banville 2000b: 209), hidden in the cargo hold of the aeroplane, brings the back back home, but *Eclipse* and *Shroud* suggest that there is now a new relation between back and face, that the back is no longer to be preserved in the twists and turns of a premodern rurality. If the back exists at all, if it is possible to preserve and maintain a contact with that part of oneself that is secreted in the back rooms in Edgeworth, in Bowen, in Beckett, then it has become necessary to look for it elsewhere. Back and face come together, in Banville and in Beckett, in that imperceptible space that Beckett imagines in his short piece 'Neither' – a space 'between two lit refuges whose doors once neared gently close, / once turned away from gently part again' (Beckett 1995: 258), the space of the interval, in which a utopian unity waits to come to consciousness. As global capital produces a global communicability, the back does not and cannot hide away in those places that modernity has not yet reached. The globalization of capital has meant that the back has become part of the face. The struggle to remain faithful to the local as opposed to the general, to distinguish between the provincial and the cosmopolitan, between home and exile, is no longer oriented by the relation between town and country, between the back road and the major thoroughfare, between the modern and the antiquated, or at least not to the same extent. Globalization tends towards a situation in which all is at once brand new and already obsolete. As a UK advertising campaign for the global bank HSBC has it – in its slogan 'the world's local bank' – globalization shapes to make the local universal.

So Banville's figuring of the relationship between Europe and Ireland takes place in a global context that was not fully available to Beckett. But if Banville is responding to the possibility of a post-nationalist Ireland in his fiction, a possibility that has come into a newly sharp focus since Beckett, it is nevertheless the case that Beckett's writing, in its blocked, agonized depiction of an unknown unity between Ireland and Europe, imagines the shape which a European Ireland might take, *avant la lettre*. If Beckett's work bears the stamp of a failed relationship between Ireland, Britain and continental Europe, if his poetics of failure and exile are determined, to a degree, by the impossibility of resolving the political contradictions of post-war Europe, then it is also the case that his writing gives a pale, utopian expression to a post-nationalist consciousness, however uncreate (see Boxall 2009: 133–99). And it is this unspoken possibility that characterizes Beckett's presence in Banville. This is not to say that the increasingly rapid globalization of culture since 1989 has allowed Banville to articulate a utopia that remains latent and unimaginable in Beckett; I would argue, on the contrary, that Banville's fiction is alive to the politically regressive consequences of globalization, just as it registers the inchoate possibilities of new communities that it harbours. But it is to suggest that Beckett's writing, as it is reflected in Banville, suggests a mode of post-national consciousness that is coming to the point of a new expression, as the boundaries that divided Europe in the immediate post-war begin to give way to new configurations. Terry Eagleton has warned against the easy assumption that European integration might resolve some of the more intractable problems of Irish nationalism. It is tempting, Eagleton (1998: 313) suggests, 'to leap suitably streamlined and amnesiac into Europe',[10] to find in a federal, corporate European culture a solution to the contradiction between Ireland's history and its relationship with modernity. But such a solution, he argues, involves not only a cultural amnesia, a loss of commitment to one's 'unspeakable home', it involves also the replacement of subservience to a national colonial power with subsumption into a new, global empire, that empire which has been theorized more recently by Hardt and Negri (2000). Banville's imagining of the relationship between Ireland and the new Europe responds to this difficulty. The challenge presented by globalization is to respond imaginatively to the possibilities for new communities and new political configurations that it creates, as Hardt and Negri (2006) have argued, while resisting the drive towards cultural uniformity and homogeneity that is the condition and the result of the globalization of capital. Banville's later fiction might be thought of partly as a response to this challenge. *Shroud* and *Eclipse*, in their peculiar relationship to one another, seek to articulate a new accommodation between Ireland and Europe, while also preserving the discrete cultural histories, both Irish and European, that are threatened with deletion by the process of post-national integration. The body that is reached for in Banville, the new relation between face and back suggested by the poetic, telepathic communication between *Eclipse* and *Shroud*, seeks to embody this possibility; it is a fragile body that emerges intact but protoplasmic from the collapsing boundaries of the new Europe. This body may still not yet be thinkable; it might still reside in the Blochian dimension of the not yet conscious. But it is this attempt to articulate a still unknowable unity emerging from the tectonic shifts in the global geopolitical landscape that is Banville's ethical and political response to the dangers and the possibilities of globalization. And it is in Beckett's writing, in Beckett's barely readable, barely thinkable articulation of an uncreated relation between face and back, that Banville sees the first stirrings of this new body, at home in the world.

Notes

1. This chapter is reprinted, with permission, from the author's *Since Beckett: Contemporary Writing in the Wake of Modernism* (Bloomsbury 2009).
2. In insisting that the tradition that he belongs to is one that is 'manufactured' by himself, Banville draws attention to this fusion in his work between Irish and wider European literary traditions, saying that 'I feel part of my culture. But it's a purely personal culture gleaned from bits and pieces of European culture of four thousand years' (Sheehan et al. 1979: 80). Powell outlines the critical debate that has emerged over whether Banville should be considered part of an Irish or of a European tradition. See Powell (2005: 199–201).
3. See Banville (2000a).
4. See Heinrich von Kleist (1988: 63), where the line is translated as 'And who except myself's Amphitryon'. See also Molière (1907: 399), where the line is translated 'And who, besides myself, may this Amphitryon be?'
5. For an elaboration of Bloch's theorization of the relationship between the 'not-yet conscious' and the 'utopian function' in art and aesthetics, see Ernst Bloch, 'The Conscious and Known Activity within the Not-Yet-Conscious, the Utopian Function', in Bloch (1988: 103–41).
6. For another essay in which Deleuze and Guattari expand their theory of 'faciality', see Gilles Deleuze and Félix Guattari, 'Year Zero: Faciality', in Deleuze and Guattari (1988: 167–91).
7. De Man does not have an essay by the title 'Effacement and Real Presence', but the title that is perhaps suggested here is 'Autobiography as De-Facement', in Paul de Man (1984: 67–81).
8. For a robust critical assessment of the impact of the Celtic Tiger economy on Irish cultural formations, see Kirby, Gibbons and Cronin (2002) and Coulter and Coleman (2003). See also Kiberd (2005).
9. For Virilio's influential analysis of the relation between speed and politics, see Virilio (1986).
10. Eagleton's argument for the importance of maintaining fidelity to nationalist specificity under post-national, global conditions is starkly opposed to Richard Kearney's (1997) enthusiastic embrace of the possibilities of post-nationalism, in his book *Postnationalist Ireland: Politics, Culture,* which emerged at about the same time as Eagleton's.

References

Banville, J. (2000a), *God's Gift: A Version of* Amphitryon *by Heinrich von Kleist*, Oldcastle: The Gallery Press.
Banville, J. (2000b), *Eclipse,* London: Picador.
Banville, J. (2002), *Shroud*, London: Picador.
Beckett, S. (1973), *Murphy*, London: Picador.
Beckett, S. (1983), *Disjecta*, ed. Ruby Cohn, London: Calder.
Beckett, S. (1992), *Nohow On*, London: Calder.
Beckett, S. (1994), *Molloy, Malone Dies, The Unnamable*, London: Calder.
Beckett, S. (1995), *Complete Shorter Prose*, ed. S. E. Gontarski, New York: Grove Press.
Beckett, S. (2006), *Complete Dramatic Works*, London: Faber & Faber.
Bloch, E. (1988), *The Utopian Function of Art and Literature: Selected Essays*, trans. Jack Zipes and Frank Mecklenburg, Cambridge, MA: MIT Press.
Boxall, P. (2009), *Since Beckett: Contemporary Writing in the Wake of Modernism*, London: Continuum.
Coulter, C. and S. Coleman (2003), *The End of Irish History? Critical Reflections on the Celtic Tiger*, Manchester: Manchester University Press.
Cronin, M. (2002) 'Speed Limits: Ireland, Globalisation and the War against Time', in P. Kirby, Luke Gibbons and Michael Cronin (eds), *Reinventing Ireland: Culture and the Celtic Tiger*, 54–66, London: Pluto.
Deleuze, G. and F. Guattari (1988), *A Thousand Plateaus: Capitalism and Schizophrenia*, trans. Brian Massumi, London: Continuum.
de Man, P. (1984), *The Rhetoric of Romanticism*, New York: Columbia University Press.
Eagleton, T. (1998). *Crazy John and the Bishop and other Essays on Irish Culture*, Cork: Cork University Press.
Hardt, M. and A. Negri (2000), *Empire*, Cambridge, MA: Harvard University Press.
Hardt, M. and A. Negri (2006), *Multitude: War and Democracy in the Age of Empire*, London: Penguin.
Kearney, R. (1997), *Postnationalist Ireland: Politics, Culture, Philosophy*, London: Routledge.
Kiberd, D. (2005), 'The Celtic Tiger: A Cultural History', in Declan Kiberd (ed.), *The Irish Writer and the World*, 269–88, Cambridge: Cambridge University Press.
Kirby, P., L. Gibbons and M. Cronin (eds) (2002), *Reinventing Ireland: Culture and the Celtic Tiger*, London: Pluto.
Kleist, H. von (1955), 'Über das Marionettentheater', in Heinrich von Kleist, *Gesammelte Werke*, 384–92. Berlin: Aufbau-Verlag.
Kleist, H. von (1988), *Amphitryon*, in Heinrich von Kleist (ed.), *Five Plays*, trans. Martin Greenberg. New Haven, CT: Yale University Press.
Knowlson, J. (1996). *Damned to Fame: The Life of Samuel Beckett*, London: Bloomsbury.

Molière (1907), *Amphitryon*, in *The Plays of Molière*, trans. A. R. Waller. Edinburgh: John Grant.

Powell, K. T. (2005), '"Not a son but a survivor": Beckett... Joyce... Banville', *The Yearbook of English Studies*, 35: 199–211.

Sheehan, R., J. Banville and F. Stuart (1979), 'Novelists on the Novel: Ronan Sheehan Talks to John Banville and Francis Stuart', *The Crane Bag*, 3 (1): 76–84.

Virilio, P. (1986), *Speed and Politics: An Essay on Dromology*, trans. Mark Polizzotti, New York: Semiotext(e).

Part two

Literary engagements

3

'The vain thing menaced by the touch of the real': John Banville as a precursor to Henry James

Darren Borg

If, as Jorge Luis Borges asserts in his essay 'Kafka and His Precursors', 'Every writer *creates* his own precursors' ([1951] 2007: 201), in the sense that every reading of a writer is a kind of *rewriting*, and subsequent authors fashion the peculiarities of their precursors through a process of interpretive imitation, then we might regard John Banville as a precursor to Henry James. Banville himself says in an interview with Hugh Haughton that 'I see [James] as the first real modernist. … In a way he was a strain of modernism I wish we had followed. I think we're scrambling now to catch up with James's modernism, but we decided for whatever reason to follow Joyce and Beckett into experimentalism' (Haughton and Radley 2011: 865). Banville's Irish influences have long been the focus of the criticism of his novels, but after the publication of *Mrs Osmond* (2017), a comparison with James is unavoidable. *Mrs Osmond* nevertheless seems the natural culmination for Banville of a lifetime of studying the Master, and the novel unites many of the aspects of Banville's reading of James. In his interviews and essays, Banville has indicated a certain aesthetic stance similar to that of James, and has demonstrated a notable interest in literary theory, so that an approach such as that of Borges raises a number of significant questions: How does Banville's work revise our understanding of James's fiction? Or his criticism? Is Banville's distinction between the two strains of modernism useful or artificial? How do Banville and James treat similar thematic material, such as the growth of sensibility, consciousness or subjectivity? Is James's unique point of view Banvillean? An examination of Banville's interpretation of James, that is – in a Borgesian sense – Banville's *influence* on James, reveals the idiosyncrasies of the former author in the latter's work. In particular, Banville's peculiar treatment of the theme of alienated subjectivity in works such as *The Untouchable* (1997) and *Shroud* (2002) may be glimpsed in James's mature works, such as *The Ambassadors* (1903) and *The Golden Bowl* (1904), and Banville's subtle use of the uncanny brings similar aspects of James's 'The Jolly Corner' (1909) into relief. These Banvillean qualities of the Master's work we would not perceive in the same light had Banville not been *Banville*.

The Henry James whom we come to know through Banville emerges not only from *Mrs Osmond* and his other fiction but also from Banville's interviews and non-fiction writings. James, as the quotation above indicates, stands apart from Joyce and Beckett, according to Banville, because the Irish writers practice a form of 'experimentation'. But what does 'experimentation' mean? To be sure, James's mature style was experimental. James himself writes in 'The Art of Fiction', 'Art lives upon discussion, upon experiment, upon curiosity, upon variety of attempt, upon the exchange of views and the comparison of standpoints' ([1884] 1984: 44–5). James can rightly be seen as the first real modernist because he is concerned with the *representation* of experience; his psychological method of storytelling takes into account the artifice of so-called objective representations of life. James, indeed, takes as his starting point the novel's essential subjectivity: 'A novel is in its broadest definition a personal, a direct impression of life: that, to begin with, constitutes its value, which is greater or less according to the intensity of the impression' ([1884] 1984: 49–50). The 'direct impression of life' that James tries to capture in his works distinguishes his style from the realism of other late-nineteenth-century writers, whose work focuses on the material conditions of life. The realist presumes that the material world the novelist describes may be isolated from the individual consciousness that perceives it; accordingly, the realist writer attempts to represent the material world undistorted by the peculiarities of individual perception. But for James, the material depends for its significance on an organizing consciousness that makes meaning out of it. In his famous exchange with H. G. Wells, James thus complains that the realism of writers like Wells and Arnold Bennett omits the 'interest':

> When the author of 'Clayhanger' [Bennett] has put down upon the table, in dense unconfused array, every fact required to make the life of the Five Towns press upon us and to make our sense of it, so full fed, content us, we may very well go on for the time in the captive condition, the beguiled and bemused condition, the acknowledgment of which is in general our highest tribute to the temporary master of our sensibility. Nothing at such moments … may be of a more curious strain than the dawning unrest that suggests to us fairly our first critical comment: 'Yes, yes; but is this *all*? These are the circumstances of the

interest – we see, we see; but where is the interest itself, where and what is its centre and how are we to measure it in relation to *that*?' (Ellman and Feidelson 1965: 319)

James recognizes that meaning resides not in the object of representation but in the subject's *relation* to it. The realist overlooks the fact that, in the very attempt to provide an unmediated representation of the world, the writer must necessarily select, arrange and interpret the world *for* the reader. In other words, there can be no unmediated representation of the world within language, and the realist's description simply provides one particular *account* among many possible accounts of the material conditions of life. As James writes in his preface to *The Portrait of a Lady*, 'The house of fiction has in short not one window, but a million – a number of possible windows not to be reckoned, rather; every one of which has been pierced, or is still pierceable, in its vast front, by the need of the individual vision and by the pressure of the individual will' ([1908b] 1953: 46). James is the first great theorist of this modernist insight, and in his works – in his major phase in particular – he practices a method that locates significance in a particular subject's relationship to the world.

While Banville, in identifying James as 'the first real modernist', acknowledges the importance of James's pioneering method, he nevertheless sets James apart from other modernists, principally Joyce and Beckett. Banville assigns James a unique branch of modernism characterized by James's distinctive *manner* of rendering life through the consciousness of his subjects. Banville sees himself following James's line of modernism:

> I would go back to Henry James, who caught in a far more serious way than Joyce did, for instance, the sense of what it is actually to be conscious. Because when you read those late novels of Henry James you're wading through this fog that is exactly like life, whereas in Joyce you know exactly what Bloom is thinking, you know exactly what all these people are doing. (Haughton and Radley 2011: 865)

Although Banville here reduces – unjustly – Joyce's variety of techniques to a singular, transparent method, James's late style unquestionably differs from Joyce's, most notably Joyce's particular mode of stream-of-consciousness. But it is Banville's comparison here of the experience of reading James to 'wading through this fog that is exactly like life' that seems to place James in the narrower *impressionist* tradition within modernism, a line of writers that might include Joseph Conrad and Ford Madox Ford, among others. The impressionist recognizes the subjective nature of narrative; indeed, many impressionists take subjectivity itself as the theme of their narratives. In a sense, the impressionist attempts to correct the problem of realism by attempting to describe personal experience more accurately, with all of its distortions intact. An impressionist narrative thus often withholds understanding and, through a variety of techniques, represents the disordered consciousness of the individual. In his article 'On Impressionism', Ford describes the method's function:

> I suppose that Impressionism exists to render those queer effects of real life that are like so many views seen through bright glass – through glass so bright that whilst you perceive through it a landscape or a backyard, you are aware that, on its surface, it reflects the face of a person behind you. For the whole of life is really like that; we are almost always in one place with our minds somewhere quite other. (Hueffer [1914] 2012: 276–7)

The 'fog', to use Banville's term, of consciousness is made up of these mental images like the face in the glass and other thought processes or memories that interfere with direct, unmediated perception of objects. Accordingly, many of one's experiences remain unincorporated into one's general interpretation of the world, and the object-in-itself persists in its obscurity. This obscurity, Banville contends, marks James's fiction to a much greater degree than it does the fiction of Joyce and other 'experimental' writers.

Banville explains in an earlier interview that he views works of art (of which not every novel is an instance) as 'closed'. As opposed to an 'open' novel in which the author interprets the object *for* the reader, a closed novel emphasizes the *absolutely unknowable* nature of the object by revealing the mediation of subjectivity. James, he argues, focuses on the psychological encounter with an essential mystery at the centre of life:

> To me the work of art is always closed. It doesn't invite the reader, or listener, in. ... James has managed to make novels that were psychologically profound but which were also closed works of art. There is a profound mystery about the best of Henry James' books, even though they are perfectly comprehensible. The object itself stands in its own mystery. And I – I suppose I have been following that line, the Jamesian line rather than the Joycean line. Because I think Joyce is a dead end. (Schwall 1997: 17)

The closed novels of James, according to Banville, preserve the mystery behind appearances in a way that Joyce fails to do. Works such as James writes *alienate* the subject; they withhold meaning and make the world unfamiliar. Indeed, Elke D'hoker notes the resemblance of Banville's theory to the Russian formalist notion of *ostranenie*, or defamiliarization. In her book, *Visions of Alterity: Representation in the Works of John Banville*, D'hoker argues that Banville challenges the assumptions on which an objective point of view is founded in order to give the representation of the object a queer, unreal quality: 'Banville suggests that by taking objects out of their characteristic surroundings, and by placing them in an exciting new light, an unusual, even uncanny, dimension of reality may be revealed' (2004: 81). *Ostranenie* refers to this process by which a work of art draws attention to perception itself. Victor Shklovsky, who develops the theory of *ostranenie* in his book *Theory of Prose*, believes the purpose of art to be the experience of this very transformation of the object into the image. 'By "estranging" objects and complicating form', Shklovsky writes, 'the device of art makes perception long and "laborious". The perceptual process in art has a purpose all its own and ought to be extended to the fullest. *Art is a means of experiencing the process of creativity. The artifact itself is quite unimportant*' ([1925] 1991: 6). Banville echoes Shklovsky in his essay 'Survivors of Joyce':

> Far from allowing us to know things with any immediacy, art, I believe, *makes things strange*. ... This is not such a mystical, not such a high-falutin process as it may seem, this interiorisation of things, this taking into us of the world, of all that stuff out there which is not ourselves. It happens all the time, continuously, in art. And its result is a different order of understanding, which *allows* the thing in its thereness, its outsideness, its absolute otherness. (1990: 78)

Works such as those of James, which Banville considers 'closed', then may be described as impressionist works that circumscribe the object and take instead as their subject matter the meaning-making process. Closed works, in other words, represent being in the world without assimilating the essence of reality.

While Banville unquestionably admires Joyce, he asserts that James accomplishes the task of art far better than Joyce. Isolating the object-in-itself requires that the artist not appear to attach his or her own significance to it, and even in Joyce's greatest work, Banville detects the author attempting to impose his own truth: '*Ulysses* seems to me a completely closed work, but one that is trying to be open. Take the Molly Bloom monologue in the end. I hate it. It is completely fraudulent. Technically, it's ... miraculous. But it is a fraud as well' (Schwall 1997: 17). Remarkably, even when Banville speaks high praise of Joyce's ability to disguise himself, we find Banville referring to a passage from James to illustrate *Joyce's* greatness. 'Joyce', says Banville, 'was never silent, but he was certainly cunning. He was the supreme escape-artist, a Houdini of the word. ... Under the guise of an all-accepting humanism, Joyce created an impenetrable fortress, an edifice like that in which Maggie Verver finds herself immured in *The Golden Bowl*' (1990: 80). The passage to which Banville refers is the well-known 'pagoda' metaphor from James's novel: 'It had reared itself there like some strange, tall tower of ivory, or perhaps rather some wonderful, beautiful, but outlandish pagoda, a structure plated with hard, bright porcelain, coloured and figured and adorned, at the overhanging eaves, with silver bells that tinkled, ever so charmingly, when stirred by chance airs' ([1904] 1983: 299). James, who largely disapproved of the first person, employs free indirect discourse here and permits neither his character nor himself to occupy the first-person point of view in the narration. The impregnability of the image derives in part from the artist's refusal to intervene and permit the narrative to adhere to a discrete subject position. Moreover, each of the adjectives in the passage – 'strange', 'wonderful', 'beautiful', 'outlandish' – supplants its predecessor as each fails, one after the other, to contain the meaning of 'it'. The description thus hovers between subject and object as the artifice of language becomes apparent. This James – the Banvillean James – is less the author of 'a personal, a direct impression of life' than the author of an *indirect, mediated* impression.

The strange inaccessibility of the truth behind appearances often leads James's characters to become suspicious about the basic assumptions on which they act out their lives. Maggie Verver becomes ever so slowly aware of her husband's affair. The meaning of their circumstances becomes finally for her subjective. She and her rival, Charlotte, sometimes seem to contend for the privilege of defining their situation. James, following Maggie's growing consciousness as the roles of the two women reverse, compares 'the deluded condition' to a cage:

> Even the conviction that Charlotte was but awaiting some chance really to test her trouble upon her lover's wife left Maggie's sense meanwhile open as to the sight of gilt wires and bruised wings, the spacious but suspended cage, the home of eternal unrest, of pacings, beatings, shakings, all so vain, into which the baffled consciousness helplessly resolved itself. The cage was the deluded condition, and Maggie, as having known delusion – rather! – understood the nature of cages. She walked round Charlotte's … and saw her companion's face as that of a prisoner looking through bars. ([1904] 1983: 465–6)

The prisoner in the cage, first Maggie and then Charlotte, witnesses the world but misperceives its significance. The cage, like Banville's 'fog' of consciousness, represents the subject's partial understanding of the world. Maggie manages to escape her cage by taking over the role of interpreter of the circumstances after her discovery of Amerigo's adultery. In not confronting Charlotte about the affair, Maggie withholds her discovery of it. Charlotte thus continues in her deluded state. In other words, authenticity becomes the site of a power struggle between *versions* of the truth. In *The Golden Bowl*, Charlotte loses this contest. In their final confrontation, Maggie knowingly plays along with Charlotte's delusion as they observe the others at cards. Maggie assumes supremacy, remaining, herself, impregnable: 'Side by side, for three minutes, they fixed this picture of quiet harmonies, the positive charm of it and, as might have been said, the full significance – which, as was now brought home to Maggie, could be no more, after all, than a matter of interpretation, differing always for a different interpreter' ([1904] 1983: 476). This conflict of interpretations between Maggie and Charlotte underscores James's modernist tendency, in Banville's view, to 'make things strange' by focusing not on the world itself but on the interior process of understanding that occupies the subject in a strange encounter with a situation whose meaning is obscure. Thus in *Mrs Osmond*, Banville echoes James's metaphor of the 'house of fiction' as Isabel Archer contemplates her own changed understanding: 'She had been allowed to live along, happily, in the house of herself, which, as she acknowledged now, was no more substantial in dimensions than a doll's house' (2017: 15).

Lambert Strether, the protagonist of James's *The Ambassadors*, undergoes a transformation of consciousness similar to Isabel Archer's and Maggie Verver's. Strether goes to Paris on an errand to retrieve his fiancée's son, Chad Newsome, whose mother fears he has come under the spell of a 'wicked woman' ([1903] 1994: 44). Strether's time in Europe exposes him to a broad range of experiences, and he comes not only to sympathize with Chad but also to believe he, Strether, has failed to live his own life. As in *The Golden Bowl*, James narrates the story in the third person, but follows the consciousness of Strether as he comes to recognize the artifice of his previous life. At one point in the novel, Mrs Newsome, weary of Strether's deferrals, sends a second wave of emissaries to complete the task. The new ambassadors, Chad's sister Sarah Pocock, her husband Jim and Jim's sister Mamie, perceive the situation differently. The Pococks' provincial interpretation of the situation comes into conflict with Strether's and, as in *The Golden Bowl*, the main character's version must compete with an alternate reading of events. Consequently, Strether begins to doubt the authenticity of his own view:

> Was he, on this question of Chad's improvement, fantastic and away from the truth? Did he live in a false world, a world that had grown simply to suit him, and was his present slight irritation … but the alarm of the vain thing menaced by the touch of the real? Was this contribution of the real possibly the mission of the Pococks? … Had they come in short to be sane where Strether was destined to feel that he himself had only been silly? ([1903] 1994: 214)

The conflict of interpretations throws Strether's nascent self-certainty – the 'vain thing' – into strangeness, and his former view of life – what he imagines momentarily as the 'real' – becomes a threat to his new sense of identity. The moment passes, however, and James continues, 'He glanced at such a contingency, but it failed to hold him long' ([1903] 1994: 214). What is 'real' becomes a matter of interpretation. The significance of the situation is subjective; there is no essential meaning beneath the surface, or, as Banville says, 'the object itself stands in its own mystery' (Schwall 1997: 17). Strether's 'touch of the real', indeed, is nothing more than a function of language, of the subject-object division that characterizes consciousness. Banville's Henry James tells the story of the modern subject's confrontation with this unassimilable aspect of the world, and his recurrent theme is the subject's intuitive grasp of its own profound alienation.

Yet something more sinister lurks beyond this realization. Seemingly in order to emphasize the incompatibility of realities experienced by different sorts of persons, Banville, in *Mrs Osmond*, devotes a large section of the novel to Osmond's point of view. He writes, 'It did not trouble him to any appreciable extent that his wife had been let in on his paltry secrets. In truth, he considered them not as secrets so much as – what? Discretionary withholdings? Pragmatic suppressions?' (2017: 183). Osmond's euphemisms indicate not only a conflict of interpretation but the shameless willingness to manipulate appearances that enables him to seduce and control Isabel from the beginning. As James writes of him in *The Portrait of a Lady*, it is 'pose' that defines him above all else. There are those, in other words, whose own images of themselves require that they 'read' others into their own stories and thus convert them into inauthentic 'portraits' of themselves. James's protagonists' alienation from the 'real' makes their anxious navigation of the world all the more perilous since deceitful individuals such as Isabel's Osmond or Maggie Verver's Charlotte, who have mastered the art of deception, lie behind the faces we hold most dear. Much of Banville's own work explores the same theme, but before James could influence Banville, Banville had, as Borges says, to *create* his own precursor; he had to define James for himself. Banville is not unlike his own character Victor Maskell from *The Untouchable*, who claims to have 'invented' the artist Nicolas Poussin. Maskell, an expert on Poussin, says,

> One might say, I have invented Poussin. I frequently think this is the chief function of the art historian, to synthesize, to concentrate, to *fix* his subject, to pull together into a unity all the disparate strands of character and inspiration

and achievement that make up this singular being, the painter at his easel. After me, Poussin is not, cannot be, what he was before me. ... I saw in Poussin a paradigm of myself. (1997: 311–12)

As with Victor Maskell, it is Banville's own rendering of Henry James which influences him; Banville prefigures James by synthesizing, concentrating and *fixing* him as the storyteller of the alienated subject.

Banville's novels *The Untouchable* and *Shroud* address the self's mistrust of its own inauthenticity on multiple levels. Each takes as its protagonist a fictionalized version of a historical figure who himself led a double-life. Victor Maskell of *The Untouchable* is Banville's reinvention of Anthony Blunt, the art historian who proved to be a Soviet spy, while Axel Vander, the protagonist of *Shroud*, is Banville's version of Paul de Man, the literary critic who was posthumously exposed as an anti-Semite who had written pro-Nazi articles for a Belgian newspaper. While Banville's earlier works, such as *Doctor Copernicus* and *Kepler*, also take historical figures as their main characters, *The Untouchable* and *Shroud*, more than any other of the author's works, complicate the notion of the self because Banville not only makes his characters masquerade as other people but also combines figures. Victor Maskell, for instance, possesses aspects of the early life of the Irish poet Louis MacNeice, and Axel Vander's story shares some details with the life of Marxist theorist Louis Althusser. These other selves do not round out Banville's characters but rather serve as fragments of identity which invade and haunt their principal selves. The Irish past of Victor Maskell, for example, lends another dimension of inauthenticity to the character as he conceals his Irishness along with his espionage. And Axel Vander is haunted in *Shroud* by the wife he may have murdered, one of the elements of Althusser's life that Banville includes. The alternate selves, in other words, function in a similar fashion to the 'fog' of consciousness that Banville discerns in the works of Henry James.

Like Strether in *The Ambassadors* and Maggie in *The Golden Bowl*, Banville's protagonists become disoriented by their manifold identities and begin to question themselves. Derek Hand, in his book *John Banville: Exploring Fictions*, writes a description of Banville's work that coincides perfectly with Banville's own assessment of James:

> The story he tells is one in which his protagonists come to understand the limitations of the human imagination's engagement with the real world. All of his writing is an attempt to delineate this strain and tension at the heart of the modern condition. It is a crisis permeating all levels of his characters' experience

and existence, so that the reality of the self, others, the world, are questioned and interrogated. (2002: 1)

Banville's duplicitous characters crave a unified, coherent self but find their attempts to define themselves confounded by the peculiar sense of play-acting that derives from the decentred nature of subjectivity. Banville, however, accomplishes his purpose in his own manner. Unlike James, Banville employs the first person in his narratives and presents them as the fictional memoirs of his characters. While James's use of free indirect narration emphasizes decentredness by evading or hovering between discrete subject positions, Banville's use of the first person demonstrates the very displacement that founds the Cartesian subject. His characters strive to isolate an essential core of selfhood as they weave their long narratives, yet they inevitably lament the absence of the transcendent, true self they seek. Victor Maskell declares in *The Untouchable*, 'I shall strip away layer after layer of grime – the toffee coloured varnish and caked soot left by a lifetime of dissembling – until I come to the very thing itself and know it for what it is. My soul. My self' (1997: 9). Yet even in this declaration, there lies an element of disingenuousness – the next sentence begins, 'When I laugh out loud like this ...' (1997: 9). Maskell's extreme unreliability and multiple masks ultimately prevent even him from locating the 'thing itself'. In *The Newton Letter*, the narrator undergoes a similar self-examination after being searchingly observed by the character Ottilie. Kersti Tarien Powell, in '"The answer ... is yes and no": John Banville, Henry James, and *The Ambassadors*', writes, '[The narrator] does not want her to know him, as this will force him to subject himself to his own self-scrutiny. His attitude indicates his need to privilege himself over others, but, more importantly, it emphasizes an essential vacuity in him' (2015: 313). And Axel Vander begins his narrative in *Shroud* by announcing, 'I am going to explain myself, to myself, and to you' and that 'the name, my name, is Axel Vander, on that much I insist' (Banville 2002: 4–5); the reader nevertheless learns in the course of Vander's narrative that even the name Axel Vander belongs not to the narrator, whose real name we never learn, but to the man whose identity he has appropriated. Thus, Banville exposes the pretence of the 'I' and the deficiency that it conceals. The 'real' self is a function of language, and the discursive nature of the subject precludes the wholeness or immediacy the characters seek.

Banville's characters experience the uncanny sensation of a divided self when they sense the mediation that gives them a false sense of self-certainty. The feeling of pleasure Victor Maskell derives from the viewing of artwork eludes him as he loses the security of a coherent identity:

> I know, and who should know better, that art is supposed to teach us to see the world in all its solidity and truth, but in those years it was the possibility of transcendence, even for the space of a quarter of an hour, that I sought after repeatedly. … And yet, the magic never quite worked. There was something wrong, something too deliberate, too self-conscious, in these occasions of intense contemplation. A suspicion of fraudulence always attended the moment. I seemed to be looking not at the pictures, but at myself looking at them. (Banville 1997: 287–8)

Maskell seeks the authentic behind the artifice but fails to find it. His contemplation of the object of art indeed reinforces his own alienation; his 'I' becomes the representation of a representation, and the transcendence he seeks evades him. In *Shroud*, Axel Vander undergoes a similar experience. Gazing at his reflection in a mirror, Vander says,

> I had the sensation then, as so often, of shifting slightly aside from myself, as if I were going out of focus and separating into two. I wonder if other people feel as I do, seeming never to be wholly present wherever I happen to be, seeming not so much a person as a contingency, misplaced and adrift in time. My true source and destination are always elsewhere. (Banville 2002: 44)

Vander's reflection here functions as his uncanny double; that is, the episode falls within a long tradition of doubling in literature that reaches its height in the gothic romance and continues into impressionist fiction and beyond. Otto Rank conducts one of the first psychoanalytic examinations of the double in his book *The Double: A Psychoanalytic Study* (1914). Rank identifies the double in stories by E. T. A. Hoffman, Jean-Paul, Adelbert von Chamisso, Oscar Wilde, Guy de Maupassant, Edgar Allan Poe and Dostoyevsky. To Rank's list may be added works by James Hogg, Robert Louis Stevenson, Henry James and Joseph Conrad. Rank observes in a number of these stories that the double functions as a herald of death and a disturbance of the sexual instinct. Rank associates the double with early religion's identification of the shadow with one's soul and concludes,

> The thought of death is rendered supportable by assuring oneself of a second life, after this one, as a double. As in the threat to narcissism by sexual love, so in the threat of death does the idea of death (originally averted by the double) recur in this figure who, according to general superstition, announces death or whose injury harms the individual. (Rank [1925] 1979: 85)

The double as it occurs in impressionist fiction, however, suggests not death but the absence of an essential part, or an impenetrable aspect, of oneself. Conrad's narrator in 'The Secret Sharer', for instance, says, 'Part of me was absent. That mental feeling of being in two places at once affected me physically as if the mood of secrecy had penetrated my very soul' ([1910] 2007: 32–3). Freud, in his essay 'The Uncanny' (1919), accounts for this difference by tracing the origin of the double not to early religion but to the early stages of psychic development. Freud argues that notions of the soul as the immortal double 'have sprung from the soil of unbounded self-love, from the primary narcissism which dominates the mind of the child and of primitive man. But when this stage has been surmounted, the "double" reverses its aspect. From having been an assurance of immortality, it becomes the uncanny harbinger of death' ([1919] 1955: 235). The double, in other words, is the individual's *ego*, originally founded at the outcome of the Oedipus complex, projected outward. This seemingly coherent 'I' represents only part of the psyche but serves as the self in everyday life. In a sense, it is a necessary fiction that allows the individual to function and perform his or her role in civilized society. Its appearance *outside* of oneself, however, suggests to the individual his or her own fictitiousness and generates the peculiar uncanny dread associated with the double. In *Mrs Osmond*, for instance, Isabel avoids her reflection in mirrors, and tells her friend Henrietta, 'Nothing is as uncanny as the look of one's own eyes peering out of a glass' (Banville 2017: 117).

From a Lacanian standpoint, the double evokes an even earlier period of development, before language, that of the mirror stage, in which the child identifies with the *imago* and subsequently gains a coherent sense of self. In his 'Mirror Stage' essay, Lacan argues that the child assumes 'the armor of an alienating identity' ([1949] 2006: 78). The double in literature thus represents the spectral image that suggests to the individual his or her decentred notion of self. The real self, prior to this phase, evades both imaginary and symbolic representation.

Victor Maskell and Axel Vander share this experience, albeit to a lesser extent, with Spencer Brydon, the protagonist of James's story 'The Jolly Corner' (1908). In 'The Jolly Corner', Brydon, who has lived a life abroad, returns to his childhood home and pursues his double through the passages of the old, empty house. Brydon imagines this double as the version of himself that he might have become had he stayed in New York. Brydon himself displays remarkable self-certainty at the outset of the story: 'I know at least', he says, 'what I am' ([1908a] 2004: 294). The crisis of the story occurs at the end when Brydon encounters his alter ego. James, writing in his characteristic style, follows Brydon's thought process in the third person. As Brydon comes upon his double, James writes,

> Horror, with the sight, had leaped into Brydon's throat, gasping there in a sound he couldn't utter; for the bared identity was too hideous as *his*, and his glare was the passion of his protest. The face, *that* face, Spencer Brydon's? – he searched it still, but looking away from it in dismay and denial, falling straight from his height of sublimity. It was unknown, inconceivable, awful, disconnected from any possibility – ! He had been 'sold', … : the presence before him was a presence, the horror within him a horror … . Such an identity fitted his at *no* point, made its alternative monstrous. A thousand times yes, as it came upon him nearer now – the face was the face of a stranger. ([1908a] 2004: 312)

As in his novels, James's narration inhabits the thoughts of his character without embodying them in the first person, displacing the subject of consciousness. Consequently, Brydon *and* his double occupy the third person, even while the reader is made aware of the character's interior reaction to the double. Brydon identifies with the figure initially, and it inspires horror as he recognizes its familiarity and simultaneous alterity: '*That* face, Spencer Brydon's?' The adjectives that describe the figure mark it as undefinable; it is 'unknown, inconceivable, awful, disconnected from any possibility', and, finally, 'monstrous'. Brydon's final assessment – 'the face was the face of a stranger' – remains ambiguous. Does he notice a difference here? Or does he now consider *his own* face strange? In the manner of an impressionist, James *defamiliarizes* the object and accentuates the mediation of subjectivity. As with Banville's characters, the double becomes a reminder of the self's contingency and part of the myriad thoughts, memories and illusions that cloud the mind.

Banville is himself a double of sorts, as many have noted, being the author of a number of mystery novels under the pseudonym Benjamin Black, but his mimicry of James in *Mrs Osmond* adds another dimension of the uncanny to the novel. Regardless of the quality of Banville's pastiche, readers familiar with the two authors' styles must inevitably question themselves: Does this sound like James? Is it Banville, or some hybrid of the two? As Jeffrey Eugenides writes in *The New York Times* review of Banville's book, 'Throughout "Mrs Osmond," I had the uncanny feeling of recognizing its sentences as Jamesian without feeling that James had written them, as though by the very act of impersonating James, Banville had managed to illuminate how inimitable James is' (Eugenides 2017). If one takes a Borgesian approach, however, and considers *Mrs Osmond* not an imitation or a version of James, but rather the work of an important precursor,

Banville's novel provides the reader with a certain key to James's narration, disclosing perhaps its most haunting aspect, that is, its radical ambiguity and uncanniness.

John Banville formulates Henry James as the great originator of the particular modernist tradition which conveys most accurately the 'fog' of consciousness. James, for Banville, is the pioneer of the 'closed', mediated impression that never adheres to a unitary subject. To this end, James employs a number of literary techniques, most notably his taking one or two characters as his centre of consciousness and narrating their encounters with the limits of perception. Banville precedes *this* James – his personal formulation – in his own work's emphasis on the individual subject's exploration of mediation, masquerade and incoherent subjectivity. The Banvillean aspects of James's work thus surface in greater clarity and intensity than they would were Banville not a lucid *reader* of James.

References

Banville, J. (1990), 'Survivors of Joyce', in Augustine Martin (ed.), *James Joyce: The Artist and the Labyrinth*, 73–81, London: Ryan.
Banville, J. (1997), *The Untouchable*, New York: Vintage.
Banville, J. (2002), *Shroud*, New York: Vintage.
Banville, J. (2017), *Mrs Osmond*, New York: Alfred A. Knopf.
Borges, J. L. ([1951] 2007), 'Kafka and His Precursors', in Donald E. Yates and James E. Irby (eds), *Labyrinths*, 199–201, New York: New Directions.
Conrad, J. ([1910] 2007), 'The Secret Sharer', in Michael Gorra (ed.), *The Portable Conrad*, 7–46, New York: Penguin.
D'hoker, E. (2004), *Visions of Alterity: Representation in the Works of John Banville*, Amsterdam: Rodopi.
Ellman, R. (ed.), and C. Feidelson, Jr. (1965), *The Modern Tradition: Backgrounds of Modern Literature*, New York: Oxford University Press.
Eugenides, J. (2017), 'Whatever Happened to Isabel Archer? John Banville's "Mrs Osmond" Picks Up Where Henry James Left Off', *The New York Times*, 20 November. Available online: https://www.nytimes.com/2017/11/20/books/review/mrs-osmond-john-banville-henry-james-portrait-lady-sequel.html (accessed 24 June 2018).
Freud, S. ([1919] 1955), 'The Uncanny', in James Strachey (trans.), *The Standard Edition of the Complete Psychological Works of Sigmund Freud*, 218–52, London: Hogarth Press.
Hand, D. (2002), *John Banville: Exploring Fictions*, Dublin: The Liffey Press.

Haughton, H. and B. Radley (2011), 'An Interview with John Banville', *Modernism/Modernity*, 18 (4): 855-69.
Hueffer [Ford], F. M. ([1914] 2012), 'On Impressionism', in Martin Stannard (ed.), *The Good Soldier: A Norton Critical Edition*, 271-87, New York: Norton.
James, H. ([1908b] 1953), Preface to *The Portrait of a Lady*, in R. P. Blackmur (ed.), *The Art of the Novel: Critical Prefaces by Henry James*, 40-58, New York: Scribner's.
James, H. ([1904] 1983), *The Golden Bowl*, ed. Virginia Llewelyn Smith, Oxford: Oxford University Press.
James, H. ([1884] 1984), 'The Art of Fiction', in Leon Edel and Mark Wilson (eds), *Henry James: Literary Criticism*, 44-65, New York: Library of America.
James, H. ([1903] 1994), *The Ambassadors: A Norton Critical Edition*, ed. S. P. Rosenbaum. New York: Norton.
James, H. ([1881] 1998), *The Portrait of a Lady*, ed. Nicola Bradbury, Oxford: Oxford University Press.
James, H. ([1908a] 2004), 'The Jolly Corner', in John Auchard (ed.), *The Portable Henry James*, 283-318, New York: Penguin.
Lacan, J. ([1949] 2006), 'The Mirror Stage as Formative of the I Function as Revealed in Psychoanalytic Experience', in Bruce Fink (trans.), *Écrits*, 75-81, New York: Norton.
Powell, K. T. (2015), '"The answer…is yes and no": John Banville, Henry James, and *The Ambassadors*', *Irish University Review*, 45 (2): 302-19.
Rank, O. ([1925] 1979), *The Double: A Psychoanalytic Study*, trans. Harry Tucker, Jr., New York: Meridian.
Schwall, H. (1997), 'An Interview with John Banville', *The European English Messenger*, 6 (1): 13-19.
Shklovsky, V. ([1925] 1991), *Theory of Prose*, trans. Benjamin Sher, London: Dalkey Archive Press.

4

From Isabel Archer to Mrs Osmond: John Banville reinterprets Henry James

Elke D'hoker

Introduction

In a 2013 review of Michael Gorra's *Portrait of a Novel: Henry James and the Making of an American Masterpiece*, John Banville speculates on Isabel's uncertain fate at the end of James's *The Portrait of a Lady*: 'What will [Isabel] do? Will she dismiss Madame Merle from her life and confront Osmond and face him down? Will she perhaps let him have her money in return for his releasing her? Will she accept the manly blandishments of the ever-persistent Caspar Goodwood and run away with him?' (Banville 2013). While these questions have preoccupied many readers of *The Portrait of a Lady*, Banville is the first to have addressed them in a full-length sequel to James's novel. While *Mrs Osmond* (2017) is both the first sequel to *The Portrait* and the first sequel Banville has ever written, *Mrs Osmond* nevertheless fits in Banville's long-standing practice of adapting canonical literary texts to suit his own purposes. In *Adaptation and Appropriation*, Julie Sanders defines adaptation as a subcategory of intertextuality, a 'sustained engagement with a single text or source' (Sanders 4). Examples of such adaptive practice in Banville's oeuvre are *The Newton Letter*, which rewrites Hugo von Hofmannsthal's *Ein Brief*; *Mefisto*, modelled on Goethe's *Faust*; *Ghosts*, with its new take on Shakespeare's *The Tempest*; and *The Infinities*, which offers a novelistic version of Kleist's play *Amphitryon*. And even though none of these novels has the sustained stylistic imitation that characterizes *Mrs Osmond*, Banville had already performed a similar act of literary ventriloquism in Benjamin Black's Marlowe novel, *The Black-Eyed Blonde*. Nor is *Mrs Osmond* the first time Banville turns to James for inspiration: *The Sea* revisits 'The Turn of the Screw' and, as Kersti Tarien Powell's study of Banville's manuscripts has shown, *The Newton Letter* is modelled on *The Ambassadors* (2015).

As Sanders points out, adaptation can variously be a 'transpositional practice, casting a specific genre into another generic mode', an 'editorial practice … an exercise of trimming and pruning', or an 'amplificatory procedure engaged in addition, expansion, accretion, and interpolation', which is where sequels, prequels or supplements find their place (Sanders 2006: 18). What characterizes the adaptive practice across these forms, however, is that it involves a 'reinterpretation of established texts' within a new generic, cultural or temporal setting (Sanders 2006: 19). In *Mrs Osmond* too such a process of reinterpretation is at work. Although the book ostensibly picks up where James left his heroine in *The Portrait*, *Mrs Osmond* also revisits many crucial scenes from James's novel itself. Reviewers of the book have mostly remarked on the seamless continuity between *The Portrait* and *Mrs Osmond*. They praise Banville's remarkable act of 'ventriloquism' (White 2017), his 'perfect' evocation of James's characteristic 'style and prose rhythms' (Wood 2018, Eugenides 2017), his unflinching focus on the inner life of his protagonist (Battersby 2017) or the way he pays 'homage' to James (Scholes 2017) through an 'impressive recreation of [his] atmospheres and pacing' (Adams 2017).

While Banville's novel has an unmistakable Jamesian feel to it, a closer reading also reveals many significant shifts in Banville's recreation of the characters, scenes and themes of James's novel. Commenting on the different endings readers have imagined for Isabel Archer, Michael Gorra notes that 'the lives we choose for [Isabel] say more about us than they do about the character herself' (2012: 333). This certainly holds true for *Mrs Osmond* as well: Isabel's sequence of encounters with various characters from the original not only propel her story forward, they also look backward. Yet in revisiting these familiar scenes, dialogues and characters, Banville casts them in a slightly different light. Hence, they bring out Banville's own characteristic concerns as well as his own take on the moral dilemmas of James's novel. In this chapter, therefore, I propose to investigate the differences between James's Isabel and Banville's, between *The Portrait* and its sequel, so as to determine what they reveal about Banville's own worldview and preoccupations, his aesthetic practice and thematic concerns.

From psychology to representation

As Darren Borg also points out in his chapter on James in this collection, Banville has repeatedly praised James as 'the first modern novelist' (Banville 1981: 16), 'the first real modernist' (Haughton and Radley 2011), and as the inventor of 'the psychological novel' (Banville 2017b), which offers 'a kind of cloud chamber in which are tracked the tiniest particles of his characters' feelings, motives and desires' (Banville 2013). While we can certainly recognize Banville's picture of James as the author of great psychological novels which stage the drama of consciousness with unprecedented detail and authenticity, Banville's celebration of James is itself curiously at odds with his own professed abhorrence of psychology. One of his favourite quotations in this respect is Kafka's 'Never again psychology!'. Referring to this quote once again in a recent interview, he adds, 'I'm going to have that carved in marble and fixed to the wall above my desk' (Schwall 2017). Darren Borg offers a way out of this strange paradox by suggesting that 'the Banvillean James is less the author of "a personal, a direct impression of life" than the author of an *indirect, mediated* impression'. Banville's staging of a particular subject's personal perception of the world serves not so much to reveal individual consciousness as to highlight the inherent mystery of the world, the impossibility of objective representation and, Borg argues, the concomitant experience of alienation on the part of the subject. Put differently, if Banville and James share an interest in the drama of the perceiving mind, James explains the limitations of subjective perception through the personal context and psychology of his characters, while for Banville these limitations are the result of the always already mediated relation between self and world, which makes a true understanding of the world impossible. This shift in emphasis from psychology to representation also characterizes Banville's recreation of Isabel in *Mrs Osmond*. Although this sustained exploration of a female consciousness is unprecedented in his oeuvre, Banville is ultimately less interested in Isabel's 'feelings, motives and desires' than in her – quintessentially Banvillean – experience of the strangeness of the world beyond the self.

Banville's lack of interest in the psychological processes that would motivate Isabel's actions and decisions in *Mrs Osmond* is evident, first, in the way her actions are all represented as spur-of-the-moment decisions, the result of unconscious processes she hardly understands herself. Her decision, at the outset of the novel, to withdraw a large sum of money is described as an 'impulse' which causes her to be 'surprised at herself' (Banville 2017a: 26). Talking to Mr Goresby, the bank manager, similarly, she 'was surprised to hear herself add that she might stop in Paris for a day or two on the way. She frowned, and glanced aside; she could not think from where had come the idea of Paris—it had popped into her head at just that moment—and wondered at herself for it' (Banville 2017a: 25). Isabel's donation of the money to Miss Janeway's suffragist cause is also not so much an active decision as the result of a leaving the bag behind 'by mistake' (Banville

2017a: 373). Even more importantly, Isabel's scheme to 'use [her] fortune … to buy [her] freedom' from her husband (Banville 2017a: 63) and to weld his plight to that of Madame Merle is presented not as the result of a long process of agonizing thought and deliberation, but rather as something that 'fell upon me in a tearing rush' (Banville 2017a: 102), something that had 'flared up in her mind, like a tiny spot of light shining in the distance on a dark night. Was it the flame of a lantern, to lead her forward?' (Banville 2017a: 174). On the train to Rome, to give a final example, Isabel 'changed her mind, or something had changed her mind for her, she did not know which' and decides to get off in Florence instead (Banville 2017a: 228).

In the famous ellipsis between chapters 30 and 31 of *The Portrait*, James also withholds from his readers the psychological processes that have led to Isabel's accepting of Osmond's marriage proposal. Yet, after he has taken the reader by surprise in depicting the fact of the engagement, he does allow Isabel plenty of scope to justify her decision and explain her motivations. By contrast, Banville's Isabel remains as perplexed by her decisions as the reader. She lets Mrs Touchett and the Countess Gemini draw their own cynical conclusions about her 'motives' (Banville 2017a: 236, 369) and defies Henrietta Stackpole's demands for an explanation: 'What more would you wish to know? It's over. *Factum est*' (Banville 2017a: 357). The only reflection on her decision is her sudden doubt, when confronted with Osmond, as to whether she had 'the right to play the avenging angel, and with the flaming sword of her self-righteousness drive the unhappy pair of sinners, not naked into the fallen world, but all too suitably apparelled into a hell that was largely of her own devising?' (Banville 2017a: 286). In its substitution of metaphor for motivation, this example is highly characteristic of the way Banville dramatizes Isabel's consciousness through images, scenes and metaphors rather than through the psychological scrutiny of James's novel.

From modernism to postmodernism

The metaphor of the 'avenging angel' is typical too in the highly theatrical dimension it confers on Isabel's thoughts and perceptions. Indeed, dramatic images abound throughout *Mrs Osmond* as Isabel often perceives the world – certain scenes, other people, herself – through the prism of the stage. Minor characters in particular are presented in actorly terms: Miss Janeway's maid is likened to 'one of those minor but necessary characters in a drawing-room drama, who pop out from the wings to interrupt the action so that the audience may have an opportunity to shuffle their feet and lean back in their seats and cough' (Banville 2017a: 52), while Miss Janeway herself 'seemed to Isabel a primordial figure, something out of the ancient drama, one of the shroud-clad anonymous Cassandras who step forward from the chorus calmly to prophesy the sacked city, the toppling towers and the errant knight expiring in a welter of his own blood' (Banville 2017a: 66). The patron of an Italian restaurant 'flash[ed] menus at them as a samurai would his sword' and then 'bowed and beamed and backed away, wriggling his fingers before him in a comical gesture of fawning servitude' (Banville 2017a: 246, 255). Certain scenes too are likened to set-pieces from the theatre or a painting: walking across London with the bag of money, Isabel 'pictured an eye-patched brigand of the streets leaping up at her with a flashing blade held fast in his teeth and snatching the case out of her grasp and plunging back into the passing crowd as swiftly as he had come'; some characters are 'grouped there so picturesquely, they might have stepped out of the *fête galante* depicted on the wall above them'; and a day of visits is compared to 'a comedy act in the music-hall' (Banville 2017a: 31, 172–3, 89). Isabel also sees her own life in theatrical terms: 'She had always set a great store by the concept of personal independence: each life is given once, with no possibility of repetition or revision, and the individual actor on whom the vivifying gift is bestowed must play his hour upon the stage with unflagging conviction and in the full realization that there will be only an opening night, with no "run" to follow' (Banville 2017a: 111).

Such theatrical tropes are of course a fixture of Banville's postmodern prose in general. They highlight the mediated quality of perception and representation, the way these are always informed by earlier stories, images and scenes. They confer a sense of postmodern belatedness on *Mrs Osmond* and bring an inevitable parodic tinge to its re-enactment of James's modernist narrative. An interesting scene in this respect is Banville's ironic recreation of the tea scene that opens James's novel. Following that famous first line, 'Under certain circumstances there are few hours in life more agreeable than the hour dedicated to the ceremony known as afternoon tea' (James 1966: 5), James's narrator proceeds to evoke the 'perfect' circumstances in which Ralph Touchett, his father and Lord Warburton enjoy their afternoon tea. In *Mrs Osmond*, a tea scene is described at the outset of the middle section of the novel, which is focalized through Gilbert Osmond. 'This delightful ceremony, so characteristically English' is described as 'one of Osmond's more recently acquired affectations' (Banville 2017a: 193). Moreover, far from a harmless ceremony, the practice had been installed to charm Lord Warburton into marrying Pansy. 'In the midst of so much southern vehemence of temperature and light', the tea scene becomes a grotesquely absurd re-enactment of its Jamesian original: the water is lukewarm, the elderly Italian major-domo manages 'to leave in both their saucers a substantial spillage of tea as pale as a straw', and, in contrast to the civilized conversation of Ralph and Lord Warburton, Osmond and his sister engage in their favourite pastime of 'exchanging choice scurrilities' concerning their acquaintances (Banville 2017a: 194, 196). This shift in scene brings out the parodic dimension of *Mrs Osmond*, its postmodern awareness that literature does not simply represent reality but rather revisits and mediates earlier literary and aesthetic creations.

This stamp of the postmodern is also evident in the highly ironic metafictional jokes in Banville's novel. As most readers will have noticed, Henry James makes a cameo appearance in the first chapter: Isabel wonders whether he might be 'a man of the theatre, perhaps, an actor-manager' and she feels 'checked and assessed' – 'she might have been a portrait that he, the portraitist, had come upon unexpectedly, hanging on the wall of a gallery' (Banville 2017a: 19). Less obvious, perhaps, is the appearance of James's real-life friends Mr Boott and his daughter as Osmond's neighbours in Bellosguardo or the sly reference to Max Beerbohm's parody of James, 'The Mote in the Middle Distance' in the scene in Rome where Madame Merle responds to Isabel's accusations with 'the abrupt stilling of the fan she had been so vigorously manipulating, while her gaze fixed itself as if upon a mote in the middle distance' (Banville 2017a: 269, 192, 335). These ironic metafictional nudges are of a kind with the theatrical metaphors in *Mrs Osmond*: they draw attention to the inevitable belatedness of contemporary representations, informed as they are by so many earlier popular plots, literary texts and artistic scenes.

From authenticity to artifice

Still, in *Mrs Osmond*, these theatrical images, familiar though they are in Banville's oeuvre, take on an additional thematic meaning as well. Already in *The Portrait*, Gilbert Osmond and Madame Merle are associated with performance and pretence. In one of her early conversations with Isabel, Madame Merle contradicts Isabel's insistence on independence and authenticity by arguing, 'one's self – for other people – is one's expression of one's self' (James 1966: 201). It is a remark that slyly foreshadows her cunning deception of the guileless Isabel. In *Mrs Osmond,* this philosophical understanding of the self as performance is further amplified in the manifestly affected and theatrical behaviour of Serena Merle and Gilbert Osmond. The latter is depicted as an arch poseur, whose studied disdain hides feelings of jealousy and inferiority, while Merle has perfected a pose of charming smoothness that masks the cunning self-interest that lies underneath. Even Pansy, in *The Portrait* still a sweet and gentle girl, is now revealed as 'a dissembling little schemer quietly and craftily biding her time until the opportunity should come when she might kick over the traces and be her true self' (Banville 2017a: 366). In the light of these performing villains, one cannot but wonder whether Isabel's new-found theatrical tropes in *Mrs Osmond* are not to be read as a sign of her being corrupted by her husband's worldview, by his preference of posing over being, copy over original and artifice over authenticity. Reviewing her marriage to Osmond, Isabel herself wonders as much, though not in these terms:

> He took a malignant satisfaction in turning up the world's stone so as to expose to the light of day the foul things swarming and squirming underneath it. That which was disgusting he savoured in the same way, sometimes it seemed to her, as he delighted in his possessions, as though the value of the latter were enhanced by the proximity of the former. As to herself, insofar as she was possessed by him, the reverse had been the case: his proximity had left her besmirched. (Banville 2017a: 273)

The question of whether Isabel has been corrupted by her husband's immoral and inauthentic personality haunts the narrative of *Mrs Osmond* even – or especially – as Isabel slowly plots her escape from him. Hence, if in *The Portrait*, Isabel's discovery of her husband's secret spells the end of her innocence and naivety, in *Mrs Osmond*, we are led to wonder whether in buying her freedom from Osmond and binding his fate to that of Madame Merle, Isabel has not also forfeited the goodness that was so integral to James's understanding of her.

The question of Isabel's loss of virtue and authenticity is also raised in another of Banville's sly appropriations of Jamesian scenes or images. At the end of her confrontation with Osmond in Bellosguardo, Isabel feels she is facing him across 'the deepest chasm', 'at the bottom of which she seemed to hear, distantly, oh, how distantly, the shattering of a small frail discarded thing that once she had deemed so precious' (Banville 2017a: 304). While the image may suggest the definite end of her marriage, the word frail also directs us to the famous 'frail vessel' metaphor which James applied to Isabel in the New York preface to *The Portrait*. Slightly misquoting George Eliot, James says about his heroine: 'In these frail vessels is borne onward through the ages the treasure of human affection' (James xi). Perhaps then, it is this frail vessel of authentic feeling which breaks when Banville's Isabel sets out to her husband the terms and conditions of her 'reckoning' (Banville 2017a: 333).

Such speculations about the corruption of Isabel's integrity in *Mrs Osmond* are central to the question of evil which Banville puts at the heart of his novel, in a shift away from James's greater concern with virtue, purity and honour. In the autumn of 2016, Banville was a guest lecturer at the University of Chicago and the course he taught was entitled 'Henry James and the Question of Evil'. In the course abstract, Banville refers to *The Portrait* and 'The Turn of the Screw' as well as biographical facts of the James family, before concluding 'These themes and sub-themes I shall place within a wider consideration of the nature of evil, posing the question, is there such a thing as evil, or are there only evil deeds?' (Banville 2015). Banville's take on *The Portrait* is here perhaps more suggestive of his own concerns than those of James and points forward to his preoccupation with the nature of evil in *Mrs Osmond* itself.

From good to evil

In *The Portrait*, Isabel has difficulty recognizing the immoral behaviour – or nature – of Merle and Osmond. After the revelations of the Countess Gemini, 'She asked herself, with an almost childlike horror of the supposition, whether to this intimate friend of several years the great historical epithet of *wicked* were to be applied' (James 1966: 519). During her midnight vigil, similarly, she struggles to locate the nature of Osmond's crime: 'She knew of no wrong he had done; he was not violent, he was not cruel: she simply believed he hated her. That was all she accused him of, and the miserable part of it was precisely that it was not a crime, for against a crime she might have found redress' (James 1966: 425). It is only Madame Merle herself who recognizes Osmond's evil nature and reproaches him, 'You have made me as bad as yourself' (James 1966: 523). Yet, in *The Portrait*, Merle and Osmond are exceptions among a big cast of largely sympathetic characters whose human failings are set beside many more positive and endearing traits. In *Mrs Osmond*, by contrast, most Jamesian characters have come down a notch or two on the scale of coldness and corruption. I have already referred to Pansy's shift from gentleness to hardheartedness, but similar shifts can be found with regard to many other characters. If James's Countess Gemini, for all her gossiping egotism, still 'cared enough for Isabel's trouble to forget her own' (James 1966: 539), in Banville's novel her sympathy for Isabel has become 'a sort of irritated compassion – her heart, as it is said, had "gone out" to her, a venture which that tempered and well-tethered organ was rarely permitted to undertake, even in the most tragic of cases' (Banville 2017a: 191). If in *The Portrait*, the countess says of her niece, 'She's very nice, in spite of her deplorable origin. I myself have liked Pansy; not, naturally, because she was hers [Madame Merle's], but because she had become yours [Isabel's]' (James 1966: 547); in *Mrs Osmond* this has become: 'The antipathy she felt towards her niece was of the mildest order … but it could alter under the action of prolonged proximity to the girl's damply vacant personality' (Banville 2017a: 216).

Isabel's aunt, Mrs Touchett, suffers a similar treatment in Banville's novel. In *The Portrait*, she is called 'as honest as a pair of compasses' and 'never overinquisitive as regards the territory of her neighbour' (James 1966: 220). In *Mrs Osmond*, by contrast, Isabel wonders 'if this person too, like so many, so very many, others, held within her a deep well of vindictiveness and spite, of which her pose of indifference was no more than the cleverly camouflaged cover' (Banville 2017a: 231). Moreover, Banville's Mrs Touchett turns out to have known all along about the Madame Merle's immoral behaviour: 'If one were to choose one's intimate acquaintances on the state of their morals one should lead an exceedingly isolated life' (Banville 2017a: 245). She claims that hardly anyone 'would be shocked or even surprised to learn she had been your husband's mistress and mother to his child' and proceeds to tell Isabel of a similar deception on the part of her husband. As a result, Daniel Touchett too changes from a good and kind man to a deceitful philanderer, of a kind with Isabel's 'gaily improvident father', who is said to have pursued 'pretty young wives' across the continent only to be chased by 'outraged husbands' in return (Banville 2017a: 319). In such a context of generalized immorality, the great crime of Madame Merle and Gilbert Osmond in *The Portrait* comes to seem very trivial indeed. Osmond himself believes that 'a misdeed kept sunk out of sight for sufficiently long … is not a misdeed at all', but Isabel too is forced to recognize 'the mundanity of the couple's crimes' (Banville 2017a: 196, 286). Small wonder then that Banville felt compelled to invent further misdeeds so as to preserve Osmond as the arch villain of his cast of characters. In *Mrs Osmond*, therefore, Osmond is not just a dishonest manipulator who has used Isabel to further his own ends, he is also a murderer with Madame Merle as his willing accomplice.

Banville's much darker picture of human nature, governed by egotistical instincts and base desires also comes to the fore in the images of evil depravity which haunt Isabel throughout *Mrs Osmond*. Once again, a juxtaposition of scenes from the two novels brings out the unmistakable shifts in perspective. In one of the early chapters of *The Portrait*, Isabel famously defines 'her idea of happiness' as 'a swift carriage, of a dark night, rattling with four horses over roads that one can't see' (James 1966: 165). In *Mrs Osmond*, however, this metaphor has morphed into a haunting memory of a dark evening in her childhood when their carriage narrowly escaped collision with a 'carriage … painted a peculiarly unsettling deep lacquered shade of shiny black', like 'a grotesquely overgrown beetle' (Banville 2017a: 247):

> Despite the speed and confusion of the moment, Isabel caught a glimpse of the driver … a view that stamped itself for ever on her young consciousness. … His cheeks were sunken, and his skin was of a faded, yellowish cast; his hair, swept back from a high pale forehead, was also a soiled shade of yellow, and coarse, like so many twists of straw. It was his eyes, however, black and shiny as wet coal and aglow with what seemed to her malignant mirth, that struck her with the most force and fearfulness. … Why had he singled her out? What had he discerned in her that was not in her sisters? And what frightful message had he meant to convey to her? It was as if one corner of the fabric of the world had been lifted so that she might glimpse the darkness that lay underneath, the darkness and the dark things that were always there, waiting to crawl out and cling to her, and against which all her bright complacencies could offer no protection. (Banville 2017a: 248–9)

That this dark underside of life is Osmond's particular domain in *Mrs Osmond* is suggested by another of Isabel's memories, some pages later, of Osmond showing his then fiancée 'a long-disused cloacal den' at the back of his Florentine house in a scene that is certainly not there in *The Portrait* (Banville 2017a: 271–2). Many other scenes in *Mrs Osmond* seem to bear out Osmond's 'contented' observation that 'people are so very bad', 'even the most righteous-seeming among them, those whom one had taken to be the very models of virtue, [are] ready at the least temptation to descend to truly astonishing depths of depravity' (Banville 2017a: 196). Another example of this is Isabel's shifted perception of Rome in Banville's novel. An unhappily married woman in Rome, James's Isabel finds consolation in long drives through the city, 'for in a world of ruins, the ruins of her own happiness seemed a less unnatural catastrophe … and her haunting sense of the continuity of the human lot easily carried her from the less to the greater' (James 1966: 517–18). In *Mrs Osmond*, however, Rome as 'the place where people suffered' has become a place of cruelty, epitomized by 'the horror [of] the afternoon entertainments on offer at the Colosseum' (Banville 2017a: 341). It is this base cruelty, rather than a sense of shared suffering, which continues into the present as Osmond and Merle are likened to 'a pair of predators circl[ing] about their captive prey' (Banville 2017a: 342). Banville's Rome is no longer the Eternal City, but the 'Infernal City' (332), whose society takes 'a prurient delight ... in nosing out the egregious misdeeds of which it had no doubt all who were human were at times capable' (Banville 2017a: 237). Small wonder then that Banville's Isabel, confronted with this generalized baseness, no longer cares to sit and think alone at night, as in the famous midnight vigil of *The Portrait*: 'There was a time when she would have thrilled to sit like this of a darkling eve, after rain, but the darkness was thicker now, and there were things that moved in it, indistinct but unmistakable forms, like wild beasts at the mouth of a cave, which only flame could keep at bay' (Banville 2017a: 315).

The shifts in characters, scenes and metaphors from *The Portrait* to *Mrs Osmond* all point to Banville's considerably darker view of human life. If for James egotism is the great crime (Gorra 2012: 315), for Banville an overriding selfishness is the basic human characteristic. His is a worldview shaped by Nietzsche and Freud: a world of individualism, selfishness, instinct and desire. James, by contrast, retains a nineteenth-century faith in Aristotelean virtue and Kantian duty, in moral reason and conscious restraint. If in *Mrs Osmond*, Isabel nevertheless stands out as a better person than many of the other characters, it is not because she lacks egotism. On numerous occasions, indeed, she berates herself for her 'self-absorption' or 'self-regard' (Banville 2017a: 16, 53, 106). What marks her out, rather, is that she takes great care not to let her actions be guided by these baser instincts. Madame Merle and Osmond, on the other hand, are shown to have no such qualms. Returning to Banville's question of whether 'there [is] such a thing as evil, or ... only evil deeds', I would argue that *Mrs Osmond* supports the second view. Since, for Banville, egotism and self-interest govern all of human life, what matters is not *being* self-centred, but letting that narcissism govern your *acts* and instrumentalizing others to further your own desires. In other words, evil are the transgressive acts of those who fail to keep their egotistic desires and drives in check, harming other people in the process.

Banville has of course long been interested in the question of evil and Gilbert Osmond joins a long line of perpetrators explored in his fiction. Nevertheless, in taking up the case of Isabel Archer in *Mrs Osmond*, Banville also has to address James's central concern with the question of goodness. Put within the context of Banville's considerably more pessimistic view of human nature, however, this question takes on a different inflection: Does virtue still matter in a Nietzschean world, where human life is governed by selfish drives and desires? And what conception of virtue would make sense in such a world? In the final part of this chapter, therefore, I will gauge the impact of Banville's subtle shifts to the characters, scenes and worldview of James's fictional universe on the discussion of virtue that is as central to *Mrs Osmond* as it is to *The Portrait*.

From being to doing

In *The Portrait of a Lady* James's concern with virtue is primarily centred on character. As a bildungsroman, the novel traces Isabel's development as a person: from an imaginative, intelligent and independent young woman to the lady of the title. 'She had a theory', the narrator tells us early on, 'that only under this provision life was worth living; that one should be one of the best … should move in a realm of light, of natural wisdom, of happy impulse, of inspiration gracefully chronic' (James 1966: 50–1). 'It was her passionate desire to *be* just', Ralph reiterates much later in the novel (James 1966: 342, emphasis added). Several critics have argued that James's emphasis on being a good person over doing good deeds also comes across in his juxtaposition of Ralph and Osmond as characters who have both 'made a convenience of [Isabel]' (James 1966: 573), have both 'use[d] Isabel as means to their own ends, not as an end in itself' (Bollinger 2002: 144; see also Seabright 1988; Gorra 2012: 316–7). Yet the difference, as Isabel puts it, is that 'Ralph was generous and that her husband was not' (James 1966: 434). James's ethics, in other words, is an Aristotelean ethics of virtue, whereby 'what makes an action admirable is that it is the expression of an admirable character' (Seabright 1988: 313). As we have already seen, Banville, by contrast, locates evil in actions rather than in character or nature: what makes Gilbert Osmond the arch villain is not that he is more egotistical and self-serving than the other characters, but that he lets these base desires govern his actions and harms other people in the process. With regard to virtue too, I would argue, the emphasis is on actions rather than character: Isabel stands out in *Mrs Osmond* not for lack of selfishness, but for her earnest desire to act ethically, to *do* good.

In Banville's novel, more than in James's, this wish is bound up with the notion of freedom. In *The Portrait*, as is well known, Isabel's desire for independence and Emersonian self-reliance is brought short by her awareness that her life has been shaped by factors – and people – outside her own free will (Gorra 2012: 114–15). Yet, Banville's Isabel fails to be engaged by the 'neat and closely printed volume of Mr Emerson's essays', which she has brought on her travels (Banville 2017a: 227). She seems more swayed by Miss Janeway's assertion that 'freedom is first and foremost a practical matter' (Banville 2017a: 56). At the end of her conversation with that lady, she announces 'I intend to use it, my fortune – my money – to buy my freedom' (Banville 2017a: 63). In *Mrs Osmond*, the question of freedom thus takes on a less philosophical and more pragmatic dimension. Isabel is free because her fortune makes her so and she now has to figure out how to put that fortune to good ends, how to *do* good to those around her and the world at large. Talking to Myles Devenish at the end of the novels, Isabel formulates the question as follows:

> 'I have a fortune; not a great one, but a fortune, nonetheless, and I am—' she paused, and her lips twitched in an ironical small smile '—I suppose the word is "free". That being the case, there must be something to the service of which I can devote my freedom, and my fortune. I used to think my first and sacred duty was to myself, and to the working-out of my "fate" – another of those words I am no longer sure I know the meaning of, though it hardly matters, since I employ them now to myself only within the confines of quotation marks.' (Banville 2017a: 373)

This quotation illustrates Banville's shift away from the Aristotelean character ethics that dominates *The Portrait*. The 'cultivation of individual identity', the shaping of the 'good self' is no longer given pride of place it has in James's novel (Gorra 2012: 52). The emphasis comes to lie, rather, on the doing of good deeds, on the performance of a service to something or someone. Yet, Isabel is uncertain as to what this 'service' might consist of. She knows what she is no longer interested in – the virtuous self – but has as yet found no alternative. Instead, she takes Devenish to Paddington Station, to the scene that opens the novel: the spectacle of a 'grown man crying', 'copiously, helplessly, unstaunchably' (Banville 2017a: 9). Isabel is powerfully affected by the 'sorrow and abjection of the spectacle he made; it was as if he had been flayed of a protective integument, and his flaming hair were blushing for him to be so nakedly and shamefully on show' and wonders what she can do to help him. Yet she does nothing in the end. Nevertheless, the scene – and her failure to help – stays with her and comes to symbolize the ethical dilemma she faces: how to *do* good, when *being* good is, *pace* Nietzsche and Freud, no longer possible. Although *Mrs Osmond* does not give a clear answer to this dilemma, it alludes to several moral theories that might provide an alternative to James's ethics of virtue.

From an ethics of virtue to an ethics of care

Isabel's first thought after witnessing the weeping man in Paddington Station is 'it was plain that her duty lay precisely in helping such as he, the unfortunate and fallen ones of the world' (Banville 2017a: 10). The appeal to duty is a characteristic of Kantian or deontological ethics, which judges actions on their adherence to certain moral principles and laws. This moral theory too is alluded to in *The Portait*, as Isabel's decision to return to Osmond could be read as governed by a sense of duty. Banville's Osmond alludes to this when he confidently predicts that Isabel will return to him and to marriage, since her 'inflexible sense of duty, that spiritual affliction inherited from her Puritan forebears … would not allow her to abandon him and all that he represented in her life and in her fate' (Banville 2017a: 183). Isabel proves him wrong, however. This suggests that the Kantian ethics of moral duty no longer holds much force with Isabel in *Mrs Osmond*. In the Paddington scene, indeed, the moral rule of helping those in need turns out to conflict with the 'rule' of obeying servants in such practical matters as giving alms to beggars: 'The rules were the rules: they applied in both directions, downwards as well as upwards and she knew the impossibility of disobeying her servant and going to the weeping man even if it were for no more than to press a coin shamefacedly into his hand' (Banville 2017a: 10).

Isabel's second reaction to the weeping man is a feeling of deep sympathy: having recently suffered so much herself, she shares his distress and feels the urge to 'direct the cab to stop, and leap down and run back and take her place beside that poor soul and pour out her own distress upon the commonplace air; but of course she did not' (Banville 2017a: 12). Yet, however great her empathy for the man's sorrowful plight, it does not lead to action: 'What, after all, could she have done for the poor wretch? What comfort would a word of hers have brought to him? … even her silver would not have saved him, for surely he was beyond saving' (Banville 2017a: 13). An ethics based on sympathy, then, does not seem to provide a solution either.

Revisiting the scene with Myles Devenish, Isabel asks him what he would have done had he been in her place, adding, 'I'm sure you would have done something' (Banville 2017a: 375). Somewhat hesitantly, Devenish replies, 'our task, it seems to me, is to look beyond the individual case, and aim to make a world that will no longer allow of the wretchedness you witnessed in that poor man's plight'. His, clearly, is a consequentialist or utilitarian ethics, interested in providing the greatest good to the greatest number. It is a moral theory he shares with his aunt, Miss Janeway, and 'the cause' she supports. Isabel, however, can muster little enthusiasm for this – to her – abstract approach and Devenish recognizes 'that he had given the wrong answer'. When he tries to further enlist the help of Isabel – and her money – for the suffragist cause and other socialist reforms, Isabel doesn't respond: 'Isabel said nothing, nothing at all.' As these are the final words of the novel, it would seem that no moral answer has been provided to Isabel's question of how to do good.

Still earlier on in her meeting with Myles Devenish, Isabel hints at yet another moral theory. She requests permission to help him care for his aunt: 'I shall remain in London, and help you tend your aunt, if you will let me, until her struggle is over' (Banville 2017a: 374). This offer of care carries echoes of other relationships in *Mrs Osmond*, in particular Isabel's friendship with Henrietta's Stackpole and her close relationship to Staines, her maid. 'You know how I care about you and worry for your welfare,' Henrietta tells Isabel during one of their long talks and Isabel herself is moved to thank Staines 'for caring for me, as you do' (Banville 2017a: 120, 315). Although Isabel occasionally bristles under their ministrations, both relationships stand out as positive and enabling ones in a world that is, as we have seen, dominated by selfishness and greed. They point to a fourth ethical theory that is held up to scrutiny in *Mrs Osmond*: an ethics of care that locates moral significance in human relationships and in the caring for the needs of others. An ethics of care is grounded not in sympathy, which involves an extension of the self, a placing of the self in the position of the other, but in altruism, emotions and the priority of the other over the self. As philosophers such as Gilligan (1982), Held (2006), and Slote (2007) have argued, a care ethics is also premised on the primacy of affective relationships for a moral life. As such, it provides an antidote to the egotism which, as we have seen, is the basic fact of human life in *Mrs Osmond*, as well as a corrective to the central sin of using others to further your own ends and desires. Compared to the pervasiveness of this self-serving egotism in *Mrs Osmond*, the alternative evidence for an ethics of care may seem only slender, occasional and implicit. It is certainly not developed into a full-fledged moral theory or presented as a redemptive new worldview. Still, an ethics of care seems by definition to shy away from the grand gesture and the reasoned philosophy, instead remaining by necessity a matter of barely perceptible acts and moments of affective insight. Nevertheless, its presence seems relevant in a novel that, quite unlike Banville's previous novels, gives so much space to friendship, especially, if not only, among its female characters.

Conclusion

In spite of these glimpses of a relational ethics of care, however, the ending of *Mrs Osmond* seems not particularly hopeful. The word 'nothing' is repeated twice in the final line and carries a hint of Eveline's paralysis in *Dubliners* as she refuses the invitation of her lover: 'No! No! No! It was impossible' (Joyce 1992: 34). Even more uncomfortable, perhaps, are its echoes of Osmond's nihilism. In *The Portrait*, Isabel defiantly describes Osmond as 'Nobody, nothing but a very good and very honourable man', as having 'no property, no title, no honours, no houses, nor lands, nor position, nor reputation, nor brilliant belongings of any sort', which is exactly why he appeals to her (James 1966: 329, 347). In *Mrs Osmond*, however, this nothingness – Osmond is described as 'a polished nobody' (Banville 2017a: 221) – carries darker overtones as it suggests a nihilism which cares for nothing but the self. In this reading, Isabel's final 'nothing' again raises the question in how far she has been corrupted by Osmond's influence, in how far she will remain, as the title suggests, 'Mrs Osmond' in spite of her bid to freedom. To this and many other questions, the novel provides no conclusive answer. Readers coming to *Mrs Osmond* expecting closure about Isabel's fate may therefore well be disappointed. Although we know that she buys back her freedom from Osmond, we are given no clear sense of what this independent woman of means will now do with her life or her freedom. At the end of the novel, in other words, we're once again wondering, as Ralph Touchett puts it early in *The Portrait*, what Isabel is 'going to do with herself' (James 1966: 63).

In a perceptive reading of the ending of *The Portrait*, Tessa Hadley argues that its frustratingly open end reflects James's failure to imagine a life for Isabel beyond the demands of social convention: 'James has accurately recorded the inbuilt constraints, the double binds, in a "good" woman's psychology and in her language; but he has not found another voice for his woman yet. She thinks and feels beyond the conventional, but she cannot say or act: he cannot imagine it for her' (Hadley 2002: 38). For Leo Bersani, the failure is not James's but that of the realist novel as a genre: 'The very nature of the novel she appears in determines Isabel's return to Osmond ... her dream of freedom has been defeated by the limited range of possibilities for being free to the realistic imagination. Isabel *and* James can no longer imagine to what concrete use her desire for freedom might be put' (Bersani 1984: 67). Perhaps, a similar faltering of the imagination is at work in Banville's reluctance to provide his independent, intelligent and conscientious heroine with a clear path to a meaningful life. Like the Jamesian author figure in *Mrs Osmond*, Banville's instead 'leav[es] her to totter on alone' (Banville 2017a: 23). Or perhaps such a life, outside the conventions of being a mother and a wife, is still relatively uncharted territory in the contemporary novel as it continues to circumscribe women's plots along gender lines.

Nevertheless, with his elaborate portrait of an entirely sane, sympathetic and courageous female protagonist, Banville himself has strayed far in – for him – unfamiliar territory. Isabel is not just the first female protagonist in his fiction, she is also the first one to escape from the self-absorption of Banville's usual character-narrators, by engaging in meaningful and enabling relations with the characters around her. Moreover, as the subtle shifts between James's original and Banville's adaptation have shown, Banville has not just extended Isabel's fictional life with a few weeks or months. Through his introduction of such contemporary themes as performativity, individualism, feminism and altruism, he has, rather, extended her life into the present. It is up to future readers – and writers – then to carry Isabel's fate further into the future. For, as the Jamesean motto of *Mrs Osmond* suggests, Isabel's life – and the moral questions it poses – will 'be [our] business for a long time to come'.

References

Adams, T. (2017), 'Mrs Osmond by John Banville – What Isabel Archer Did Next', *The Observer*, 1 October. Available online: https://www.theguardian.com/books/2017/oct/01/mrs-osmond-review-john-banville-henry-james-portrait-lady (accessed 19 March 2018).

Banville, J. (1981), 'A Talk', *Irish University Review*, 11 (1): 13–17.

Banville, J. (2013), 'The Novel That Reinvented Fiction', *The Irish Times*, 12 January. Available online: https://www.irishtimes.com/culture/books/the-novel-that-reinvented-fiction-1.957607 (accessed 19 March 2018).

Banville, J. (2015), 'Henry James and the Question of Evil'. Available online: https://english.uchicago.edu/courses/henry-james-and-question-evil (accessed 19 March 2018).

Banville, J. (2017a), *Mrs Osmond*, London: Viking.

Banville, J. (2017b), 'John Banville: Novels Were Never the Same after Henry James', *The Irish Times*, 7 October. Available online: https://www.irishtimes.com/culture/books/john-banville-novels-were-never-the-same-after-henry-james-1.3242726 (accessed 19 March 2018).

Battersby, E. (2017), 'Mrs Osmond by John Banville: An Entertaining Homage to Henry James', *The Irish Times*, 7 October. Available online: https://www.irishtimes.com/culture/books/mrs-osmond-by-john-banville-an-entertaining-homage-to-henry-james-1.3232980 (accessed 19 March 2018).

Bersani, L. (1984), *A Future for Astyanax. Character and Desire in Literature*, New York: Columbia University Press.

Bollinger, L. (2002), 'The Ethics of Reading: The Struggle for Subjectivity in *The Portrait of a Lady*', *Criticism*, 44 (2): 139–60.

Eugenides, J. (2017), 'Whatever Happened to Isabel Archer? "Mrs. Osmond" Picks Up Where Henry James Left Off', *The New York Times Book Review*, 20 November. Available online: https://www.nytimes.com/2017/11/20/books/review/mrs-osmond-john-banville-henry-james-portrait-lady-sequel.html (accessed 19 March 2018).

Gilligan, C. (1982), *In a Different Voice*, Cambridge, MA: Harvard University Press.

Gorra, M. (2012), *Portrait of a Novel. Henry James and the Making of an American Masterpiece*, New York: Liveright.

Hadley, T. (2002), *Henry James and the Imagination of Pleasure*, Cambridge: Cambridge University Press.

Haughton, H. and B. Radley (2011), 'An Interview with John Banville', *Modernism/Modernity*, 18 (4): 855–69.

Held, V. (2006), *The Ethics of Care: Personal, Political, and Global*, New York: Oxford University Press.

James, H. (1966), *The Portrait of a Lady* [1881, 1908], London: Penguin.

Joyce, J. (1992), *Dubliners* [1914], London: Penguin.

Sanders, J. (2006), *Adaptation and Appropriation*, London: Routledge.

Scholes, L. (2017), '*Mrs Osmond* by John Banville, Book Review: A Fine Act of Literary Ventriloquism and Imagination', *The Independent*, 2 October 2017. Available online: https://www.independent.co.uk/arts-entertainment/books/reviews/mrs-osmond-john-banville-book-review-a7979376.html (accessed 19 March 2018).

Schwall, H. (2017), 'Finding a Jamesian Tone and Digging Down. Interview with John Banville'. Available online: http://www.johnbanville.eu/materials (accessed 19 March 2018).

Seabright, P. (1988), 'The Pursuit of Unhappiness: Paradoxical Motivation and the Subversion of Character in Henry James's *Portrait of a Lady*', *Ethics* 98 (2): 313–31.

Slote, M. (2007), *The Ethics of Care and Empathy*, New York: Routledge.

Tarien Powell, K. (2015), '"The answer … is yes and no": John Banville, Henry James and *The Ambassadors*', *Irish University Review*, 45 (2): 302–19.

White, E. (2017), '*Mrs Osmond* by John Banville Review –Superb Henry James Pastiche', *The Guardian*, 14 October. Available online: https://www.theguardian.com/books/2017/oct/14/mrs-osmond-john-banville-review (accessed 19 March 2018).

Wood, M. (2018), 'The Fantastic Fact', *London Review of Books*, 4 January. Available online: https://www.lrb.co.uk/v40/n01/michael-wood/the-fantastic-fact (accessed 19 March 2018).

5

Afterlives of a supreme fiction: John Banville's dialogue with Wallace Stevens

Pietra Palazzolo

In an essay on the strategy of fiction writing, John Banville stresses that the function of the artist is no longer to speak about things but 'to speak the things themselves' (Banville 1993: 108). The necessity to abandon the task of speaking *about* things reveals Banville's anti-mimetic view that the world is fundamentally unknowable, a notion of alterity that manifests itself as a pervasive tension across his oeuvre. It is the realization of the world's alterity, of its resistance to critical scrutiny, that introduces the writer's conundrum: while naturally gravitating towards the desire for self-expression in the representation of reality, one is forced to acknowledge the limits of artistic resources. Conflating Stevens's, Rilke's and Beckett's insights, Banville has stressed that poetry springs precisely from this tension between the artist's wish to say things, to go on writing and imagining, and the awareness of 'liv[ing] in a place/That is not our own' (1990: 381):

> It is out of the tension between the desire to take things into ourselves by *saying* them, by praising them to the Angel, and the impossibility finally of making the world our own, that poetry springs, and that other poetry which some of us disguise by not justifying the right-hand margins of our books. Hence the note of solitude, of stoic despair, which great art always sounds. As Beckett says: *I can't go on, I'll go on.* (Banville 1981: 16)

This conflict has pushed Banville to question the correspondence between words and things and to explore the shifting nuances of the creative process in its expressive use of language and its relation to the notion of an otherness which exceeds conventional boundaries (self/other; internal/external; speech/writing).

In questioning the mimetic notion of literary representation and the transparency of language, Banville is in sync with Stevens and Beckett when they stress the importance of the imagination in their own contexts. If for Stevens, the point of tension between romantic and modernist ideas is marked by 'an end of the imagination' (1990: 502), it is an absence that must itself be imagined, as Beckett's famously acknowledged in one of his prose works: *Imagination Dead Imagine*. In enacting the substitution of transcendental truths and 'soiled metaphors', the modern writer has to work by means of erasure and depletion – 'the world for us is flat and bare, there are no shadows anywhere' (Stevens 1990: 167) – where the act of imagining takes on new valences. As Banville stresses, the task of the artist is to create 'necessary falsehoods' which can go beyond the true/false quandary and be transformed into ritual by acknowledging their fictionality:

> A lie is only a lie when the one lied to thinks he is hearing the truth. When the liar and the listener both know it is a lie, then the lie becomes transformed into ritual. Henry James recognized this. ... Society, he tells us, lives by, can only live by, necessary falsehoods. Art is one of them – the Supreme Fiction, as Wallace Stevens calls it. (1981: 16)

It is a point that demonstrates his insight into 'modern rituals', where the relationship between the artist and his readership is based upon the acceptance of necessary fictions, or, in Stevens's words, of '[the belief] in a fiction, which you know to be a fiction, there being nothing else' (1989: 163). Banville's remarks on the significance of ritual also reveal the importance of modes of saying, beyond the distinction between content and form. For Banville, form is a 'sort of self-sustaining tension in space' that already constitutes the work of art and 'in some sense *is* the completed thing'. The task of the writer, however, is to transfer it 'into the world, where it will be manifest yet hidden, like the skeleton beneath the skin' (1993: 109). Form, then, is something that is at once imaginary and tangible, and that exists in the space between the realm of imaginative possibilities and the performative quality of language.

Wallace Stevens's aesthetic is a crucial source of inspiration for Banville's works. Banville's scientific tetralogy (1976–86) contains overt references to the systems of order that captivate, to the point of obsession, all the clear-minded heroes of the four novels. Various studies have addressed the parallels between these systems and Stevens's notion of the supreme fiction (Imhof 1981a; McMinn 1999; Ferguson 1997; Berensmeyer 1999; D'hoker 2004). The latter in Stevens, however, is not a self-contained and fixed system of order; rather, it is a constantly shifting mode of poetic elaboration that can only be grasped in motion. The tetralogy does not stage the scientists' projects *as* supreme fictions, but uses their epistemological crises to show the points of friction between their 'rage for order' (Stevens 1990: 130) and the expressive forms underlying their creative acts. If Banville's redefinition of the Stevensian concept of supreme fiction starts with his unique rendering of scientific and historical discourses in the tetralogy, as shown in Michael Springer's discussion in this volume, it is also, and more effectively, expressed in the sustained exploration of the creative process that his subsequent series and novels enact, exploring its significant links *with* the supreme fiction while also expanding on it. It is my contention that the Art trilogy extends Banville's exploration of the creative process into a contemporary elaboration of what has been defined as a 'romantic modernity' (Critchley 1997: 97), something which, as in Stevens, reflects the continuing, haunting presence of the romantic legacy for the shaping of our modernity. The term 'romantic modernity' posits itself beyond historical labelling, since it refers not to the *post-romantic* modernity of authors such as Yeats and Eliot (Bornstein 1976), but to a peculiar mode of poetic yearning – Stevens's insistence on the romantic as 'meaning always the living and … the imaginative' (1989: 220) – that cuts across generic or periodic categories. In this way my analysis will reveal an intriguing convergence between the two writers, since they both focus on the vitality of 'mode[s] of becoming' (Blanchot 1993: 398) and on the dynamic investigation of romantic and modernist aesthetics and its legacy.

Banville's appreciation of Stevens's work is best reflected in his use of imagination as inextricably intertwined with one's perceptions of things, which also calls for a need to acknowledge the supreme fiction as a necessary imaginative act that constantly re-elaborates itself. In Banville's prose fiction this urge for continual change arises from the cognitive crisis that results from a revealing encounter with the other which adjusts to individual demands, while also positing itself beyond the merely human need for consolation. This shifting view of the other is vital to delving into Banville's redrawing of some of the key concepts of romantic aesthetics (knowledge, perception, imagination) as mediated through the work of Stevens. In Banville's versions of the supreme fiction we can glimpse a trajectory that takes us from the fantastic Copernican systems of order to the more mundane attempts of Morrow (*Athena*), Alex Cleave (*Eclipse*), and Axel Vander (*Shroud*), where Stevens's grappling with the perception of the world is intertwined with a Beckettian concern with the otherness of things, and to the varying and shifting explorations of the elusiveness of material reality in Banville's latest novels (*The Sea, Ancient Light, The Blue Guitar*). My analysis will also lay the ground for the 'ghostlier demarcations' (Stevens 1990: 130) of the 'radical openness' (Hand 2002: 176) of Banville's fictional universe, as discussed in the last section of this chapter.

Towards a supreme fiction: Abstraction, transcendence, nobility

Considering Banville's work through the lens of past aesthetic projects, Joseph McMinn comments that Banville's 'postmodern myth' distances itself both from the Romantics' conception of the supreme fiction as a self-contained, 'parallel cosmos' conjured by the artist as a 'little god' and 'that modernist version of it in Stevens and Rilke' by using a language 'which does not always obey the divine imperative' (1999: 4). While I agree with McMinn's emphasis on Banville's intervention into the notion of supreme fiction, I find this overstates the contrast between Stevens and Banville. For both writers the supreme fiction expresses itself in the dynamics of the creative process and can be perceived in motion. I contend that Banville's work displays a much deeper link to key Stevensian concepts and a subtler understanding of the legacy of romantic and modernist aesthetics, as both writers are inheritors of a 'romantic modernity'. A brief overview of the centrality of the idea of supreme fiction in Stevens's oeuvre, and as directly addressed in his well-known long poem, 'Notes toward a Supreme Fiction' (1942),[1] will enhance our understanding of Banville's use of this key concept as well as of his dialogue with Stevens as a significant precursor.

Conceived as a poem about poetry, 'Notes' is divided into three sections named after the essential characteristics of a supreme fiction: 'It Must Be Abstract', 'It Must Change', and 'It Must Give Pleasure'. Despite its neat structure, the poem is perhaps one of Stevens's most evasive works. It is a poem that 'feels at once both liberated and restrained' (Vendler 1969: 168) in its oscillation between didacticism and playfulness. The title 'Notes' itself, and 'toward' rather than 'about', envisages the supreme fiction not so much as an attainable target, but a suggestion of what cannot be seen or named (Ziarek 1994: 129). The characteristic features of a supreme fiction, then, seem to dissolve into the fluidity of various manners and multifaceted moods. It is precisely in this versatile range of design, however, that the supreme fiction can be seen, as it were, 'visible or invisible / Invisible or visible or both: / A seeing and unseeing in the eye', according to the intensities it registers: 'My house has changed a little in the sun / The fragrance of the magnolias comes close / False flick, false form, but falseness close to kin' (1990: 385). It is not to be seen and yet can be perceived and lives in change, in the modifications that the poem enacts and which is triggered in the re-enactment of various readings (which suggests change through motion). Indeed, reading triggers and perpetuates the rhythms that the poem produces, as we move from abstraction, to change, and pleasure, enlarging the space of its fruition.

The demand for abstraction of the first canto, where the ephebe is incited to 'see the sun again with an ignorant eye / And see it clearly in the idea of it', without 'suppos[ing] an inventing mind as a source / Of this idea' (380), clearly alludes to man's longing for significance in the absence of certainties – 'the death of one god is the death of all' – and the necessity to restore the essential value of things and words. This is the first phase of the process of 'decreation',[2] closely related to abstraction, through which we come to see the world as uncreated. Stevens's secular use of decreation, however, entails a further stage that bestows a positive, compositional force on it (re-creation), which in 'Notes' is extended through the exploration of what changes and gives pleasure.

'It Must Be Abstract' is punctuated by playful presentations of shape-shifting figures (the giant of the weather, major man, the figure in sagging pantaloons) that never settle in any 'singular' incarnation, being 'abler in the abstract'. The figure in 'old coat' and 'sagging pantaloons' who 'confect[s] the final elegance, not to console / Nor sanctify, but plainly to propound' (1990: 389) is at once presented and dismissed, followed as it is by the powerful demand of Section Two of the poem: 'It Must Change'. In this section, the allure of change within sameness in the ordinary is presented in a graduated approach until the sparkle in the motion of 'transformation [becomes] the freshness of a world' (397–8). 'It Must Give Pleasure' redefines nature's monotonous sounds as a more tolerable cyclic repetition and a source of pleasure (405–6). In contrast to Canon Aspirin's imposing mind in canto vii, the crucial verb is here 'to discover' (403). By means of this discovery, it will be possible to find the real, 'seeming, at first, a beast disgorged, unlike, / Warmed by a desperate milk … / To be stripped of every fiction except one, / The fiction of an absolute' (404). The last lines of 'Notes' acknowledge the centrality of the 'irrational rational' and reveal feeling and mutability as essential aspects of the poetic energy,[3] perceiving the earth 'in a moving contour, a change not quite completed' (1990: 406), seen in the moment between changes, different yet not fully transformed.

What the poem thus shows is the continual process of creation, never reaching closure but constantly re-elaborating its fragmentary parts.[4] In this way, Stevens's adoption of the dialectical triad for the production of a poem that both subverts and exploits it is an active experimentation which expands the alternate possibilities of a given pattern. Already we might begin to see connections to

Banville's writing on a formal level, with its interest in what can be defined as an 'active re-elaboration' of received forms as opposed to fruitless speculating on the production of the purely 'new'. Banville's own musings on the significance of form evoked earlier aptly echo Stevens's words in 'A Note on Poetry' that 'All poetry is experimental poetry', since 'form is to be free in whatever form is used' (1989: 187, 240).

For both Banville and Stevens, the formal tension underlying the work of art embodies and bears out concerns about the role of the artist in 'a leaden time' (Stevens 1965: 63), unveiling a conflict that is political and social as well as aesthetic. Despite the charge of indifference to social and political issues of their own times, both writers use the imagination and related modes of expression as a way to access the real and not as a circumventing strategy.[5] For Stevens, the necessity for abstraction in poetry should not be conceived in contrast to the concrete or the particular but as a way of 'stat[ing] the premise of an epistemology by which even the most sensuous detail remains radically a product of abstraction' (Leggett 1987: 40).[6] The links between abstraction and the other two features of the supreme fiction in 'Notes' (change and pleasure) are crucial in preserving the world's 'most sensuous detail[s]', because in de-creating false conceptions the artist also re-creates something like a 'new knowledge of reality' (1990: 534). Similarly, Banville's use of transcendence to illuminate things, as discussed below, does not intend to evade the real but provides a way of accepting our strategies of perception in engaging with the world. Banville's fictional universe immerses the reader in the myriad of sensory impressions that interrupt the narrator's attempt to maintain a sense of totality within multiplicity. Overriding the convention of self-recollection and emplotment, his works require an active engagement with the narrators' journeys of discovery in a world of interconnected realms that are sharable and enriched with every new reading.

Although using different terms to define the shifting modes of the imagination in saying things in the work of art, Stevens and Banville believe in the supreme fiction as a necessary fiction which is inseparable from one's experience of the world. This is why the supreme fiction breaks the imagination–reality quandary in its ability to relate at once to a search for the real as well as 'the fiction of an absolute' (1989: 404) Stevens's reference to the need to yield to a 'declared fiction', 'to believe in something that we know to be untrue' (1996: 430), is expressed in correspondence with Gilbert Montague: 'We are confronted by a choice of ideas: the idea of God and the idea of man. The purpose of NOTES is to suggest the possibility of a third idea; the idea of a fictive being, or state, or thing as the object of belief by way of making up for that element of humanism which is its chief defect' (in Cook 1988: 214). His suggestion of a third idea, the idea of a fictive state, gestures towards the supreme fiction as a fictive abstract that elevates the individual's needs to a more communal level, while keeping intact the binding sense of the commonplace. Abstraction then is envisaged as a necessary condition, not for an arbitrary fiction making that exists only in the mind, but as a means of getting closer to the world we inhabit, since without the supreme fictions 'we are unable to conceive of [life]' (1965: 31).

Stevens's discussion of nobility as a key force of the imagination, and in its relation to the sharable quality of the abstract, is useful for an understanding of varying dimensions of perception in his poetry as well as in Banville's work. In the last section of 'The Noble Rider and the Sound of Words' (1942), Stevens once again avoids clear definitions, rendering the variable quality of nobility in comparison with a wave: 'As a wave is a force and not the water of which it is composed, which is never the same, so nobility is a force and not the manifestations of which it is composed' (1965: 34). Encouraging associations between an abstract concept (nobility) and the shape-shifting fluid force of water, the simile redefines our sensory perceptions of reality, shifting our focus from substance to subtlety. This conception of nobility pushes for a 'molecular' perception of things in Deleuzian terms, explored in Stevens's late poems, which is registered in motion in the shifting contours of a virtual dimension.[7] Stevens's mode of perception allows for a 'travers[ing]' between the realms of the visible and the invisible, as rendered in 'An Ordinary Evening in New Haven', introducing a play of possibilities in the permeation of 'dust[s]' and 'shade[s]': 'It is not in the premise that reality / Is a solid. It may be a shade that traverses / A dust, a force that traverses a shade' (1990: 489). The novelty and characteristic trait of this virtual space is that it is shareable, inviting the reader's participation, as in modern abstract painting,[8] precisely because it resists representation or fixed embodiment. Stevens's poetry registers, in fact, the passage from 'place' to 'occasion', since the virtual space becomes a 'real unreality', as it were, in the act of each individual's reading (the way we look at paintings or respond to a poem's varying movements), laying the basis for the theory of poetry to become the theory of life, as Stevens tirelessly observed. For Stevens, as for Banville, the task of the poet is not to provide readers with consoling tales, but to turn 'his imagination ... [into] the light in the mind of others' (1965: 25), since 'the imagination changes as the mind changes' (1989: 199). Art serves to illuminate things as if objects had a virtual energy of their own beyond the solidity of their physical contours and of fixed interpretations.

Dimensions of perception in Banville's Art trilogy

In an interview with Hedwig Schwall, Banville provides an account of the way he uses the imagination, distinguishing his art from John McGahern's:

> He [McGahern] has to fight against the imagination. He has to make things as straightforward, as square, as solid and earthly as possible; to get at truth by chopping away things. ... Don't imagine, say how it was! ... But my way of doing things is to accumulate, to set up, to set things going at such speed that they begin to glow. And the only way to do that is to elaborate and to use all the force and weight and power of the imagination. (Schwall 1997: 18)

For Banville art serves to endow things with an intensity which, though not partaking of their 'own li[ves] in the world', is triggered by the elusive presence of things themselves: 'It's the thing that keeps you writing ... that is what Art is for' (Sheenan, Banville, and Stuart 1979: 84). Yet, the contrast presented in this extract between the two writers' techniques (erasure vs. accretion) unveils a subtler understanding of the artist's use of the imagination. As Banville explains in a later interview, this method entails a way of 'be[ing] transcendent into the world, not out of it ... to make reality become reality' (Piñeiro and Banville 2015: 60). This relentless faith in the possibility of illuminating things, 'to make the world blush' (2015: 60), recalls Stevens's traversing of realms (visual, spatial, historical) in the virtual space of the poem, something which is mapped at the point of tension between the writer's 'rage for order' and the acknowledgement of reality's alterity. My analysis of Banville's Art trilogy in this section will show how his redefinition of key Stevensian concepts (supreme fiction, abstraction, nobility, the enigma of the commonplace) allows for a fruitful examination of modernist aesthetics and their significant function in the development of contemporary narrative modes. Both artists' grappling with the imagination develops through distinct phases. In Stevens, this tension between possibility and restriction is visible in the move from his early poems' musings on the mind–reality quandary to a closer adherence, in 'Notes' and his later poems, to a poetic expression that gestures towards the real as subtlety rather than object. In Banville, it is shown in the way Copernicus's and Kepler's searches for systems of order give way, in the post-tetralogy novels, to a fuller engagement with the varying phases of the creative process. I argue that the trilogy on art – *The Book of Evidence*, *Ghosts* and *Athena* (1989–1995) – extends some of the concerns presented in Banville's earlier novels, introducing the ethical nature of one's relation with the world (things, people and the work of art) and thus revealing a fuller dialogue between Banville's work and Stevens's idea of a poetry that is the poetry of life.

The novels of the trilogy trace Freddie's obsession with art, which culminates in his stealing of a painting by an unnamed Dutch master, and the murder of the maid, Josie Bell, who catches him red-handed. While in prison he starts studying Dutch painting, and becomes an expert in the field, moving to an island off the Irish coast to work as Professor Kreutznaer's amanuensis after completing his ten-year sentence, as described in *Ghosts*. The last book of the trilogy, *Athena*, set in Dublin, recalls how, after changing his name to Morrow, Freddie is asked by a dubious character, Morden, to authenticate eight paintings. In the same house where the paintings are stored he meets A., a girl with whom he starts an unlikely relationship that ends with her departure, from Morrow's life and mind (the latter especially if we recognize that she is a figment of his imagination). Banville's trilogy explores the nuances of the narrator's act of creation *after* the crisis of imagination, and thereby recalls Stevens's grappling with the idea of a fictive abstract as the poet's necessary act of adaptation to the pressure of his own time (1965: 36). The ending of *The Book of Evidence* (Freddie's prison memoir) initiates this exploration, where Freddie's task to 'bring her [Josie] back to life' is envisaged as a way of compensating for the 'failure of imagination' that made the murder possible.

The motives that engendered Freddie's failure to imagine Josie 'vividly enough' (1990: 216) derive from his obsession with art as a gateway to 'a different version of reality' (1998: 83) and his tendency to move between extremes of transfiguration and erasure. Although he feels compelled to imagine a life for the figure depicted in *Portrait of a Woman with Gloves*, a seventeenth-century middle-aged woman, in response to her insistent gaze – 'It is as if she were asking me to let her live' (1990: 105) – he is blind to the presence of the maid. In an excess of imaginative flair, Freddie envisions the painted woman as her widowed father's only consolation, giving a detailed account of her at once reticent and strict attitude. Perceived as an obstacle to his plan to set the 'woman with gloves' free, Freddie finds himself unable to develop a human response for the chambermaid, whom he first kidnaps and then murders in his car.

Yet, the confession of his failure of imagination seems to be at loggerheads with a passage that denotes 'wonder' at Josie's presence, just before delivering her the first hammer blow: 'I had never felt another's presence so immediately and with such raw force. I saw her now, really saw her, for the first time, her mousy hair and bad skin, that bruised look around her eyes' (113). As the unnamed narrator of *Ghosts* puts it: 'How, with such knowledge, could he have gone ahead and killed?' (1994: 86).[9] For Banville, knowledge is not understanding and seeing is not perception, as there is a gap between the seeing eye and the understanding mind (Schwall 1997: 15). In *Shroud*, he addresses this paradox in clearer terms: 'Some things, real things, seem to happen not in the world itself but in the gap between actuality and the mind's apprehending; the eye registers the event but the understanding lags' (2002: 352). In *Ghosts*, the gap between the eye's vision and the mind's apprehension is restaged when Freddie realizes that Flora is no longer a figment of his imagination: 'A girl, just a girl, greedy and dissatisfied. ... But this is not what I saw, that is not what I would let myself see' (239). Freddie's description of his 'essential sin', then, needs more careful consideration. His inability to see Josie as a fellow human being (different yet similar to him) only covers one aspect of his failure: the wish to appropriate the maid's otherness by superimposing his own categories on her. If, however, we understand imagination as the ability to 'invent the other' (Attridge 1999: 20–31; Derrida 1992: 311–43), in the Stevensian sense of 'discovering', then Freddie's failure can be conceived as his inability to notice Josie's singularity within sameness (similar yet different from him). Josie's radiance bespeaks the uncanny, lingering quality of something that escapes his descriptive ability; she cannot be incorporated into Freddie's imaginative patterns because she exceeds, in Levinas's terms, '*the idea of the other in me*' (1969: 50). The maid's resistance, her demand that she be treated as a fellow human being and released, reflects the moment of crisis in Freddie's imaginative ability which is epitomized in the murder, the manifestation of his inability to provide an ethical response.

If in *The Book of Evidence* the other is denied access to Freddie's art-fed cocoon of fabricated selfhood, in *Ghosts* the making of a new life in Flora is encumbered by the extravagant creations that populate the narrative – a group of castaways seeking shelter in Professor Kreutznaer's house – and the intricate play of 'worlds within worlds' (55) that it stages. As the 'little god' of his fiction, Freddie strives to make his characters real, yet both creations and creator lack the sense of 'thereness' that he sees in the old inhabitants of the island (Sergeant Toner, the civic guard, Mr Tighe, the shopman, and Miss Broaders): 'I held on to them as if they were a handle by which I might hold on to things, to solid, simple ... things, and to myself among them' (37). The title, *Ghosts*, then, refers both to his puppet-like creations with their 'disjointed, improvised air' and

Freddie himself who is 'suspended in empty air [and] weightless' (37). They are neither dead (Josie) nor alive (the islanders) but 'something in between; some third thing' (29). The book registers another failure of the imagination, as Freddie's conjuring of a world for his creatures can ultimately be reduced to the idea of the other as shelter, to live *in* them rather than to make a life for them: 'Perhaps that is all I ever wanted to do, to break open the shell of the other and climb inside and slam it shut on myself, terrible spikes and all' (238). Even the revelatory moment at the end of Part I – when Flora is seen as an 'incarnation of herself, no longer a nexus of adjectives but pure and present noun' (147) – is achieved only by a short-lived moment of detachment from the little god's conflated imaginings. *Ghosts* closes with the realization that Freddie is indeed 'only at the beginning of this birthing business' (239). The self-perpetuating world of *Ghosts*, then, must yield to subtler strategies of perception which recall Stevens's own grappling with the nuances of the fictive abstract as access to the real.

It is only in *Athena* that the encounter with the other is restructured and mediated through loss, 'solitude and making-do' (1998: 226). The narrative is taken up by Morrow – Freddie himself transfigured – who leads the reader through meandering explorations of A., the girl with whom he is in love and who suddenly leaves him. *Athena* traces an approximation to the 'ineffable mystery of the Other' (47) which rests upon Freddie's loss of A., the motive that initiates the narrative: 'Write to me, she said' (233). Presented as a lover's letter of apology and explanation, *Athena* stages the narrator's (and writer's) dilemma in the opening pages when Morrow tries to measure the extent of his sense of loss:

> I feel as I have not felt since I was a lovelorn adolescent, at once bereft and lightened, giddy with relief at your going – you were too *much* for me – and yet assailed by a sorrow so weighty, of so much more consequence than I seem to myself to be, that I stand, no, I kneel before it, speechless in a kind of awe. There are moments when I think I might die of the loss of you. … And yet at the same time I feel I have never been so vividly alive, so quick with the sense of things, so exposed in the midst of the world's seething play of particles, as if I had been flayed of an exquisitely fine protective skin. (3)

Morrow's relief at A.'s departure bespeaks his inability to respond to her as existing beyond his imaginings – 'you were too *much* for me'. Yet, he also feels a heightened exposure to the 'sense of things' and their network of relations, as if the removal of a 'protective skin' had suddenly made him alive to the complexity of 'the world's … play of particles' and of intersubjective exchange: not the idea of the other in me or in our relation to others, but the haunting quality of the other as an uncanny yet inalienable part of selfhood.

It is clear, then, that the term 'imagination' in the trilogy, the 'act of parturition' that links all the three books, goes through a series of redefinitions; it is not always reducible to the imaginative appropriation of things and people (*The Book of Evidence* and *Ghosts*), but gestures, as in Stevens, towards the making of a fiction that exposes the dynamics of differential relations and provides a more vivid sense of the real (*Athena*). As Morrow muses in *Athena*: 'Probably I am imagining, that's why it seems so real' (35). The book's many subplots all contribute to a subtle subversion of the real/unreal quandary which constantly frustrates the many quests for authenticity that intercalate the main narrative: Morrow's involvement with Morden, Inspector Hackett and Aunt Corky; the figuration of an array of 'incidental grotesque[s]' and beggars; the mirroring of Morrow's relationship with A. in the art summaries interposed with the main narrative. More than an arbitrary confusion of categories of knowledge, the book suggests a sense of the real that is inextricable from the imagined – 'the real [as] constantly engulfed in the unreal' (1965: 25) – and that is rendered in a single stroke with a sense of delight, amazement and failure. On a performative level, the varying layers of signification act as Stevens's sharable quality of the abstract, maintaining the vitality of the creative process in the act of reading and in negotiation with ever-renewing interpretations.

Things then are as they appear and yet different, as the reader is explicitly reminded in the critique of the fourth painting, the *Syrinx Delivered* (1645). Inserted almost casually towards the middle of the book, the reference to the Syrinx is a crucial underlying motif in *Athena* as well as in the trilogy and its relation to artistic creation. Depicted at the moment that immediately precedes her metamorphosis into the world of nature while pursued by Pan, the Syrinx represents 'what changes and yet endures', epitomizing the tension between the drive for transcendence and the realization that everything 'will be just as it is and yet wholly different' (105), as in Adorno's dictum paraphrased in the book. Seen in this way, *Athena* offers a stage for the illuminations of both self and world in the play of perspectives and blurring of boundaries that characterize the novel, while returning us to the enduring kernel of the world.

Art provides a multifarious space for the exploration of a reality that is not separate but intertwined with our perception of things. The interrelation of art and life (mind and world), in the fabrication of a supreme fiction is reflected in the leitmotif of the love story, an engagement with the singularity of the other par excellence which is also a perfect example of what 'changes and yet endures' (105). Morrow's desire to 'fix a single object [A.] ... in the mind's violent gaze' embodies the paradox of capturing that which is pervasive yet at the same time absent from the narrative. The sequence of encounters with A. is depicted as a complicated game of reflections in 'the moving mirror in which [Morrow] surpris[es] [him]self', as 'a goggle-eyed Actaeon' (118). A. is 'the goddess of movement and transformations', perennially fluctuant in the multiplicity afforded by the choice of the letter 'A': 'Abstract, abstracted, abstractedly, and then the variants, such as absently, and absent-minded, and now, of course, in this endless aftermath ... just: absent' (47).

A closer approximation to the singularity of this uncapturable other is possible only when Morrow's obsession with fixing her in his mind in a 'single image' fails, the eerie vividness of her 'contours' delimiting the extent of his loss: 'I see her turning slowly in the depths of memory's screen, fixed and staring, too real to be real, like one of those three-dimensional models that computers make. It is then, when she is at her vividest, that I know I have lost her forever' (219, 161). Loss, both her disappearance and the decaying image of her in his memory, is indeed a prerequisite for Morrow's new selfhood, as well as for the making of the letter-book. The fleeting nature of the force that 'operate[s]' and 'burns' in the lovers, as in the act of creation, does not allow for a stable sense of its presence, but can only be registered in its passing – 'It is a force whose action is so delicate and so fleeting we hardly feel it operating in us before it has become a thing of the past' (118). It is through the lovers that something that endures passes, and something that changes endures.

It is only in an imageless state, in Morrow's thought of the 'idea of her' (97) that A. can be glimpsed. In perceiving A. in the idea of her, he is left with a sense of her presence that goes beyond mere sight and is felt, like the filtered light of a sun that is present yet unseen through a misty morning, as an emotion that pervades his whole being: 'For, even when she was still here, still with me, if I summoned her to mind it was not she who came but only the vague, soft sense of her, a sort of vaporous cloud through which her presence gleamed like the sun unseen gleaming through a mist at morning' (97). Morrow's insistence on a vague yet permeating sense of A. reveals a series of intertextual and intra-textual resonances: the motif of the sun-God, Phoebus, in 'Notes' via Keats's *To Autumn* and the art commentary in *Pursuit of Daphne* in *Athena*. The incitation to the ephebe to 'see the sun again with an ignorant eye / ... in the idea of it' (380) enacts a metamorphosis from the sun as a 'voluminous master folded in fire' to the slumbering motion of its force suffused in 'autumn umber' (381). Speaking to and through precursors, the metamorphoses of Banville's Apollo in the art critique, experiencing loss of the object of his desire (Daphne) and his own selfhood, reverberate in Morrow's musings on A., epitomizing the artist's predicament in the making of the work of art.[10] Evoking Stevens's shift from substance to subtlety, the thought of A. engenders a passage from the fixity of image-making to feeling; a sense of the real that is mediated through the unreal.

Banville's proximity to the aesthetics of Stevens acquires a new significance in the novels, especially from *Athena* onwards, where the desire to tell, write, and go on is echoed in the narrators' quests, enhanced, as it were, by their performative quality. *Athena*'s focus on modes of perception which are multiple and sharable is enacted by a number of strategies underlying the performative valence of its narration and in the 'play of differences' (*différance*) that make signification possible (Derrida 1981: 26–7). Morrow's attempt to respond to A., his absent interlocutor, is characterized by a dynamic interplay between speech and writing (Derrida 1976: 61–5), as his utterance is inseparable from the attempt to explore varying dimensions in his encounter with the 'flicker[ing] and shimmer[ing]' otherness of A. (48). The constant shift between second- and third-person pronouns when addressing A. – 'And yet you, she – both of you!' (89) – enacts the merging of modes of telling and narration epitomized in the book's opening and closing lines: 'My love ... listen. I have things to tell you' (1); 'Write to me she said ... I have written' (233).

The effects of analogy add a further layer of signification to the differential levels of perception deployed in *Athena* through the use of simile, a peculiar trait in Banville's writing (as discussed in Michael Springer's work in this volume) which also pervades Stevens's poetry. If, on the one hand, the mode of analogy employed by Banville seems to support a denial of coincidence in the idea that everything is like everything else, reworked in various ways in his novels, it is also, on the other hand, a means to extend its effects in the richer ensemble of tunes that reverberate in his fictional universe. Unlike metaphors which offer a more defined adherence between tenor and vehicle, similes 'impose an additional cognitive burden to the listener' (Glucksberg and Keysar 1990: 16) for the way in which they highlight the terms of the comparison. Morrow appraises the 'soft sense' of A. as 'a sort of vaporous cloud ... [which] gleamed like the sun unseen gleaming through a mist at morning' (97). The double simile encourages a series of possible associations in the chain of signification of A. Promoting analogy with the literal properties of the vehicle, rather than to its symbolic qualities as in the case of metaphor, the simile returns the idea of A. to the perception of material reality: the insubstantial, porous quality of clouds, and the suffused light of the sun filtered through mist. The passage from image to feeling, or from product to subtlety, highlighted above is revealed in action through ever-renewing interpretations of the simile in the experience of reading (Stevens 1989: 170), its effect heightened by a sharp focus on the process of comparing. It also creates a play of resonances within and between works, providing the occasion, for both narrators and readers, to be 'plagued with coincidences' (Banville 2005: 97).

Writing from after the end: John Banville's 'series writing'

The discussion of key Stevensian concepts in the first part of this chapter provides the platform for the exploration of Banville's redefinition and experience of fiction making and writing alterity. Furthermore, it also paves the way for consideration of subtler links to the 'radical openness' that characterizes Banville's 'elaborate fictive universe' (Murphy 2018: 20). Banville's use of these concepts acquires further significance in its relation to the making of the work of art and the tension between desire (the writer's wish to go on) and absence (the irreducible alterity of the world). Taking a cue from Stevens's elaboration on the evasive notion of the supreme fiction as the poetry of life and as the multifarious embodiment of the tension between openness and overlaid pattern, it is possible to trace some of the unique characteristics of contemporary sequence writing. Stevens's insistence on the vitality of the concept of the supreme fiction and its resistance to being fixed within defined patterns, makes it a crucial point of departure for an examination of Banville's own exploration of the artistic process in the novel as the poetry of life beyond genre distinctions (Banville 1981: 16). In his refusal to define the supreme fiction, Stevens seems, in a letter to Hi Simons, to anticipate the extent of its influence on future generations of writers:

> As I see the subject, it could occupy a school of rabbis for the next generations. In trying to create something as valid as the idea of God has been … the first necessity seems to be breadth. It is true that the thing would never amount to much until there is no breadth or, rather, until it has all come to a point. (1966: 435)

For Stevens, the grappling with the 'enigma' of a supreme fiction becomes a stage for the predicament of the artist torn between 'the poetry of the idea' and the poetic text. In addition, the characteristics of a supreme fiction clearly go beyond the borders of 'Notes' both thematically – 'it is confined to a statement of a few of those characteristics' – and structurally, in the sense that it is a first attempt in a wider search for breadth that includes poetry as an idea, and not just as a mode of expression. Until future generations try 'to create something as valid as the idea of God has been' the poetry of 'Notes' seems to be the only possible way to glimpse the lingering absence of a poetic energy (Rilke's and Stevens's focus on the value of saying) that exceeds the written word (the said). The peculiar stylistic tension of 'Notes' coincides, in fact, with a change in form: the long poem. Thus, Stevens's concern with the expression of poetic writing in the early 1940s results in the adoption of a form that promotes engagement, both on the part of the poet and the reader, leaving space for creative improvisation in the 'Theatre of Tropes' that it stages. The long poem is both a way of moving forward, in the unfolding of new stories and feelings, and of folding back to its own (hi)stor(ies), revealing 'traces of an unexpected genealogy' (Stevens 1965: 50).

The appeal of 'Notes' depends precisely on the contrast between overlaid pattern and liberated manner that the long poem engenders, which contributes to the making of this poem as a landmark in Stevens's career and a model for future generations (Gelpi 1985). Michael Davidson considers 'Notes' to be 'one of the primary models for contemporary poets in their attempt to move beyond the single, self-sufficient lyric to the 'poem of a life' (1985: 146). Indeed, considering poetry in its enlarged sense of creative writing, as Banville does, one can see how Davidson's study of the legacy of Stevens's work on contemporary poetry can be extended to much post-war fiction for its tendency to use a structured yet porous form, like the sequence of novels (Connor 1996: 136–9), a practice also repeatedly found in twenty-first-century fiction.[11] The sequence has been used in a variety of ways until recent times, finding perhaps its extreme example in the oxymoronic and chiastic prose of Beckett's *Trilogy* (1950–2) and in the 'creative expansiveness' (Gontarski 1996: xvii) of *Nohow On* (1980–3). Yet despite such stylistic openness, what has stimulated critics' and writers' attention alike is that both the long poem and sequence writing permit a higher degree of attention to variation within continuity, which is manifested in the reworking of themes as well as in the forms' unique ways of interrogating their own condition of possibility. In this way the unfolding of the sequence, just like Stevens's 'Notes', is pitched against existing narrative styles and projected into a description of a space which is yet to come, at once self-contained, as a product, and open to the alterity of the writing process. It is in this sense that the sequence resists embodiment while presenting multiplicity of perspectives, just like the playful appearance of shape-shifting figures in 'Notes'.

In Banville's fictional universe, the sense of totality is created not only by the intertextual relations to concepts and ideas expressed by a range of literary and philosophical precursors, but also by a pattern of intra-textuality (or cross-referencing) that characterizes his novels. Manifesting itself both in terms of narrative voice (a kind of *retour de personnage*) and adoption of interlocking thematic and narrative units, intra-textuality is particularly relevant to our discussion, since, more than buttressing ontological connections, it can be conceived as a peculiar challenge to narrative closure. Far from aiming at arbitrary fragmentation and unending deferral of meaning, however, this challenge aims to engage with some sort of textual continuity that is reflected in the habit of writing novel sequences. Indeed, a series embodies a textual paradox that defers closure while gesturing towards the formation of a whole, 'reminding us of the incompleteness of any ending', as Steven Connor has suggested, yet 'produc[ing] in the reader the expectation of totality' (2002: 1). In Banville, sequence writing provides a fertile link to works that interrogate their own form and that make of the tension between totality and fragmentation an intriguing point of departure. In this way the sequence conflates genres and expands writing; it exists in the open endings of each book, a pattern which is always liable to interruption and discontinuity.

The re-elaboration of material is a process that occurs not only in the novel sequences (the science tetralogy, 1976–86; the Art trilogy, 1989–95), but also in the books that – though connected – were published outside of a formal sequence (*Eclipse,* 2000, *Shroud,* 2002, and *Ancient Light,* 2012), and in the fictions that stand alone. Hence the possibility exists for Banville's books to be read both in sequence or by themselves, at times engendering more unexpected connections with the later novels. This has led critics to postulate the existence of other unofficial series, exploiting, as it were, the highly intra-textual quality of his fiction that is revealed, most intensely, in liminal texts.[12] Banville's own comments on the making of his sequences evince what Steven Connor identifies as the ability of the sequence to move 'forward by its way of arising out of itself' (7). The Art series, for instance, came about in random fashion with Banville's realization of the return of Freddie's voice while writing the first chapter of *Ghosts*: 'I couldn't get past that first chapter. And then … that voice just began to speak again. And when I finished that book I realized there had to be a third one. It had to be an arch shape, with *Ghosts* as a kind of central stone. But I'm not sure I was right; maybe *Athena* was one book too many' (Banville 1981: 13). This passage seems to hint at an underlying lack of control on the part of the author to the extent that the Art trilogy seems as much a result of Banville's improvisation as of the wish to adopt a patterned triadic frame with '*Ghosts* as a kind of central stone' and *Athena* as the concluding novel. In spite of its supposedly cohesive function, *Ghosts* is transitional and adopts a non-linear movement that returns the reader to its beginning with 'little god['s]' musings on having 'achieved nothing' and being 'locked in the same old glass prison of myself' (236). Similarly, *Athena* registers the typical openness of the series more radically, since the 'too many [concerns of] ... one book' break into the narrative space of later novels. The re-elaboration of a series of characters that escape the narrator's control and appear as 'marginal' (outcasts and beggars in the 'theatre of the streets') across *Athena*, *Eclipse* and *Shroud* is central to the economy of the main narrative (Morrow-A., Alex-Cass-Axel), as I have shown elsewhere (Palazzolo 2005: 219–25). This is because they embody a residual quality of the writing of otherness explored at greater length through figures (Cass, Magda) that inhabit a 'median plane' (Banville 2002: 332).[13]

Such improvisation is not confined to the Art trilogy, and even the planned sequence – the science tetralogy – seems to escape the writer's jurisdiction at some crucial junctures. Originally conceived as a series on four great scientists (Copernicus, Kepler, Newton and Einstein), the tetralogy elicits a sense of totality while at the same time escaping the boundaries of the sequence in which the works are supposedly contained. The third novel, *The Newton Letter: An interlude,* introduces a shift in the design of the series, moving from the fictional biography of historical figures (Copernicus and Kepler) to more compelling concerns with the epistemological crisis of knowledge as epitomized by the narrator's disbelief in the possibility of completing his biography of Newton.[14] The shift, both in generic form and point of view, functions as an apt 'interlude' to the series, as the subtitle stresses, starting an inquiry into the dynamics of writing – and sequence writing – that will become central in Banville's subsequent series and later fiction. Acting as a transitional work within Banville's oeuvre, *The Newton Letter* reflects the significance of textual openness which is restaged, once again, in the last book of the tetralogy, *Mefisto*. Again, this is not a book on Einstein, as originally planned, but on the interplay of chance and order in the life of Gabriel Swan, a present-time scientist. His desire to find order and harmony in the randomness of life is constantly undermined in the narrative not only with a back-to-back revisitation of the events in Part II, but also with an ending that favours becoming over stable identity. The image of Gabriel waiting to see his 'almost mended' new face after recovering from the injuries he suffered in the fire points to yet another beginning: 'I want no protectors now. I want to be, to be, what, I don't know. Naked. Flayed. A howling babe, waving furious fists. I don't know' (Banville 1987: 234).

It is clear, then, that Banville engages the reader with a series of interlocking works that can be enjoyed both individually and as parts of a whole, with each new novel functioning as a 'variation on a theme' (Hand 2002: 176). His latest book to date, *Mrs Osmond* (2017), reopens the game of possibilities not only in dialogue with Henry James, but also for the openness of its Banvillean conclusion, as demonstrated in Elke D'hoker's lucid analysis of the novel in this volume.

Banville's indebtedness to Stevens's work has provided a useful measure for pinpointing the ways his fiction fashions a unique narrative style that is both nurtured by the influence of its predecessors and yet projects its own vision into a kind of 'new synthesis'. It has also shown how the journeys traced by the many narrator-writer figures populating Banville's fiction can be illuminated in a world of interconnected realms both within the narrative and in the 'extended wings' (Stevens 1990: 70) of his interlocking works. Like Stevens's elevation in the appreciation of the evanescent reality of the work of art glimpsed in his last poem, 'As You Leave the Room', Banville's writing does not enclose but passes *through* each new beginning, *as if* 'nothing has been changed except what is / Unreal, as if nothing had been changed at all' (1989: 117).

Notes

1 First published separately by the Cummington Press (1942), 'Notes' was included in *Transport to Summer* (1947) as the closing poem.
2 Adapted from Simone Weil's *La Pesanteur et La Grâce* where she defines it as 'making pass from the created to the uncreated' and opposes it to destruction which is the 'making pass from the created to nothingness', the term 'decreation' is crucial to Stevens's elaboration of a theory of poetry as theory of life in modern times (Weil ([1948] 1987). Roy Harvey Pearce (1980: 287) unveils the multilayered functions of the process of decreation 'first as a condition of the working of imagination, then as a process, and finally as an integral component of poetic realization'.
3 In 'The Irrational Element in Poetry', Stevens discussed the irrational as both part of nature (the weather's will to change, for example) and man (as in unpredictable changes of poetic energy) and explains that the changes 'reflect the effects of poetic energy; for where there are no fluctuations, poetic energy is absent' (1989: 232).
4 The coda about the soldier is not conceived as a proper closure to 'Notes'; see Vendler (1969: 205).

5 Written just as the United States entered the war, 'Notes' evokes Stevens's concerns about the role of the artist in 'a leaden time' as the world 'does not move for the weight of its own heaviness' (1965: 63). Stevens's emphasis on the necessity for poetic abstraction is a means to endure and preserve the tension between the 'imperative of a war' and the wish 'to return to the humdrum world of peace' (Longenbach 1991: 253). In Banville, the shift from the Irish context of *Nightspawn* and *Birchwood* to the more international settings of the science tetralogy and later novels is not a flight from the sociopolitical situation of his country, rather it expands the examination of the epistemological questions raised in a previous work in a critique of forms of historical and cultural representations (Palazzolo 2005: 58–9).

6 See also Longenbach's link between Stevens's insistence on the necessity for the abstract and the Abstract expressionists' call for 'art that made sense of "the present world upheaval" in a language transcending the barriers of nationality and class' (253).

7 For critical accounts of Deleuze's theory of human sensory experience, see Daniel W. Smith (1996: 29-56) and Brian Massumi (1996: 217–39).

8 As Stevens considered, it is 'a subtlety in which it was natural for Cézanne to say: "I see planes bestriding each other and sometimes straight lines seem to me to fall"' ([1951] 1965: 174).

9 For an intriguing analysis of the ethical implications of Freddie's act, see Elke D'hoker (2002: 23–37).

10 I have discussed the metamorphoses of Apollo in *Athena* in 'Desire, Pursuit, and Loss: The making of *Athena*', *Journal of Comparative Literature and Aesthetics*, 40 (3) (2019).

11 Among the works that appeared both before and after Banville's series are A. S. Byatt's quartet of novels (*The Virgin in the Garden*, *Still Life*, *Babel Tower*, *A Whistling Woman*, 1978-2002), Roddy Doyle, *The Barrytown Trilogy* (1987–91), Paul Auster's *The New York Trilogy* (1985–87), Margaret Drabble's trilogy (*The Radiant Way*, *A Natural Curiosity* and *The Gates of Ivory*, 1987–91), Pat Barker's *The Regeneration Trilogy* (1991–95), Cormac McCarthy, *The Border Trilogy* (1992–98). It is also important to consider how works can function as interlocking narratives within a wider fictional universe, as in David Mitchell's idea of 'a sprawling macrocosm' (in Dillon 2011: 5), or in the radical openness of Banville's works within and beyond the series.

12 *The Untouchable* has often been considered as the last book of an art 'tetralogy' (1989–1997) (Hand 2002: 157; Imhof 1981: 9; Tournay 2001: 12; D'hoker 2002: 12), or even as the opening novel of a trilogy with *Eclipse* and *Shroud* (1997–2002). Similarly, although conceived as separate books, *Eclipse* and *Shroud* display a highly interlocking structure which is extended to *Ancient Light* (2012), making the three books a recognizable series about Cass Cleave.

13 In *Shroud*, Cass is rendered as unknowable: 'She would not be known; there was not a unified, singular presence there to know. She was one of those creatures – Magda was another such – who exist on a median plane between the inanimate and the super-animate, between clay and angels' (Banville 2002: 332).
14 Kersti Tarien's study (2002) of the development of Banville's fiction through a detailed analysis of his manuscripts is relevant here.

References

Attridge, D. (1999), 'Innovation, Literature, Ethics: Relating to the Other', *PMLA*, 114: 20–31.
Banville, J. ([1976] 1990), *Doctor Copernicus*, London: Minerva.
Banville, J. ([1981] 1990), *Kepler*, London: Minerva.
Banville, J. ([1982] 1999), *The Newton Letter*, London: Picador.
Banville, J. ([1986] 1987), *Mefisto*, London: Paladin Grafton Books.
Banville, J. ([1989] 1990), *The Book of Evidence*, London: Minerva.
Banville, J. ([1993] 1994), *Ghosts*, London: Vintage International.
Banville, J. ([1995] 1998), *Athena*, London: Picador.
Banville, J. ([1997] 1998), *The Untouchable*, London: Picador.
Banville, J. (1981), 'A Talk', *Irish University Review*, John Banville Special Issue, 11 (1) (Spring): 13–17.
Banville, J. (1993), 'Making Little Monsters Walk', in Clare Boylan (ed.), *The Agony and the Ego: The Art and Strategy of Fiction Writing Explored*, 107–12, London: Penguin.
Banville, J. (2000), *Eclipse*, London: Picador.
Banville, J. (2002), *Shroud*, London: Picador.
Banville, J. (2005), *The Sea*, London: Picador.
Berensmeyer, I. (1999), *John Banville: Fictions of Order, Authority, Authorship, Authenticity*, Heidelberg: Universitatverläg.
Blanchot, M. (1993), *The Infinite Conversation*, trans. Susan Hanson, Minneapolis: University of Minnesota Press.
Bornstein, G. (1976), *Transformations of Romanticism in Yeats, Eliot, and Stevens*, Chicago, IL: University of Chicago Press.
Connor, S. (1996), *The English Novel in History 1950-1995*, London: Routledge.
Connor, S. (2002), 'Prosecutions: John Banville's Frames Trilogy', *Contemporary British Fiction Lecture*, London: Birkbeck College, (Autumn), unpublished paper.
Cook, E. (1988), *Poetry, Word-play and Word-war in Wallace Stevens*, Princeton, NJ: Princeton University Press.
Critchley, S. (1997), *Very Little…Almost Nothing: Death, Philosophy, Literature*, London: Routledge.

D'hoker, E. (2004), *Visions of Alterity: Representation in the Works of John Banville*, Amsterdam and New York: Rodopi.

D'hoker, E. (2002), 'Portrait of the Other as a Woman with Gloves: Ethical Perspectives in John Banville's *The Book of Evidence*', *Critique* 44 (1) (Fall): 23–37.

Davidson, M. (1985), 'Notes beyond the *Notes*: Wallace Stevens and Contemporary Poetics', in A Gelpi (ed.), *Wallace Stevens: The Poetics of Modernism*, 141–60, Cambridge: Cambridge University Press.

Derrida, J. ([1972] 1981), *Positions: Jacques Derrida*, trans. by Alan Bass, Chicago, IL: The University of Chicago Press.

Derrida, J. (1976), *Of Grammatology*, trans. Gayatri Chakravorty Spivak, Baltimore, MD: Johns Hopkins University Press.

Derrida, J. (1992), 'Psyche: Invention of the Other', in Derek Attridge (ed.), *Acts of Literature*, 311–43, New York: Routledge.

Dillon, S. (ed.), (2011), *David Mitchell: Critical Essays*, Canterbury: Gylphi.

Ferguson, G. (1997), *Modernist Influences on the Fiction of John Banville*, unpublished D.Phil. thesis, Jordanstown: University of Ulster.

Gelpi, A. (ed.), (1985), *Wallace Stevens: The Poetics of Modernism*, Cambridge: Cambridge University Press.

Glucksberg, S. and Keysar, B. (1990), 'Understanding Metaphorical Comparisons: Beyond Similarity', *Psychological Review* 97: 3–18.

Gontarski, S. E. (1996), 'The Conjuring of Something out of Nothing: Samuel Beckett's "Close Space" Novels', Introduction to Samuel Beckett, *Nohow On: Company, Ill Seen Ill Said, Worstward Ho*, vii-xxviii, New York: Grove Press.

Hand, D. (2002), *John Banville: Exploring Fictions*, Dublin: Liffey Press.

Imhof, R. (1981a), 'John Banville's Supreme Fiction', *Irish University Review*, John Banville Special Issue, 11 (1) (Spring): 52–86.

Imhof, R. (1981b), 'My Readers, That Small Band, Deserve a Rest: An Interview with John Banville', *Irish University Review*, John Banville Special Issue, 1 (1) (Spring): 5–12.

Leggett, B. J. (1987), *Wallace Stevens and Poetic Theory: Conceiving the Supreme Fiction*, Chapel Hill, NC and London: University of North Carolina Press.

Levinas, E. ([1961] 1969), *Totality and Infinity: An Essay on Interiority*, trans. Alphonso Lingis, Pittsburgh, PA: Duquesne University Press.

Longenbach, J. (1991), *Wallace Stevens: The Plain Sense of Things*, Oxford: Oxford University Press.

Massumi, B. (1996), 'The Autonomy of Affect' in Paul Patton (ed.), *Deleuze: A Critical Reader*, 217–39, Oxford: Blackwell.

McMinn, J. (1999), *The Supreme Fictions of John Banville*, Manchester: Manchester University Press.

Murphy, N. (2018), *John Banville*, Lanham, MD and London: Bucknell University Press.

Palazzolo, P. (2005), Writing Alterity: John Banville and His Encounter with the Work of Wallace Stevens and Samuel Beckett, unpublished D.Phil. thesis, Colchester: University of Essex.

Palazzolo, P. (2019), 'Desire, Pursuit, and Loss: The Making of *Athena*', *Journal of Comparative Literature and Aesthetics*, 40 (3).

Pearce, R. H. (1980), 'Toward Decreation: Stevens and the Theory of Poetry', in Frank Doggett and Robert Buttel (eds), *Wallace Stevens: A Celebration*, 286–307, Princeton, NJ: Princeton University Press.

Piñeiro, A. and J. Banville (2015), 'The Evidential Artist: A Conversation with John Banville', *Nordic Irish Studies*, 14: 55–69.

Schwall, H. (1997), 'An Interview with John Banville', *The European English Messenger*, 6 (1): 13–19.

Sheenan, R., J. Banville and F. Stuart (1979), 'Novelists on the Novel. Ronan Sheenan Talks to John Banville and Francis Stuart', *The Crane Bag*, 3 (1): 76–84.

Smith, D. W. (1996), 'Deleuze's Theory of Sensation: Overcoming the Kantian Duality', in Paul Patton (ed.), *Deleuze: A Critical Reader*, 29–56. Oxford: Blackwell.

Stevens, W. ([1951] 1965), *The Necessary Angel: Essays on Reality and the Imagination*, New York: Vintage Books.

Stevens, W. ([1954] 1990), *The Collected Poems*, New York: Vintage Books.

Stevens, W. (1966), *The Letters of Wallace Stevens*, Ed. Holly Stevens, New York: Alfred A. Knopf.

Stevens, W. (1989), *Opus Posthumous: Poems, Plays, Prose*, Ed. Milton J. Bates, New York: Alfred A. Knopf.

Tarien, K. (2002), *The Textual and Thematic Evolution of Banville's Fiction*, unpublished D.Phil. thesis, Oxford: University of Oxford.

Tournay, P. (2001), 'Into the Heart of the Labyrinth: The Pursuit of Mannerist Traditions in John Banville's *Athena*', *Miscelánea: A Journal of English and American Studies* 24: 12–25.

Vendler, H. (1969), *On Extended Wings: Wallace Stevens' Longer Poems*, Cambridge, MA: Harvard University Press.

Weil, S. ([1948] 1987), *La Pesanteur et la Grâce* (Paris: Plon, 1948), *Gravity and Grace*, trans. E. Craufurd, London: Routledge.

Ziarek, K. (1994), 'The Other Notation. Stevens and the Supreme Fiction of Poetry', in *Inflected Language: Toward a Hermeneutic of Nearness*, Albany, NY: State University of New York Press.

6

Effacing the subject: Banville, Kleist and a world without people

Rebecca Downes

'I suppose we all begin by imitation,' said Banville on writing what he claims were bad imitations of Joyce's stories before beginning to find his own voice as a writer (Friberg 2006: 200). But, if in his early years he did his best to shrug off the anxiety of influence, in recent times, he has readily embraced imitation, writing in the voice – or with the pen – of other writers, most notably Henry James with *Mrs Osmond* (2017) and (as Benjamin Black) Philip Marlowe with *The Black-Eyed Blonde* (2014). This is consistent with his abandonment of the failed quest for authenticity as a major concern and of a general shift away from the aesthetics of failure that characterizes his early novels. *Maskenfreiheit*, the fashioning of the self through the medium of the mask, has been a staple theme throughout Banville's oeuvre. The premillennial novels are all structured around a tension between the self as constituted by ostensibly inauthentic masks and a persistent nostalgia for the idea of an essential self, the quest for which is always a failed endeavour. However, the latter notion is gradually relinquished in later novels, which are distinguished by a more celebratory embrace of imitation and semblance.

Stylistically, a broadly postmodernist aesthetics characterized by negation, irony and failure give way in Banville's postmillennial novels to a more expansive prose style that emphasizes expression and affirmation. This is concomitant with an increasing interest in the alliance between creativity and mortality. Although anxieties around selfhood are still a concern in the late period, the focus is no longer on the fractured subject of modernity and the failed quest for a reality beyond appearance. Grief and loss are the major themes of the postmillennial works, and there is a new attention to the integral role played by mutuality and shared experience in the art event and a fidelity to the expressive and communicative capacities of poetic language. The thematic centrality of loss and death procures a liberation from the impasse of the 'I' persecuted by its own sense of inauthenticity and an abandonment of the quest for a putative unmediated reality beyond appearance.

During this period of transition that roughly spans the first decade of the new millennium, Heinrich von Kleist's *Amphitryon* (1807) occupies an extraordinarily dominant position in Banville's work. He wrote a stage version set during the Irish 1798 rebellion under the title *God's Gift*, which was staged in 2000, the same year he published the novel *Eclipse* in which the play figures as a major intertext. It is referenced in the next two novels, *Shroud* (2002) and *The Sea* (2005), as well as in his 2012 novel *Ancient Light*, and is the main source text for *The Infinities* (2009), which was intended as a novelistic reworking of the play. In a 2010 interview, Banville called it 'one of the greatest dramas of Western literature' (Owens 2010). His engagement with Kleist goes back at least as far as the publication of *Mefisto* (1986), which draws on Kleist's famous essay on the marionette theatre. He also adapted two more of Kleist's plays for the Irish stage – *The Broken Jug* (1994a) and a version of *Penthesilea* entitled *Love in the Wars* (2005) – but his obsessive return to *Amphitryon* warrants particular attention. Although Kleist also wrote prose, it is as a dramatist that he matters to Banville. This is somewhat ironic, because Banville's novelistic appropriations are far superior in their philosophical scope and aesthetic achievements than his dramatic adaptations, which are minor additions to his oeuvre. The novel, and more specifically the novel of ideas, is his *métier*. In fact, it is Banville's incorporation of dramatic tropes into his novels and particularly his creative appropriations of *Amphitryon* in the immediate postmillennial period that see him move on from the failed quest for authenticity played out through repeated stagings of the crisis of representation. It is the affective qualities of language rather than its representative function that interests Banville in these later novels. I use the term 'affective' here to distinguish the event qualities of the fiction, which incorporate both semantic and somatic elements, from the semiotic or textual object and to denote a capacity to alter subjects and thus to bring about changes in reality, however modest.

From the semiotics of the text to the aesthetics of the event

Banville draws on physics and painting in the science tetralogy and the Art trilogy, respectively, as analogues for the work of writing; and acting, in the postmillennial period, is another artistic cognate. The use of theatrical tropes such as dramatic monologue, the familiar references to the circus and the commedia dell'arte in *Eclipse* and *Shroud*, the observation of the Greek unities in *The Infinities* and, crucially, the adoption of *Amphitryon* as a major intertext across the postmillennial period underline the performative aspects of these novels, drawing the focus away from the semiotics of the text to the aesthetics and erotics of the event. While this is related to the thematics of love in Banville's late work, my interest here is in the art event as erotic in the broadest sense insofar as it is an experience that is intersubjective and sensory.

The event of reading and the contract between the reader and the text began to particularly interest Banville around the millennium and its aftermath. Like his narrators, Banville is accomplished in *Maskenfreiheit*, so when he speaks in the first person, outside of the novels, a certain degree of invention, which is not to say untruth, is to be expected. He freely blurs the frontier between life and art, reality and illusion. It is not surprising then that he should invoke the myth of the sirens in an anecdote about his first encounter with 'the golden world of art' (Banville 2007: 24). The fragment he describes is of a young girl skipping school when she catches the strains of her classmates singing and presumably undergoes a spiritual awakening. Banville suggests that it was he, rather than the girl in the story, who had a small epiphany, an experience of 'time-out-of-time' (25). He likens it to 'a sense, as one has in dreams, of clearly remembering a place where I have never been, a place that is at once strange and wholly familiar. … It is the world as I know it, ordinary and everyday, yet somehow immanent with inscrutable significance' (25). Whether or not it is a conjured simulacrum, a place where he has indeed never been, the fragment serves as a synecdoche for his late aesthetics. All the attributes are there: the rapturous moment, the sense of self-loss, the distortion of temporality and, crucially, the focus on the work's effect on the reader rather than its formal qualities or narrative content – the work in question was, he notes, 'hardly more than a religious pamphlet' (24). The content of the fiction in the story, like the narrative content of his own work, is secondary to the intensities it produces for the reader and merely thematizes the more ephemeral event qualities of the work, its affective force.

Banville's novels are replete with uncanny moments where time appears to speed up or stand still or instances when his characters seem strangers to themselves. Such moments are also central to Kleist's play, in which Amphitryon, a general in the Theban army, is usurped by the god Jupiter who, in the guise of her husband, seduces Amphitryon's wife Alkmene. In a parallel action, Jupiter's son Mercury transforms himself into Amphitryon's servant Sosias and holds back the dawn for an hour in order to facilitate his father's tryst. Both Sosias and Amphitryon return from battle to find their identities stolen by these doppelgänger impostors. A comedy of errors ensues, before Jupiter concedes to Amphitryon at the end of the play. The effacement of the central character provides a framework that constellates Banville's abandonment of the self-relation as a central concern with his configuring of the novel as a performative intersubjective event and his turn to death as his major theme.

The plot of the play provides Banville with an apt framework for *Eclipse*, given that he set out to write 'a book with no real centre'. Interviewed on the novel's publication, he bemoaned the necessity of having a plot with human agents. 'I think of myself as a posthumanist writer – for me, human beings are not the centre of the universe', he claimed and acknowledged 'a move toward emptying of content' (Wallace 2000). However, this should not be understood as a drive for formal purity. It is not form that Banville opposes to content but force. Banville's use of drama as an analogue to emphasize the event qualities of his novels is evidence of his interest in the experiential and temporal aspects of the art experience. He is a consummate stylist and his art aims above all at exercising and experiencing linguistic power, which is thematized in the crossovers, penetrations and usurpations within the fiction.

The repeated dismantling of coherent identity through a proliferation of substitutions in *Amphitryon* echoes features of Banville's broader oeuvre, which has long incorporated strategies of repetition, increasingly operating according to its own internal rhythms and affective significances. Banville has always remodelled and reused names and characters, reinterpreted themes and revisited ideas. His fictional world is highly reflexive, constituted by the honing of metaphors, the moulding, sculpting and polishing of a world, renewed and refined by a series of successive reworkings. Full of echoes and half-quotes, the novels build on a tropology amassed over the course of his literary career. Twins, the circus, the red-haired stranger and the commedia dell'arte are all quintessential Banvillean tropes that recur throughout his oeuvre. His characters are all variations on a small troupe of types and they become increasingly defined as types as the variations proliferate. This is especially apparent in his late trilogy, *Eclipse*, *Shroud* and *Ancient Light*, in which the proliferations of echoes and doubles becomes vertiginous. By the middle and late phases of his career, the corpus tends towards a vast phantasmagoria of simulacra.

This referential depletion should not, however, be ascribed to the disintegration of the sign and the kind of postmodern playfulness that to some extent characterizes his earlier works and indeed exemplifies the preoccupation of a host of late-twentieth-century writers, literary theorists and philosophers with the breach of the semantic link between word and world. As the work turns towards mortality as its major theme, the focus shifts away from an exploration of the limitations of figural language and on to a more celebratory interrogation of linguistic power. As the characters of classical drama were masks for the gods, Banville invites us to think of his characters, particularly in the late work, as less than, or more than, or certainly not quite, human. Like the figures of Greek drama, the circus, the commedia dell'arte or the characters of myth, they can be read as a series of masks for the Dionysian energies of the work of art. Banville's staging of subjectivity as unstable and dynamic in his reworkings of *Amphitryon* reveal a free force of life that connects subjects to one another, to external objects and, crucially, by virtue of its traversal of the margins of the self-conscious subject, to finitude and death. This transmission of life in the artistic encounter is not confined to the narrative content of the fiction or to the work of creation but is continuous and dynamic. The artwork, in this sense, should not be considered a fossil of the creative energies that brought it into being. Banville's late aesthetic repeatedly presents life as something that is manifested in encounters and interconnections and the artwork as participating in a vast network of relations. The tenuous and dispersed life of the work of art is made apparent in the emphasis that is placed on the contract between the reader and the novel, a category that comes increasingly to interest Banville in the postmillennial period. Banville plays with this contract to draw attention to the transaesthetic event of the artwork, which constitutes its relation to death. Considered in this dynamic sense as the transmission of force, poetic language is not a pale impression of a more profound, authentic reality beyond appearance, but an autonomous *becoming*.

Kleist's play is full of crossovers, substitutions and traversals of boundaries. The limit condition is central to his art, and in *Amphitryon* the god's usurpation of the man is figured as a loss of self in the very literal sense, whereby Amphitryon is figured as living beyond his own death:

AMPHITRYON: I am unhappy, I am smitten down,
    The blow destroys me, there is nothing of me left.
    I am already buried and my widow
    Already mated with another husband. (III.3)

Banville carries over this configuration of death in *Eclipse*, which opens with Alex Cleave, an actor by profession, in retreat from public life having fallen into a crippling self-consciousness and 'corpsing' on stage during a production of Kleist's play just as he is about to deliver the pivotal line 'Who, if not I, is Amphitryon?'. After four decades the actor has 'died in the middle of the last act' (2001: 11), and 'with funereal tread' he makes 'a grave, unsteady exit' before the curtain comes down, 'ponderous and solid as a stone portcullis' (90). This mirrors the opening of the novel, in which Cleave experiences an uncanny bodily invasion: 'I was accustomed to putting on personae but this, this was different' (3). This alteration in the character of the double from the actor's mask to a strange irreconcilable other is the event, repeated in various configurations throughout the novel, that underlines the temporalization of the problem of authenticity. The cleavage – evidence of Banville's fondness for nomenclative punning – into before and after marks the shift from self-fashioning to the unravelling of the self. With this unwanted intrusion, the question of the authenticity of the subject becomes the problem of accepting temporal existence and confronting the fact of death.

For the greater part of the novel, Cleave is embarked on a melancholic and often humorous self-elegy. The 'weight' or 'ballast' that has descended and eclipsed his light, 'as if something had plummeted past the sun, a winged boy, perhaps, or falling angel', is heavily alluded to as the weight of mortal awareness (3). His invocation of Dante on the opening page as he remarks on a cold that is both 'infernal' and 'paradisal' sets off a series of allusions to the afterlife (3). He begins to feel spectral himself and thinks, 'Perhaps I have at last become my own ghost' (55). Later in the novel, he declares, 'For I have died, that is what has happened to me' (167). This mock triumphalism in the face of what is apparently a rather pedestrian mid-life crisis is heavily ironic and typical of Banville's comic impulses, not least because to declare oneself dead is inherently to affirm that one is alive. The irony of Cleave's proleptic pronouncement of his death underlines the inauthenticity of his narrative but also draws a distinction, crucial to Banville's late art, between reference and utterance. The contradiction lies in the gap that opens up between *what* he says and *that* he says it. Here it is the disintegration of the sign through referential depletion that keeps the subject intact within the *mise en abyme* of language, safely at a distance from real mortal existence, the pain of alienation being much less acute than that of death. The ironic consciousness thus configured procures a safe enclave from the reality of time and death, a suspension of the self in the artifice of language conceived as a set of self-referential tropes. It is a doubling that promises an illusory immortality by infinitely reflecting the subject in the mirror of his self.

But Cleave's dramatic monologue not only underlines the split into speaker and subject and the fall into temporal consciousness. Irony, in Banville's work, is not merely an endless playing out of postmodern alienation but a distancing strategy that introduces elements of shock and humour. Such elements block emotive responses to character and situation so that the pleasures and the pathos of the text are explicitly those of language and are at least partly sundered from plot and the human drive for meaning. It is a Brechtian strategy that draws attention to the relation between the reader and the text and to the temporal event of reading. The novel is replete with episodes that resist interpretation, atmospheric fragments imbued with significance but which seem superfluous to the production of meaning within the semiotic system of the text. Whole pages are devoted to exorbitant pastoral descriptions, dream sequences, scraps of memories, many of which do nothing to drive the plot, thin as it is, or in some cases constitute dead ends in the narrative and actively disrupt coherence.

Shortly into the novel, Cleave recalls the moment when he first knew he would be an actor. Nothing remarkable is contained in the vignette that follows. It is merely a lucid description of a childhood encounter with an old woman peddling mushrooms. There is no dialogue, no crisis, but what is accented, much like the siren song of Banville's professed inauguration into the world of art, is how the scene moved the young boy: 'Something surged in me, an objectless exultancy. A myriad voices struggled within me for expression. I seemed to myself a multitude. I would utter them, that would be my task, to be them, the voiceless ones!' (11). This 'objectless exultancy' is the affirmative pole of the unbinding of word and world, which is diametrically opposed to the negative power of irony. The fracturing of the subject here does not take the form of the torturous self-relation but is an ecstatic rupture into multiplicity. The subject shorn of the illusion of self-presence becomes an inventor. The shattering of the illusion of self-presence acquires a more capacious, creative character, an expansive splintering open rather than an erasure or a self-cancelling reflexivity. The episode thematizes the role of elaborate description in Banville's art, which is to create an affective experience often unfettered to character and situation.

This is very different to description in realist fiction and is closer to the classical art of *hypotyposis* discussed by Roland Barthes in his essay 'The Reality Effect'. Barthes (1986: 142) connects modern realism, which always, albeit to varying degrees, contains 'useless detail' that serves no direct function in the production of meaning, to the beautiful in classical rhetoric. The latter, although extraneous to narrative function, has a *ceremonial* function and is intended to impress and incite admiration. Barthes distinguishes this from modern realism in which the function of superfluous detail is to signify the real by not meaning anything. What does not *mean* but merely *is* signifies life: 'what is alive cannot not signify – and vice versa' (146). But life in this reductio ad absurdum is a paradoxically moribund category, signalled by an empty sign that operates only as an absence or placeholder, and indeed Barthes positions realism as a median stage in 'modernity's grand affair', which he claims is 'to empty the sign and infinitely to postpone its object' (148). What is lost, according to Barthes, in the move from classical rhetoric to realism is the suffix '*Let there be*' and with it the 'luster of desire' that attends the ceremonial style (147, 146). Banville admits that 'let there be' with his narrator-artists, all immoderate impresarios, opulent embellishers whose lavish musings are hyperbolically infused with pathos. Their speech acts are performative rather than constative. Intentionality is not expunged here as it is in realist description, and life is not so much *signified* in the superfluity of the semantic content as *aroused* in the reader. It is this aesthetic force, this force of life erupting in the aesthetic event, that abides even through the patina of Cleave's ironic insouciance. What Banville's art aims at is an apprehension of this life freed from human context, an 'objectless exultancy' that arises out of the transmission of *desire* rather than meaning or sense.

Vivid pastoral descriptions feature more prominently in this novel than in any of Banville's other works, and they serve to collapse, intermittently, ironic distance. Rather than dramatizing a distance between self and world, the emphasis is on immersion and thrilling proximity. In one such scene, Cleave, far from being alienated from nature, declares, 'never in my life, so it seems, have I been so close up to the very stuff of the world, even as the world itself shimmers and turns transparent before my eyes' (Banville 2001: 49). The deconstructive critique of romanticism regards the preoccupation with nature in romantic literature as a desire for temporal stability, and Banville parodies this wistful desire for permanence in the Art trilogy. But the depictions of nature in *Eclipse* are very different from the still tableaux of the earlier art novels. All is movement and flux, and the narrative is replete with episodes in which the putative distance between the speaking subject and the world onto which he gazes collapses in a prose style that is sumptuous and limpid, imbued with a ceremonial resplendence. The focus is not on emptying the sign of referential content but on infusing it with a superabundance that exceeds and even deflects reference. The overt performativity of Banville's writing shifts the focus away from reference and towards the power of expression, the capacity to transmit excitations that cannot be called emotions or feelings because what is in question transcends the personal and the psychological and exists 'in itself'. These intersubjective energies of the work of art are the affects of which Deleuze and Guattari (1987: 9; 1994: 169) call Kleist the exemplary artist. It is not certain the extent to which Banville is familiar with Deleuze's writings, although he does reference Deleuze's writings on the cinema in *Ancient Light*. Rather than reading Banville through a Deleuzian lens, however, I consider them both as participants in a certain strand of aesthetic theory that can be traced back to Nietzsche and further back again to Kleist, for whom the work of art is not a representation of reality but participates in reality. Rather than being the product of a pre-existing subject, art is subject forming. Its intensities are, in this sense, presubjective and impersonal. This is why Deleuze and Guattari (1994: 169) call affects the 'nonhuman becomings of man'. It is in its capacity to produce affects and thus to offer an ecstatic mode of experience which transcends the bounds of the human subject that Banville's fiction relates to death.

This has little to do with plot. Plot is always of lesser importance to Banville than style and although the pathos of plot may echo and augment the pathos of style, in many instances Banville deliberately places them at odds. In a deep state of grief after Cass's death, Cleave remarks, 'The tragedians are wrong, grief has no grandeur. Grief is grey' (Banville 2001: 191). But the affective intensity of the novel does not follow this trajectory. Despite the more restrained and deeply sad notes in the book's final section, there is a certain continuity and even ironic humour that underlines the divergence of pathos from plot when, in reply to Miss Kettle's 'I'm sorry for your trouble', out of automatic courtesy, Cleave breezes, 'Oh, it's no trouble' (196). His melancholic self-absorption throughout the narrative is no, or not much, less affecting than his grief over his daughter's death in the final section. Nor is affect, in this sense, something ephemeral that cannot be captured by consciousness or grasped by close cognitive attention to the language. The power of the text comes from the manner in which it affords an affective experience and an apprehension of life force that does not arise within the self and cannot be contained within the individual. Affect is the flux and flow of life's intensities endowed with substantive, independent and sharable existence. It is not something that happens outside of language or that is so fleeting that it dissipates before coming to consciousness. Banville's art is a perfect rejoinder to such suppositions. The ceremonial character of his prose, its implicit 'let there be', commands a slow sort of attention and creates an intensity of affect that is not rationalized away by a consciousness that lags behind a visceral receptivity.

'Who, if not I?': The death of the other

However, it is not his own death that Cleave must ultimately confront but that of his daughter Cass, whose suicide he learns of at the end of the penultimate 'act'. The solar eclipse that attends the news of Cass's death is the organizing aesthetic principle around which the novel coheres; everything portends that occultation. The use of 'now' with the past tense augurs the cessation of becoming and the pure presence that Cleave ostensibly desires, a temporal subsidence that is foreshadowed when the time of narration and the interior time of the narrative become blurred: '[N]o, no, that is now, not then; things are running together, collapsing into each other, the present into the past, the past into the future' (167). This all anticipates the denouement and the overarching anachronism of Cleave's prescient, albeit unconscious, grieving for Cass. The apparitions of a woman that he witnesses throughout the novel, vague at first, but becoming more distinct as the narrative progresses, mirror the living presence of the caretaker's daughter Lily, who, unbeknownst to Cleave for the first section of the novel, has taken up residence in the house. When he discovers that she is living there, Cleave waits for the moment when she and the ghost will coincide, when the apparition will descend on her 'like the annunciatory angel, like the goddess herself, and illumine her with the momentary benison of her supernatural presence' (124). A transposition between Cass and Lily is implied during the eponymous eclipse and just before the news of Cass's death arrives. In an eerie scene at the circus, a malevolent clown hypnotizes Lily, prompting Cleave to come to her rescue and to claim: 'My name is Alexander Cleave, … and this is my daughter' (187). This mirrors the incident that began the unravelling of his life, and it marks a closure of sorts, a collapse of ironic distance and an answer to the question: '*Who if not I,…?*' (89). Although in his brief return to the stage Cleave attains the unselfconscious grace he so desires, it brings not the quietude of self-presence but self-loss and pain: '[I]t was as if a drop of the most refined, the purest acid had been let fall into an open chamber of my heart' (187). The implied conflation of Lily and Cass and the conjunction of night and day and of dark and light in the eclipse are figures for the collapsing of boundaries in the death space of art.

All the novels of the postmillennial period have an Orphic character. Mourning and mortality are their central preoccupations. All Banville's protagonists of this period must confront their own mortality as well as their grief in the wake of the other's death. In *The Sea*, immersed in grief after losing his wife, Max Morden is left with the same question as that which faced Alex Cleave in *Eclipse*: 'Who, if not myself, was I?' (Banville 2006: 217). As soon as the question arises, however, it is reformulated as two further questions: 'Who was to know me, if not Anna? Who was to know Anna, if not I?' (217). This makes explicit the shift away from the alienated central subject exiled in the interiority of the self-relation to a more dynamic subject constituted by the limit condition and by the other.

Numbed by grief, Alex Cleave and Max Morden invoke the events of the past in order to feel what they cannot feel directly or intensely enough in the present, and in both novels the reality of these past events is ambiguous. In *Eclipse*, just as he is about to be told of Cass's death, Alex has a sudden recollection of an outing the pair made when she was a child. She was wearing a dress 'made of layer upon layer of some very fine, translucent, gauzy stuff' (Banville 2001: 162). They encountered a group of drunk young men, one of whom had a bleeding hand and who splashed blood on Cass's dress. They returned home, Cass changed out of the dress and both of them refused to make any account of it to Lydia. An uneasy intimacy between Alex and Cass is implied throughout the late trilogy, and her literal haunting of him is a ghostly supplement to the complex emotional hold she has always maintained over him. Alex, attempting to assimilate the memory, cannot situate it in time, hence, in reality:

> I think now that what had happened had happened out of time, I mean had happened somehow not as a real event at all, with causes and consequences, but in some special way, in some special dimension of dream or memory, solely, and precisely, that it might come to me there, as I stood in the hall, in my mother's house, on an evening in summer, the last evening of what I used to think of as my life. (163)

This 'special dimension' in which dream and memory mingle is the realm of art, where the sublimations of the imagination take shape. They gain concretion, not as pale impressions of reality but as distillations and intensifications. This conceit is further developed in *The Sea*, in which Max Morden's exile into the past is ambiguously figured as an insubstantial pageant conjured by his grief-stricken imagination. However, Banville, borrowing from Henry James's *The Turn of the Screw*, guards against determinate interpretations and reductive psychological readings with a twist in the book's closing section, which posits the ostensible fiction as real. This forces the reader into an irresolvable ambiguity making it impossible to determine reality from illusion. This shuts down any division between dream and memory, sign and signified. It deflects attention from the representative function, drawing the reader out of the events depicted *in* the work to the *event of the work itself*. The power of *The Sea* lies neither in its realist nor its metaphorical account of grief but in the way it captures the very texture of grief on a level that is independent of both the order of representation and that of the symbolic.

Banville has speculated that the grief in *The Sea* may have been a delayed manifestation of his own grief for his mother and father, both of whom died when he was in his thirties ('Being John Banville' 2008). He remarks of his novel *Mefisto*, written in the aftermath of his parents' deaths: 'For the first time, out of whatever extreme of distress it was that I was in, I began to let things happen on the page which my conscious, my waking, mind could not account for' (Banville 2012b: 370). In a shift from the rigid formal structuring of the three preceding science novels, the prose style in *Mefisto* is looser, more sinuous, and in *The Sea*, where grief is dealt with directly as the central theme of the novel, this fluid style is more pronounced. Banville observes that 'part of being an artist is not being able to feel in time. … I feel after the event', he claims, 'long after the event' ('Being John Banville' 2008). The emotion in Banville's highly wrought prose is not raw, but this is not to say it is diluted or weakly reproduced. On the contrary, it is too strong, too concentrated, to be raw emotion. The stylistic rendering of the self-abandon of the newly bereaved is far too artistically refined to be unconscious as it was in *Mefisto*, but its contrivance does not diminish its force. Art for Banville is not a representation, but a refinement and an intensification, of life. This is why the past holds such a fascination for him and why he consistently portrays it as more vivid than the present, as paradoxically *more present*. In the shifting planes of Banville's fiction, the distant figures of the past and the ephemeral figments of dreams echo and often usurp present reality as the gods do in *Amphitryon*.

Nonhuman becomings

In his 2005 essay 'Fiction and the Dream', Banville declares that the 'writing of fiction is far more than the telling of stories. It is an ancient, an elemental, urge which springs, like the dream, from a desperate imperative to encode and preserve things that are buried in us deep beyond words' (2012b: 372–3). This appeal to depth should not be reduced to that psychological slogan 'the return of the repressed', not least because it exceeds the merely personal, but also owing to Banville's long-standing allegiance to Kafka's maxim 'Never again psychology!' Elsewhere, he remarks: 'Of course, my books are about life – what other subject is there? – but life is so much more than psychologising'

(McKeon 2009). Art, for Banville, is precisely the opposite of psychologizing, which delimits the sublimations of the imagination by reducing them to the personal. Banville is not interested in the codification of life through art but in its intensification and its transformation. The vitalist aesthetics that emerges in his late period presents a conception of life as a force that flows beyond and between subjects and out of which forms, including the forms of art, emerge. The life of art is not a coded representation of the life of the artist but exists *in itself*. The artist-narrator of Banville's 2015 novel *The Blue Guitar* (172) spells it out: 'Trans-this and trans-that, all the transes, that's what I was after, the making over of things, of everything, by the force of concentration, which is, and don't mistake it, the force of forces. The world would be so thoroughly the object of my passionate regard that it would break out and blush madly in a blaze of self-awareness'.

Banville repeatedly describes the artist's role as witness bearer and the work of art as a matter of revealing the world, of describing things so attentively and in such detail that they blush: 'When we blush, or when the object blushes, it is at its most vulnerable but it is also at its most sensitive and it gives up something of itself that otherwise would be held inside' (Bigsby 2011). To make an object blush is not only to confer intensity but to endow it with consciousness, and in Banville's art objects are frequently endowed with uncanny life, poised on the precipice of animation: a house has 'a tense and watchful aspect' (Banville 2003, 13); an armchair sits 'braced somehow and as if about to clamber angrily to its feet' (Banville 2012a: 27); pieces of furniture stand 'sullenly at attention ... like almost living things' (Banville 2001: 16). Inordinately effusive on the minutiae of weather conditions, Banville is a connoisseur of the pathetic fallacy. But if the apparently inanimate world is brought to life, the animate characters that populate his novels are regularly represented as not quite human. They are often thinglike, lapidary, even mechanistic, or figured as otherworldly, as gods, ghosts or angels. Such ontological mutability is part of the work's playfulness, but it is a serious play that blurs the supposedly inviolable border between animate and inanimate and between life and death. It undermines the stability of forms and opens onto a dimension in which life is not proper to persons or bound to forms but is dynamic and nomadic.

The late trilogy is characterized by multiple surrogacies, substitutions and duplications. *Shroud*, published two years after *Eclipse*, focuses on Cass's relationship with the academic Axel Vander, with whom she consummates by proxy her illicit desire for her father. Her catatonic absences from the later novel correspond to her spectral presence in *Eclipse*. Cass, for her part, is a surrogate of sorts for Vander's wife Magda. The situation gets even more convoluted in the third novel of the trilogy *Ancient Light*, in which Alex Cleave returns to acting to play the lead role in a biopic of Axel Vander, and a further series of mirrorings ensues. This multiplication of doubles and proxies accentuates the manner in which the characters are presented as ciphers, their actions not self-willed but generated out of forces, particularly erotic forces, acting through them. This finds its highest expression in *The Infinities*, which along with the late trilogy is Banville's take on the ancient Greek *Dionysia*, during which competing dramatists each presented a set of three tragedies and a satyr play in honour of the god. *The Infinities* is a satyr play in novelistic form, an irreverent burlesque centred on the gods' intervention in human affairs, full of Dionysian chaos, sexual humour and deviant merriment.

As previously mentioned, *The Infinities* is directly based on *Amphitryon*, and the tale it tells of the interpenetration of the mortal world and the deathless realm of the gods is an eminent conceit for Banville's exploration of the transaesthetic event of the artwork and its relation to death as the experience of traversing the limits of bound identity. The narrator is Hermes, son of Zeus, who casts himself as the inventor of this fictional world. However, as the novel progresses his voice transforms into old Adam's comatose dream. The narrative voice is highly ambiguous, slipping from one voice to another 'like a Möbius strip' so that, in another Jamesian turn of the screw, it becomes impossible to determine who has conjured up who, if the gods are figments of Adam's dream or the human world is a mere folly for the god's amusement (Downes 2017: 27). With this narrative device, Banville accomplishes his aim of writing a book with no real centre. The conflicting energies of the work are embodied by the gods: the lusting Zeus who, as in Kleist's play, takes on human form to satisfy his lust for Adam's daughter-in-law, Helen; Hermes, the psychopomp, charged with escorting Adam to the afterlife; and the god Pan, whose intervention signals Adam's last minute 'panic' and grants his wish for '*one last time among the living*' (Banville 2009: 288). It is these currents that animate the human cast and move the action along. Nothing is permitted to settle in this novel of shapeshifters and impersonators, and the reader is required to hold open multiple possibilities, to accommodate temporal aberrations, breaches of the law of individuation, interpenetrating worlds and traversals of narrative planes. Its ruling element is air and the prose is buoyant, dilated with metaphor and tumid vivacity.

The radical decentring of the subject here is not a dualism but a fractal dynamic. It is the liberation of experience from the self-enclosure of individual existence. To the question of who speaks, we might answer, after Deleuze (1990: 141), 'the fourth person singular', the nomadic, impersonal voice of the artwork freed of the gravitational weight of the bound body. The *Amphitryon* schema of embodying, or being usurped by, the gods is an obvious figure for the inhabitation of character, the propulsion of plot, and the simultaneous doubling and erasure of the self that is required of the writer, and indeed the reader, of fiction. And Banville's fable about dying is also an interrogation of the processes and purposes of making art. Nietzsche (1995: 214), whose influence is evident throughout Banville's oeuvre, recognized that our desire for art is rooted in a deep-seated yearning to traverse the bounds of individuality and to experience, for an instant, another mode of being that perhaps is death: 'There are moments and, as it were, sparks of the brightest, most ardent fire in whose light we no longer understand the word "I": there beyond our being something exists that in those moments becomes a here and now, and that is why we long with all our hearts for bridges connecting the here and the there.' These moments are ubiquitous in Banville's art. Throughout his works, narrative plotting is subordinate to digressions, episodic divergence, rapturous moments, and instances of self-overcoming. In such episodes, time is not linear; in these empty pockets of 'timeless time', life and death inhere simultaneously (Banville 2001: 169). It is in these moments of self-forgetting that the shackles of reflexive consciousness are loosened and the illusoriness of a unified, atomized subject is revealed, and life, ecstatic and dispersed, is released.

In *The Infinities*, the rapturous moment dilates to encompass the duration of the novel. The entire fictional space is an interval of grace that celebrates life. By contrast to the plaintive tragedies of the immediate postmillennial years, this is not an Orphic venture. Its orientation is not from life to death but rather the opposite. The novel's Dionysian comedy brings death into the heart of life. Banville has often expressed the view that 'real art is perfectly useless' (Ehrenreich 2005: 51), like old Adam's body of equations, 'a vast and gorgeous gewgaw the joy of which was its utter inutility' (Banville 2009: 262). However, in these death-obsessed works, there are signs perhaps of a more serious project, that of making acquaintance with the fact of death. Banville's reworkings of *Amphitryon* repeatedly figure the art experience as one that, in its most intense moments, risks the stability of the self. This is what Banville (1994b) finds so compelling in Kleist, who 'turned the world upside-down, and in the process shook out of it precious secret things: in doing so he left himself no place to stand'. Kleist lived in close proximity to death, taking his own life at the age of thirty-four. Although he is one of the most respected figures in German literature, he has remained largely neglected in the English-speaking world. In the alternative world of *The Infinities*, it is his compatriot and contemporary Goethe who has been forgotten, while 'the sublime Kleist' is commemorated. Precursorship is not unidirectional, and just as Kleist has contributed to Banville's development as an artist, these works not only rescue an important artist from relative obscurity but present the practice of art as a collective endeavour.

References

Banville, J. (1986), *Mefisto*, London: Minerva.
Banville, J. (1994a), *The Broken Jug*, Oldcastle: The Gallery Press.
Banville, J. (1994b), 'Kleist: Neglected Genius', *The Independent*, 14 October. Available online: https://www.independent.co.uk/arts-entertainment/kleist-neglected-genius-tomorrow-in-the-deutsche-romantik-season-at-the-south-bank-john-banville-1442756.html (accessed 12 February 2014).
Banville, J. (2000), *God's Gift*, Oldcastle: The Gallery Press.
Banville, J. (2001), *Eclipse*, London: Picador.
Banville, J. (2003), *Shroud*, London: Picador.
Banville, J. (2005), *Love in the Wars*, Oldcastle: The Gallery Press.
Banville, J. (2006), *The Sea*, London: Picador.
Banville, J. (2007), 'Alternative Worlds', in Brendan Flynn (ed.), *The Clifden Anthology*, 24–6, Co. Galway: Clifden Community Arts Week.
Banville, J. (2009), *The Infinities*, London: Picador.
Banville, J. (2012a), *Ancient Light*, London: Penguin.
Banville, J. (2012b) 'Fiction and the Dream' in Raymond Bell (ed.), *Possessed of a Past*, 365–73, London: Picador.
Banville, J. (2015), *The Blue Guitar*, London: Viking.
Banville, J. (2017), *Mrs Osmond*, London: Viking.
Barthes, R. (1986), 'The Reality Effect', in *The Rustle of Language*, trans. Richard Howard, 141–8, Oxford: Basil Blackwell.
'Being John Banville' *Arts Lives* (2008) Dir. Charlie McCarthy, [TV programme] RTÉ 1, 17 January.
Bigsby, C. (2011), 'In Conversation with John Banville', *#New Writing*, 16 December. Available online: http://www.newwriting.net/feature/in-conversation-with-john-banville/ (accessed 20 June 2012).
Black, B. (2014), *The Black-Eyed Blonde: A Philip Marlowe Novel*, London: Mantle.

Deleuze, G. (1990), *The Logic of Sense*, trans. Mark Lestor, ed. Constantin V. Boundas, London: The Athlone Press.

Deleuze, G. and F. Guattari (1987), *A Thousand Plateaus: Capitalism and Schizophrenia*, trans. Brian Massumi, Minneapolis, MN: University of Minnesota Press.

Deleuze, G. and F. Guattari (1994), *What Is Philosophy?*, trans. Hugh Tomlinson and Graham Burchill, London: Verso.

Downes, R. (2017), 'Death and the Impersonality of Style in John Banville's *The Infinities*', *Nordic Irish Studies*, 16: 21–36.

Ehrenreich, B. (2005) 'Ben Ehrenreich Talks to John Banville', in Vendela Vida (ed.), *The Believer Book of Writers Talking to Writers*, 43–58, San Francisco, CA: Believer Books.

Friberg, H. (2006), 'John Banville and Derek Hand in Conversation', *Irish University Review*, 36 (1): 200–15.

Kleist, H. ([1807] 2004), *Amphitryon*, in David Constantine (ed. and trans.), *Kleist: Selected Writings*, 66–134, Indianapolis, IN: Hackett.

McKeon, B. (2009), 'John Banville, The Art of Fiction No. 200', *The Paris Review*, Available online: https://www.theparisreview.org/interviews/5907/john-banville-the-art-of-fiction-no-200-john-banville (accessed 14 February 2014).

Nietzsche, F. (1995), *Unfashionable Observations*, trans. Richard T. Gray. Stanford, CA: Stanford University Press.

Owens, J. (2010), 'John Banville: The Powells.com Interview', 5 April. Available online: http://www.powells.com/post/interviews/john-banville-the-powellscom-interview (accessed 5 June 2012).

Wallace, A. (2000), 'A World without People', *The Irish Times*, 21 September.

7

The limits of simile: Rilke, Stevens and Banville's scepticism

Michael Springer

In a talk he gave in 1980, John Banville identified the creation of art as arising from two contradictory conditions: our inescapable need to make the world significant; and our inescapable uncertainty about the relation of any significance we can possibly make to anything other than the interior of our own heads. He uses two poets to exemplify these contrasting situations: Rilke, 'prais[ing] the world to the Angel', the first; and Wallace Stevens the second, with his insistence on the foreignness of this world to all of our meaning. That he poses them as opposite is unexceptional, if one focuses on the tenor and tone of their work. But considered philosophically, Rilke and Stevens can appear to be two sides of a single coin. One can understand why this is so by considering instances of their work as responses to scepticism. Both Rilke and Stevens are preoccupied with if, and how, the significance humans are able to give to their world relates to the external world, rather than simply itself. Stevens is austere in his scepticism. As 'The Snow Man' puts it, there is a 'nothing' in the world, which a shriving of significance allows one to see (or even to be). Rilke's response takes off in precisely the opposite direction: if we're the only ones who signify, then 'everything here apparently needs us'. While they respond to this perception in diametrically contrasting ways, however, they are both ultimately idealists.

This is obviously a view of Rilke that runs counter to the many that emphasize his concern with immanence. Such readings focus on his claims regarding the importance of the world, of the here and now. But they miss the way the here and now is mediated, through speech and conceptual transformation: 'Earth, isn't this what you want: to arise within us, / *invisible*? Isn't it your dream / to be wholly invisible someday? – O Earth: invisible! / What, if not transformation, is your urgent command?' Rilke turns the inevitability of mediation into a virtue and a cause; he does not evade it. This explains why, like all fanaticisms, his is a function not of certainty, but doubt. Rilke appears to take in both the consideration of this scepticism and the realization that the very posing of its possibility undermines any hope one might have of being able to overcome it. The response is therefore the recognition of the need to continue in one's signifying endeavours in full awareness of their possibly solipsistic nature. Caught in some sort of limbo between terrestrial specificity and transcendental angelic realms, we persist in translating the former to the latter. Rilke's preoccupation with justifying and clarifying the relation between the works of intellect and the material world indicates the extent to which he considers it to be in need of such substantiation. The *Duino Elegies* are, in this sense, an apology for *poiesis*.

In that series of poems, the final explanation of, and justification for, attempts to make our world significant is the obscure felt imperative to do so. The poet feels that this world is calling him to enchant it, and this feeling is taken to be sufficient reason to persist in doing so. The feeling obviously doesn't resolve the scepticism (or at least not on its own terms), but it does give the poet some sort of justification for bracketing it from consideration in respect of these kinds of activities. Thus, the passion of the avowals of the complementarity between spirit and nature must be considered within the larger frame of the philosophical awareness of the shakiness of any such foundation. While Rilke is ardently invested in the world, he is intellectually also disjoint from it. The 'task' of poiesis may work from the immanent, but it aims for the transcendent. Therefore, while Banville is not wrong to claim that, 'despite his constant urge toward transcendence, Rilke was thoroughly of our world' (Banville 2013), the vacillation between transcendence and immanence is slightly more complicated than the phrasing portrays it to be.

There is a section from the *Duino Elegies* Banville has cited so frequently as to make it appear something of a mantra:[1]

> Are we, perhaps, here just for saying: House,
> Bridge, Fountain, Gate, Jug, Fruit tree, Window, –
> possibly: Pillar, Tower? ... but for saying, remember,
> oh, for such saying as never the things themselves
> hoped so intensely to be.

And in line with the frequency with which these lines are alluded to, they are also framed in significant ways. The general tenor of Banville's direct, non-fictional statements about Rilke's significance for him as an author is well captured by his claim, 'Whenever I ask myself what art might be, and why I try to make art,

I think of those lines' (Imhof and Banville 1981). As with my emphasis on the doubt underpinning Rilke's insistence, this points to a situation of uncertainty: the questioning of the meaning and purpose of the endeavour one has made one's life's work. Rilke is crucial to Banville not because he provides a simple solution, but because he shows a way of engaging with a complex impossibility of one. This is demonstrated by the earnestness of the way in which Rilke is invoked, enlisted at the very foundation of art – the fundamental justification. The sentiment quoted above is again typical. Banville frequently cites Rilke as a source he turns to for these most profound of aesthetic considerations.

In a review of Mark Harman's translation of *Letters to a Young Poet*, Banville describes the ninth Duino Elegy as 'a beautiful answer' to the question of why we 'persist in our humanness'. In this chapter, I explore in greater detail what he means by this through an analysis of *Doctor Copernicus*. As I demonstrate, the novel's implied response to scepticism has much in common with Rilke's. I then compare this with *Eclipse*, to argue that Banville comes to see that Rilke's 'answer' to scepticism in fact simply begs the primary question. Banville's recognition of this in turn leads him, in his later novels, to inflect this solution with an irresolvable irony that brings him much closer in outlook to Wallace Stevens.

Kepler, written immediately after *Doctor Copernicus*, is arguably Banville's most Rilkean book – or at least the most explicitly so: the epigraph is taken from the *Duino Elegies*, and there are direct quotations and intertextual references throughout it (Berensmeyer 2000). But this is not necessarily a virtue for my purposes. As Elke D'hoker (2004) notes, Kepler appears to succeed in his Rilkean endeavour better than does Copernicus. Intent as I am on demonstrating how the shortcomings of the Rilkean position are exacerbated in the development of Banville's career, Copernicus's failures are more instructive than Kepler's success. Rilke's significance for Banville has also usually been discussed with primary reference to the later novel (Berensmeyer 2000; D'hoker 2004; Kenny 2009) – unsurprisingly, given its emphasis on the intertextual links. Shifting focus to *Doctor Copernicus* therefore allows for a broader delineation of the development of Banville's understanding of and response to Rilke's work through the course of his career, in line with the aims of this chapter.

Doctor Copernicus

This disillusionment with the possibility of knowledge, and attendant meditations on the nature of human intellection and figuration, is the central subject of *Doctor Copernicus*. The attempt to access – and hence, necessarily, the faith in – ultimate truth instigates the astronomer's attempt to replace the Ptolemaic system, which offers self-consciously expedient explanations of the motion of the planets in line with inherited orthodoxies regarding the divine mathematical harmony of the cosmos in order to 'save the phenomena'. Brudzewski, a defender of the system Copernicus seeks to replace, observes that astronomy 'does not discern your principle thing, for that is not to be discerned' (Banville 1999: 35). As Elke D'hoker (2004: 29) notes, in ascribing to Brudzewski the view that '[w]e are here and the universe, so to speak, is there, and between the two there is no sensible connection', Banville 'clearly tries to give these scholastic beliefs a Postmodern flavour by emphasising the limits of knowledge they try to observe'.[2]

Throughout the novel two attitudes to thought and its implications for human being are consistently contrasted, the one represented by Copernicus, the other to some extent by the Scholastics, but more properly by Copernicus's older brother Andreas. In this opposition, Copernicus's longed-for transcendental knowledge, unsullied by materiality and free of its means of expression, is counterpointed by an acceptance of embodiment and a recognition of the inescapable implications of this for any possible form of knowledge. These contrasting attitudes are perhaps most clearly illustrated by their proponents' attitudes to names. For Copernicus, the arbitrariness and messiness of designation is a source of dissatisfaction and anxiety, captured in a Heraclitean meditation on the name of the River Vistula: '[T]he name was the same, but the name meant nothing. ... it was at once here and there, young and old at once, and its youth and age were separated not by years but leagues. He murmured aloud the river's name and heard in that word suddenly the concepts of space and time fractured' (Banville 1999: 20). His goal is hence to access a mode of knowing that transcends the linguistic. In an argument with a fellow astronomer he states, 'I believe not in names, but in things' (Banville 1999: 36). Among the Scholastics with whom he disagrees, his teacher Canon Wodka expresses the opposing view most succinctly: 'I believe that the world is *here* ... that it exists, and that it is inexplicable. ... [T]heories are but names, *but the world itself is a thing*' (23; emphasis original). Ultimately, Copernicus comes to see himself as having failed in his attempt to transcend the signifier, as having merely formulated further names. However, Banville's approving citation of Rilke's *Duino Elegies* would indicate that the author's attitude to the nature of names is rather more complex, as is evidenced by the treatment of embodiment and sensation and the implications of these for subjectivity in *Doctor Copernicus* and other novels.

Indeed, the significance of the question of embodiment in this respect is signalled in the section immediately following Canon Wodka's assertion that 'the world itself is a thing': 'On Saturdays in the fields outside the walls of the town Caspar Sturm instructed the school in the princely art of falconry. The hawks, terrible and lovely, filled the air with the clamour of tiny deaths. Nicolas looked on in a mixture of horror and elation. … Compared with their vivid presence all else was insubstantial. They were absolutes' (23). The physical force of the image is compounded by the implication of Nicolas's erotic attraction to Caspar Sturm: 'Nicolas watched him watching his creatures and was stirred, obscurely, shamefully', and he later ejaculates on waking from a dream in which '[m]onstrous hawklike creatures were flying on invisible struts and wires across a livid sky, and there was a great tumult far off, screams and roars, and howls of agony or of laughter' (24). A connection is implied between eroticism and mortality throughout this passage, first hinted at in the polyglot pun of the hawks' filling the air with 'tiny deaths' and stated more explicitly in the description of Nicolas's ejaculation as 'a kind of exquisite dying' (24). This link clarifies the contrast between the two attitudes described above. The longing for the transcendent is a desire precisely for the unchanging, the deathless, whereas mortality is the inescapable condition of embodied being, and this point underpins Nicolas's motives in adopting the course of action he eventually does.

The contrary to Nicolas's striving for disembodied, transcendental changelessness is provided by his older brother Andreas, who most clearly figures embodied human being in the novel. Dissolute, sensual and impatient of theorizing, Andreas inhabits the physical world with no longing for an absolute elsewhere, and figures to some extent as Nicolas's inverted double, as his animus. Indeed, when on his deathbed, disillusioned with his life's work and despairing of his earlier ambitions, Nicolas conjures Andreas in a hallucination: this is made explicit: '[Y]ou have said that you are dreaming me … . That is why I am here, because at last you are prepared to be … honest' (238). In this hallucination, the vision of Andreas points out to Nicolas, 'I was that which you must contend with. … I was the one necessary thing, for I was there always to remind you of what you must transcend. I was the bent bow from which you propelled yourself beyond the filthy world' (240). Providing an assessment of Nicolas's life and work, he tells him he has missed 'the thing itself, the vivid thing, which is not to be found in any book, nor in the firmament, nor in the absolute forms.' He continues, 'It is that thing, passionate and yet ordinary, that thing which is all that matters, which is the great miracle. You glimpsed it briefly in … others … and turned away, appalled and … embarrassed' (241).

The characterization of the prized object of the epistemological effort as 'ordinary' is an indication of how certain of Banville's preoccupations follow those of Wittgenstein and Cavell, for example, concerning the inaccessibility of the ordinary to certain modes of thought, which I shall touch on later in this chapter. The conception of the relation of embarrassment to this ordinary, however, seems original.

Embarrassment is accorded very close scrutiny on many occasions in Banville's oeuvre, and imbued with especial force and intensity. Andreas has earlier said to Nicolas, 'It was always your stormiest emotion, that fastidious, that panic-stricken embarrassment in the face of the disorder and vulgarity of the commonplace, which you despised' (238). And in *The Sea*, Max Morden remarks on his and his wife's discomfort on her being diagnosed with cancer,

> I realized what the feeling was that had been besetting me since I had stepped that morning into the glassy glare of Mr Todd's consulting rooms. It was embarrassment. Anna felt it as well, I was sure of it. Embarrassment, yes, a panic-stricken sense of not knowing what to say, where to look, how to behave … . It was as if a secret had been imparted to us so dirty, so nasty, that we could hardly bear to remain in one another's company yet were unable to break free, each knowing the foul thing that the other knew and bound together by that very knowledge. From this day forward all would be dissembling. There would be no other way to live with death. (Banville 2005: 22)

This depiction emphasizes those aspects of the emotion that, rather than relating exclusively to a relatively thin veneer of social observance, stem from some deeper, more primary of our modes of engagement with the world. Such would certainly be consistent with the references to it in *Doctor Copernicus* and *The Sea*. The connection between embarrassment and death underscored in these two novels points towards a specific view of the embarrassment in question. Namely, that it is an embodied response to the abject. Significantly – given my characterization of Andreas as representing a form of embodied being from which Nicolas attempts to flee – in the hallucination scene in which the reference to embarrassment appears, Nicolas says to Andreas, 'You are death', to which Andreas characteristically replies, 'O that too, brother, that too, but that's of secondary importance' (Banville 1999: 237). This is only consistent: mortality and finitude are the necessary and inevitable correlatives of embodied being, its horizon and organizing principle; Nicolas's aspiration after the transcendent and absolute is also a desire for changelessness.

There is, however, an indication that Nicolas undergoes some transformation on his deathbed. At the very end of the book, in the formulation, 'This was dying, yes, this was unmistakably the distinguished thing' (237), the parallelism in the verbal formulation with the object of his lifelong preoccupation – 'the vivid thing', 'the principal thing' – is clear.³ And indeed, this dimension of death is gestured at within the very first pages of the novel: when Nicolas's mother dies in his early childhood, she is described, in the free indirect, as being 'utterly, uniquely still, and seemed in this unique utter stillness to have arrived at last at a true and total definition of what she was, her vivid self itself' (5). The motif is reiterated in the scene of Nicolas's *petite morte* following his dream about the hawks, in which 'his self shrank together into a tiny throbbing point' as he is 'poised on the edge of darkness and a kind of exquisite dying' (24). Taken together, these descriptions imply the irony of Nicolas's project: self-coincidence consists in absolute self-dispersal, and the closest he can hope to get to the absolute knowledge he desires is in ceasing to be a subject of knowledge, in the becoming of an object.

There is in this depiction a further connection to Rilke's work, and one that is intimately tied up with the notion, so frequently quoted by Banville, of the human duty to bring the world to life within us through an aesthetic engagement with it. In *The Notebooks of Malte Laurids Brigge*, a central focalization of the young poet's anxiety and loathing of Paris are his meditations on the nature of death in the modern city (Rilke 2009). In counterpoint to his grandfather's death, which is intimate, familial, immediate, Malte considers death in the modern city, like life, to be commodified, inextricable from systems and technologies that render it alien and unapproachable. There is also however, in addition to such technological causes, a moral dimension to this alienation, exactly analogous to that implicit in the imperative mood of the *Duino Elegies*, and many other of Rilke's poems (perhaps most emphatically 'Archaic Torso of Apollo': 'You must change your life'[4]): 'Who cares about a well-made death these days? No one. Even the rich, who could afford to die in well-appointed style, are lowering their standards and growing indifferent; the wish for a death of one's own is becoming ever more infrequent. Before long it will be just as uncommon as a life of one's own' (Rilke 2009: 4).

The notion of such a being towards death and the comportment towards the world implied by the *Duino Elegies* are analogous: both register a sense of responsibility towards the fundamentally other, and both premise a project of subjectivity on this responsibility. For example, at the very end of the ninth Duino Elegy, having concluded that the point of our being human has to do with the fact that 'Earth' and its things appear to need us to become themselves, Rilke claims that death itself, 'our intimate companion', is the 'holiest inspiration' of this transfiguration. A just, a morally answerable, mode of being is one in which embarrassment before the abject is transformed into acceptance, and this acceptance is seen as providing the basis for a transformation of the self. This is similarly captured in Andreas's claim that '[w]e know the meaning of the singular thing only so long as we content ourselves with knowing it in the midst of other meanings .... It is not the thing that counts, you see, only the interaction of things.' Such a stance – as espoused by Andreas here, as espoused by Rilke – corresponds to Stanley Cavell's idea, exemplified for him especially well by Beckett's work, of the ordinary as a goal, as something to be achieved (Cavell 1976). In her chapter in this volume, Pietra Palazzolo discusses this trait in Wallace Stevens's work with reference to the poet's idea of 'nobility', and elaborates it with Deleuze's idea of the 'virtual', and the transcendental empiricism he derives from this. Brian Massumi's (2002) ideas on the logic of relation capture something similar to what Andreas is after in this formulation: the objective as existing only and always in its interaction with a subjective, and hence inconceivable in and of itself. The 'goal', in Cavell's sense, is to overcome the desire to access the world in some way other than the indeterminate, event-based manner this vision of objects and subjects as fields of intensity implies – to be content with mediated immanence, and not long for immediate transcendence. (This is ultimately Wittgenstein's idea of philosophy as a therapy for the pathology of being unable to desist from desiring a form of knowledge that is unattainable.) A central aspect of such an undermining of metaphysical thinking is a reconfiguration of the mind–body problem, and Banville's extrapolation of Rilke's ideas, and his treatment of the question of beauty, are of great interest in this respect.

As mentioned above, beauty and the perception of it are among the most prominent and striking aspects of Banville's work, in both theme and form. The density and gloss of the writing and the acuity of perception is matched by the consistent preoccupation of the protagonists and narrators with order, harmony and clarity. While the overt theme of the science tetralogy is epistemological, of the Art trilogy ethical, and of later novels such as *Eclipse*, *Shroud*, *The Sea* and *Ancient Light* existential, the ultimate goals and achievements of these apparently disparate categories are all consistently depicted as being most properly conceived of as beauty. To qualify this no doubt unhelpfully generalizing claim, I should emphasize that I take the understanding of beauty espoused by Banville's work to be rooted in a specific perception of the nature and implications of embodied being. Simply put, beauty is depicted as a certain sensory, perceptual relation to the world and other people, a certain comportment of embodiment. While the Art trilogy explores the ethical dimensions of this conception of beauty, and the science tetralogy the epistemological, it is implied that the paradigm example of it, at least in a contemporary Western cultural configuration, is that of art and aesthetic discourse surrounding it. The significance of Rilke's exhortation for Banville's understanding of art stems precisely from this perception: the directive to allow things to come to life within us, to perceive things in such a way that they, and we, are redeemed in the perception, is an exact analogue of the corollaries of the idea of beauty put forward in Banville's work.

A passage from *Doctor Copernicus*, in which a solution to a problem presents itself to Nicolas, demonstrates this especially well:

> Calmly then it came, the solution, like a magnificent great slow golden bird alighting in his head with a thrumming of vast wings. It was so simple, so ravishingly simple, that at first he did not recognise it for what it was. … He turned the solution this way and that, admiring it, as it were turning in his fingers a flawless ravishing jewel. It was the thing itself, the vivid thing. (Banville 1999: 83–5)

Given the earlier characterization of the hawks as 'an absolute' of embodiment, the fact that the solution is here figured as a bird is significant, as is Nicolas's passivity in the process. His admiration is depicted as a tactile, sensory involvement, and his initial response is also described in terms applicable to the apprehension of an object of beauty: it is 'ravishing' and 'ravishingly simple', the repetition further emphasizing the extent of the subject's passivity in the occurrence, and alluding to the idea of beauty discussed above.

Such an understanding of beauty in one respect runs directly counter to a Kantian view. While it does indeed propose a disinterested interestedness, the emphasis on embodied perception inverts the prioritizing of the mental side of the mind–body dichotomy implied by the Kantian idea of the conceptual intimations of order underpinning the phenomenon.[5] In this respect Banville's attitude is explicit: the novels consistently depict intellection, or at least certain aspects of it, as a disruptive, destructive faculty. The apparitions of beauty that suddenly illuminate the narrative occur despite, not because of, the protagonists' mental life. This distrust of intellection, and of a humanity defined on the basis of it, helps account for the tinge of misanthropy and self-loathing that mark out so many of his narrators. Freddie Montgomery, for example, while determinedly getting drunk, muses,

> It was not just the drink, though, that was making me happy, but the tenderness of things, the simple goodness of the world. This sunset, for instance, how lavishly it was laid on, the clouds, the light on the sea, that heartbreaking,

blue-green distance, laid on, all of it, as if to console some lost suffering wayfarer. I have never really got used to being on this earth. Sometimes I think our presence here is due to a cosmic blunder, that we were meant for another planet altogether, with other arrangements, and other laws, and other, grimmer skies. I try to imagine it, our true place, off on the far side of the galaxy, whirling and whirling. And the ones who were meant for here, are they out there, baffled and homesick, like us? No, they would have become extinct long ago. How could they survive, these gentle earthlings, in a world that was meant to contain *us*? (Banville 2001d: 24)

The painterly metaphor ('how lavishly it was laid on'), and through it the positing of an organizing agency, by way of which the narrator here engages with the scene implies a (perhaps ironic) engagement with the natural world by analogy with the modes of engagement with a work of art. Such a relation of work of art and natural world serves further to substantiate the inversion of the Kantian schematization of beauty: where for Kant the aesthetic dimension is the natural world, subsequent aesthetic discourse adopts the terms applied there, primarily beauty and the sublime, to characterize the relation to the work of art. With an attitude such as Freddie Montgomery's spelt out above, in which the natural world is posited as being *as if* a work of art in order to apply aesthetic categories to the original aesthetic object, the inversion is complete. Montgomery's statement in *Ghosts* (2001c) sums the matter up rather succinctly: 'Nature did not exist until we invented it one eighteenth-century morning radiant with Alpine light.'[6]

The solicitude expressed for the 'gentle earthlings' bespeaks a tenderness and affection for the world of objects and the physical directly proportional to Freddie's implicit disenchantment with '*us*'. Later in the novel Freddie puts the matter more bluntly: 'Here is a question: if man is a sick animal, an insane animal, as I have reason to believe, then how account for these small, unbidden gestures of kindness and of care?' (Banville 2001d: 43).[7] Andreas's criticism of Nicolas's desire to transcend the physical must be read with this schema in mind: his aversion to the physical constitutes an aesthetic-moral failing, a rejection of the possibility of coming to terms with the world. In light of this reading, there is a profound irony in his consistently stated credo that 'knowledge must become perception' (his alternative to the prevailing orthodoxy of formulating theory to 'save the phenomena'). The novel implies that exactly the reverse is the case, that perception must become knowledge, or rather, that perception itself *is* knowledge.

This vision of subjectivity and awareness is afforded further prominence by the striking and frequent use of simile throughout the oeuvre, as has been thoroughly demonstrated by Joseph McMinn (2006). Connected to, and very often a central aspect of, the sharpness of the observation and presentation of sensory perception, simile and metaphor function to enact the form of understanding, the form of apprehension of the world, indicated (in the implied failings of Nicolas Copernicus's life's project, for example) as being the appropriate response to our nature and condition. As McMinn (2006: 148) puts it, in the neo-Romantic sense in which he understands simile to function in Banville's work, 'analogy is not so much a figure of speech, but a way of seeing and experiencing the world'. Importantly, metaphor and simile serve to provide insight and understanding by way of a purely perceptual intuition of similitude and analogy, and the characters who use them are presented as obtaining some specific form of access to the world through the use of such figures. For example, when Nicolas's father dies, his grief is described as being 'the shape of a squat grey rodent lodged in the heart' (Banville 1999: 12) and in this way – through the positing of the equivalence of a sensory with a non-sensory experience, and hence the obtaining of some purchase on the inexplicable and inarticulable – some grasp is obtained on an otherwise inconceivable entity. Rather than being predicative, this procedure enacts the metaphorical carrying over of the sensory to the non-sensory, the known to the unknown. The structural analogy with the process Rilke exhorts is clear: to 'say' the world in such a way that it is transfigured, 'invisible', in the saying of it.

> these Things,
> which live by perishing, know you are praising them; transient,
> they look to us for deliverance: us, the most transient of all.
> They want us to change them, utterly, in our invisible heart,
> within – oh endlessly – within us!

Perhaps ironically, it is in this process that perception and knowledge are most closely conjoined.

An apt example of the frequent density of simile in the writing, as well as its role in the subject's apprehension of the world, is provided in the following passage from *Eclipse*:

> This is how I wake now, sliding warily out of sleep as though I had spent the night in hiding. ... I have a deep dislike of mornings, their muffled, musty texture, like that of a bed too long slept in. ... I have come to think of my life as altogether like a morning's interminable passing; whatever the hour, it is always as if I have just risen and am trying to get a grip on things. (Banville 2001b: 28)

The specific context of the comparison – waking in the morning – is expanded to serve as an analogy of the narrator's life in general, in which his continuously 'trying to get a grip on things' proceeds by way of such an apprehension of likenesses. Precisely as McMinn claims, therefore, the function takes on a far more fundamental role in the character's cognition of himself and his world than the merely figural.

A related aspect, because similarly based on the perception and organization of qualia, is Banville's idiosyncratic use of adjectives. Among the most notable of these are the strings of numerous, often unpunctuated, adjectives, which produce a vivid sense of the process of a character's gradual apprehension of a given thing or situation through an agglomeration of properties: 'a magnificent great slow golden bird' (Banville 1999: 83), 'cool and smooth and moist', 'cold and calm and distant', 'a fleeting, sidelong, faintly smiling look' (Banville 2001b: 58, 58, 71). There is also his use of obscure, technical or specialist lexemes to denote a specific quality ('velutinous', 'cinereal', 'oleaginous'), drawing attention to the sensory manifold and the character's inhabitation of and response to it – as well as to the characters' connoisseurship of language. This conjunction of perceptual acuity and ornate, baroque diction indicates the way in which the world is known, perhaps primarily, through language, and the extent to which the knowledge of a thing consists in the knowing of its name, as Walter Benjamin (1986) would attest. The following passage from *The Sea* serves well to demonstrate various of these aspects, as well as the characteristic density of adjectives and adverbs and the ways in which they are linked to perceptual clarity:

> It was one of the last days of that summer's heat-wave, the air like scratched glass, crazed by glinting sunlight. Throughout the afternoon long gleaming motor cars kept pulling up outside and depositing yet more guests, heron-like ladies in big hats and girls in white lipstick and white leather knee-high boots, raffish pinstriped gents, delicate young men who pouted and smoked pot, and lesser, indeterminate types … sleek, watchful and unsmiling, in shiny suits and shirts with different-coloured collars and sharp-toed ankle boots with elasticated sides. Charlie bounced among them all, his blued pate agleam, pride pouring off him like sweat. Late in the day a huddle of warm-eyed, slow-moving, shy plump men in headdresses and spotless white djellabas arrived in our midst like a flock of doves. (Banville 2005: 105)

Nevertheless, however rich this faculty may be or skilled and insightful such characters in the manipulation of it, it is ultimately presented as providing insubstantial, and perhaps even illusory, succour, precisely at those moments of greatest subjective strain and import. Such a failure of simile to provide meaning frequently occurs in connection with questions of identity and selfhood. Alex Cleave, who claims to be trying to achieve 'the pure conjunction, the union of self with sundered self' (Banville 2001b: 70), when trying to explain to his wife the reason for his retreat to the seaside house in which he grew up, reaches the following impasse:

> The incident with the animal in the wintry gloaming was definitive, though what it was that was being defined I could not tell. I saw where I was, and I thought of the house, and knew that I must live there again. ... Such seeming absence of human agency was proper also; it was as if ...
> 'As if what?' my wife said.
> I turned from her with a shrug.
> 'I don't know.' (2–3)

More to the point, understanding based on simile or analogy is depicted as preventing any possibility of self-coincidence, of full inhabitation of one's being, and thus of any full and authentic engagement with the world and other people such as that urged by Rilke's admonitions. In *Athena* (Banville 2001a), Morrow observes, 'Ah, this plethora of metaphors! I am like everything except myself,' while Max Morden similarly notices 'everything for me is something else' (Banville 2005: 138).

Ultimately, hence, the capacity of similitudinous apperception to provide a basis for knowledge and action proves limited, and it is this limitation that leads to the prominent foregrounding of the matter of nouns and naming in *Doctor Copernicus*. As discussed above, Nicolas, considering his entire life's work as having consisted in 'merely an exalted naming', sees this as a failure, but this pessimistic view of designation can be contrasted with one that falls in line with Rilke's idea of praising the world to the Angel. In this view, naming is an act of communion, an engagement with the quiddity of a thing. The valorization of this dimension is indicated by Andreas in the deathbed scene: 'What shall we call it ... the quest for truth? Transcendent knowledge? Vanity, all vanity, and something more ... the cowardice that comes from the refusal to accept that the names are all there is that matter, the cowardice that is true and irredeemable despair' (Banville 1999: 240). As with the moral and redemptive valence implied in the exhortatory phrasing of Rilke's (1987) ninth Duino Elegy, the depiction of this question emphasizes its moral aspects – what *ought* we to do, given the way we are constituted? Andreas's description of Nicolas's attitude as 'a kind of cowardice' outlines what such a moral dimension may consist in, but the point is made emphatically in the Art trilogy.

The Art trilogy details Freddie Montgomery's murder of a young woman and his subsequent attempt to atone for his act. He envisions this as an effort of imagination: understanding his murder as being predicated on a failure to fully register his victim's being – 'because ... he does not see her properly' (Banville 2001d: 266) – he views his proper atonement as consisting in an imaginative revivification. 'Prison, punishment, paying his debt to society, all that was ... merely how he would pass the time while he got on with the real business of atonement, which was nothing less than the restitution of a life' (267). This does not refer, as probably goes without saying, to a literal restoration of the girl's life. Rather, such resuscitation takes the form of a task of the imagination: seeing his lack of imaginative engagement as that which has made it possible for him to kill the young woman, he comes to understand the possibility of redemption as consisting in the achievement of a mode of engagement with the world and others sufficiently animated by imagination to preclude the possibility of such violence.

The solipsistic nature of this 'solution' marks its limitations, and is perhaps an intentional irony, given that the penance itself remains profoundly narcissistic. Nevertheless, insofar as it can be said to be achieved, the following epiphany may be taken to be the moment at which this occurs:

> And as she talked I found myself looking at her and seeing her as if for the first time, not as a gathering of details, but all of a piece, solid and singular and amazing. No, not amazing. That is the point. She was simply there, an incarnation of herself, no longer a nexus of adjectives but a pure and present noun. ... And somehow by being suddenly herself like this she made the things around her be there too. ... I felt everyone and everything shiver and shift, falling into vividest forms, detaching themselves from me and my conception of them and changing themselves instead into what they were, no longer figment, no longer mystery, no longer a part of my imagining. (321)

The displacement of the self that allows for the other to be apprehended not as an impediment to be removed nor as a tool to be annexed to the protagonist's own purposes – Banville's characters' habitual attitudes – but as an independent and self-contained subjectivity can be read as equivalent to the requirement to fully imagine the other that is proposed at the outset of the effort. The irony, of course, is that this is made possible by her ceasing to be 'a part of [his] imagining', by his relinquishing of any attempt to shape or structure her being to his own ends or according to his own preconceptions, and simply perceiving her – a point that chimes with, and is subject to precisely the same irony as, Copernicus's dictum that 'perception must become knowledge'.

Such a depiction of the possibility of true perception as consisting in a divestment of preconfigured cognitive schemata and imaginative constructions obviously has much in common with the thinking about the question of 'the ordinary' in post-Kantian philosophical endeavour. Robert Pippin (2003: 344) sums this up well as involving

> the appeal to a more original, less distorted experience of the human things as such, as human, not as artificially constructed through the lens of some theory. In a word, that word that has circulated so much in twentieth-century thought; in Husserl on the life-world; in Heidegger on pre-predicative experience, being-in-the-world, and the everyday; in the later Wittgenstein, Austin, Cavell (and through Cavell's insistence, found anew in Emerson and Thoreau); and recently in two books by Stanley Rosen: an appeal to 'the ordinary' as a way of bypassing, avoiding, not refuting the supposedly reductionist, skeptical, disenchanting, enervating trajectory of modern naturalism.

As Montgomery puts it in the epiphany quoted above ('And as she talked'), the precise point of the experience is that it was 'not amazing', but simply itself. Stanley Cavell's (1976) position with respect to figuration and imagination spelt out in his essay on *Endgame* has a great deal in common with that implied by Montgomery's epiphany and my understanding of the use and treatment of simile throughout the oeuvre. Indeed, this concern is announced as early as the epigraph to *Doctor Copernicus*, taken from Stevens's (1972) 'Notes toward a Supreme Fiction': 'You must become an ignorant man again. / And see the sun again with an ignorant eye, / and see it clearly in the idea of it.' Like Cavell and Stevens, Banville is acutely aware of the contradictory, and hence impossible, nature of such an undertaking – a contradiction perfectly exemplified in the desire that 'perception become knowledge': it involves the desire to conceive of something without conception, to know without knowledge of. While such a view would conceive of true knowledge as being ostensive – if a certain specific form of ostention, a 'thou' rather than a 'that' – even within the moment of ostention a supreme fiction intervenes. Significantly, the closing lines of the section from which the epigraph to *Doctor Copernicus* is taken read, 'Phoebus was / A name for something that never could be named. / … // There is a project for the sun. The sun / Must bear no name, gold flourisher, but be / In the difficulty of what it is to be'.

Among the most fundamental of such supreme fictions is that of the self.[8] At the conclusion of the passage in which M. relates his epiphany, when he feels 'everyone and everything detaching themselves from me and my conception of them and changing themselves instead into what they were', he asks – mournfully, as the following discussion will demonstrate – 'And I? Was I there amongst them, at last?' (Banville 2001c: 321). Such meditation on the insubstantiality, absence or fraudulence of the self is a recurrent motif in the three novels, and indeed in almost all of the author's subsequent ones. Freddie Montgomery, for example, anticipating his arrest and incarceration thinks wistfully:

> First there would be panic, and then pain. And when everything was gone, every shred of dignity and pretence, what freedom there would be, what lightness! No, what am I saying, not lightness but its opposite: weight, gravity, the sense at last of being firmly grounded. Then finally I would be me, no longer that poor impersonation of myself I had been doing all my life. I would be real. I would be, of all things, human. (Banville 2001d: 138)

Importantly, being 'human', and by implication fully moral, is predicated on ceasing to impersonate something, or someone, and becoming one's true self. To praise the world to the Angel, to achieve a 'saying such as things hoped never so intensely to be', one must first be able to say oneself, the first of the 'pair of lovers' involved in such communion, in such a way. But if one's self is a fiction, the best any such saying can aspire to is an exalted naming, the ministrations of a supreme fictiveness. In contrast to Rilke, Stevens in his notion of a supreme fiction appreciates, in line with theorists who emphasize the overcoming of metaphysically inflected systems of thought, that one can only begin to do this by 'perceiving the idea / Of this invention, this invented world'.[9] One cannot tell the Angel of things, but only of our constructions of them, the roles they play in our fictions. The Rilkean answer thus simply recapitulates the problem, asking for an access to the real that, because impossible, runs the risk of devolving into another arbitrary ideology of the transcendental basis of the name, such as exemplified by Nicolas in *Doctor Copernicus*. It is for this reason that Banville gravitates towards a more complex and problematic view of the matter as his career progresses. Coming in his later novels to adopt a stance far closer to that of Wallace Stevens, Banville's grappling with the quandaries of scepticism takes on the paradoxical quality identified in the philosophical considerations of how such extraordinary apparatuses as ourselves may hope to access the ordinary, 'plain sense of things'.

Notes

1. For example Sheehan, Banville and Stuart (1979), Imhof and Banville (1981), Banville (1981, 1983, 1990).
2. The same point is made in Hand (2002: 71–4).
3. The allusion to the description of his own expected death attributed to Henry James by Howard Sturgis ('at last, the distinguished thing') is also unmistakable (Edel 1968). In this volume, Darren Borg and Elke D'hoker explore Banville's response to Henry James.
4. Berensmeyer (2000) shows how the imperative exerted by the painting in *The Book of Evidence* has a similar effect, but in the opposite direction, enjoining Freddie to restore the life of the girl.
5. I have in mind here Kant's idea of beauty as consisting in the pleasure that arises from the experience of the harmonious interaction of the imagination and understanding, and the way this in turn hence prioritizes the cognitive aspects of the phenomenon. Cf. Kant (1987: 20–32), Budd (1998: 6).
6. The allusion to Oscar Wilde here is also clear: 'For what is Nature? Nature is no great mother who has borne us. She is our creation. It is in our brain that she quickens to life. Things are because we see them, and what we see, and how we see it, depends on the Arts that have influenced us. … They did not exist till Art had invented them' (Wilde 1909: 42). Such allusions provide further support for the contention that Banville's work is concerned with a tradition of thinking about art and its relation to other aspects of human thought and activity.
7. While it is important to take account of the various aspects of the unreliability of the narrators pronouncing such judgements, the tenor of the opinion expressed is sufficiently similar to those of most of Banville's protagonists to warrant the claim that it exemplifies relatively broad concerns, rather than simply the psychopathy of a specific character.
8. Pietra Palazzolo's chapter in this volume discusses the significance of Stevens's idea of the supreme fiction for Banville in detail.
9. Stevens, 'Notes toward a Supreme Fiction'. And as Palazzolo's chapter shows, these inventions are perpetually being updated and inflected, so the fiction is a necessarily ongoing one.

References

Banville, J. (1981), 'A Talk', *Irish University Review*, 11 (1) (Spring): 13–14.
Banville, J. (1983), 'Place Names: The Past', in Tim Pat Coogan (ed.), *Ireland and the Arts*, 62–5, Dublin: McNamara Press.

Banville, J. (1990), 'Survivors of Joyce', in A. Martin (ed.), *James Joyce: The Artist and the Labyrinth*, 73–81, London: Ryan.
Banville, J. (1999), *Doctor Copernicus*, London: Picador.
Banville, J. (2001a), *Athena*, in *Frames Trilogy*, 417–601, London: Picador.
Banville, J. (2001b), *Eclipse*, London: Picador.
Banville, J. (2001c), *Ghosts*, in *Frames Trilogy*, 194–415, London: Picador.
Banville, J. (2001d), *The Book of Evidence*, in *Frames Trilogy*, 1-192, London: Picador.
Banville, J. (2005), *The Sea*, London: Picador.
Banville, J. (2013), 'Study the Panther!' *New York Review of Books*, 3 January. Available online: http://www.nybooks.com/articles/archives/2013/jan/10/study-panther/?pagination=false (accessed 30 July 2017).
Benjamin, W. (1986), 'On Language as Such and on the Language of Man', in Peter Demetz (ed.), Edmund Jephcott (trans.), *Reflections: Essays, Aphorisms, Autobiographical Writing*, New York: Schocken Books.
Berensmeyer, I. (2000), *John Banville, Fictions of Order: Authority, Authorship, Authenticity*, Heidelberg: Universitätsverlag C. Winter.
Budd, M. (1998), 'Delight in the Natural World: Kant on the Aesthetic Appreciation of Nature: Part I: Natural Beauty', *British Journal of Aesthetics*, 38: 6.
Cavell, S. (1976), 'Ending the Waiting Game: A Reading of Beckett's *Endgame*', in *Must We Mean What We Say?*, 107–49, Cambridge: Cambridge University Press.
D'hoker, E. (2004), *Visions of Alterity: Representation in the Works of John Banville*, Amsterdam: Rodopi.
Edel, L. (1968), 'The Deathbed Notes of Henry James', *The Atlantic*, June. Available online: http://www.theatlantic.com/past/docs/unbound/flashbks/james/jnote.htm (accessed 30 July 2017).
Hand, D. (2002), *John Banville: Exploring Fictions*, Dublin: The Liffey Press.
Imhof, R. and J. Banville (1981), 'An Interview with John Banville', *Irish University Review*, 11 (1): 5–12.
Kant, I. (1987), *Critique of Judgment*, trans. Werner S. Pluhar, Indianapolis, IN: Hackett.
Kenny, J. (2009), *John Banville*. Dublin: Irish Academic Press.
Massumi, B. (2002), *Parables for the Virtual: Movement, Affect, Sensation*, Durham, NC: Duke University Press.
McMinn, J. (2006), '"Ah, This Plethora of Metaphors! I Am Like Everything Except Myself": The Art of Analogy in John Banville's Fiction', *Irish University Review*, 36 (1) (Spring-summer): 134–50.
Pippin, R. (2003), 'The Unavailability of the Ordinary: Strauss on the Philosophical Fate of Modernity', *Political Theory* 31 (3) (June): 335–58.
Rilke, R. M. (1987), *Duino Elegies: IX*, in *The Selected Poetry of Rainer Maria Rilke*, trans. Steven Mitchell, New York: Random House.
Rilke, R. M. (2009), *The Notebooks of Malte Laurids Brigge*, trans. and ed. Michael Hulse, London: Penguin.

Sheehan, R., J. Banville and F. Stuart (1979), 'Novelists on the Novel: Ronan Sheehan Talks to John Banville and Francis Stuart', *The Crane Bag* 3 (1): 76–84.

Stevens, W. (1972), *The Palm at the End of the Mind*, ed. Holly Stevens, New York: Vintage.

Wilde, O. (1909), 'The Decay of Lying', in R. Ross (ed.), *The Complete Writings of Oscar Wilde* (Vol. VII), 3–57, New York: The Nottingham Society.

8

John Banville and Hugo von Hofmannsthal: Language, mundane revelation and profane sacrality

Joakim Wrethed

Descending from a bourgeoisie Viennese family, Hugo von Hofmannsthal was a literary prodigy practically born into the midst of the artistic and intellectual prosperity of turn-of-the-century Vienna. When his poems began to appear, *Jung Wien* intellectuals were 'struck by a new star in their midst ... whose lyric poems, in their breadth of expression and classical poise, conjure the spirits of Goethe and Hölderlin' (Hofmannsthal 2005: vii). In his introduction to Hofmannsthal's *Selected Tales* (2007), J. M. Q. Davies draws attention to an impressive list of *fin de siècle* Viennese artists, scientists and writers who all in their respective fields would come to influence the modernist movements and the intellectual life of a great part of the twentieth century. Davies refers to 'a galaxy of early Modernist talent – Klimt, Schiele and the other Secessionists; Schnitzler, Bahr, Hofmannsthal and their fellow "Young Vienna" writers; Freud, Mach, Mahler, Richard Strauss and Schönberg' (Hofmannsthal 2007: 7). A golden throne seemed to be waiting for the young poet and prose fiction writer, but after some form of creative crisis Hofmannsthal abandoned poetry and the short story form to work mainly with drama, for instance as Richard Strauss's librettist in operas such as *Der Rosenkavalier* and *Elektra* (Hofmannsthal 2005: xii). The crisis has been compared to the one that afflicts the speaker in Hofmannsthal's famous 'Lord Chandos Letter', which fictionalizes a loss of faith in language's expressive power. Possibly, this explains Hofmannsthal's move towards the theatre and the opera, 'which with [their] many metalanguages could approach Wagner's ideal of the *Gesamtkunstwerk*, the total work of art, more closely than other literary forms' (Hofmannsthal 2007: 28–9).

As concerns the connection between John Banville and Hofmannsthal, the most prominent philosophical idea that has undoubtedly been carried over into Banville's prose fiction is precisely this scepticism towards the capacity of language to capture the 'world'. Even though Hofmannsthal himself denies having received the idea from any specific theorist or philosopher (Hofmannsthal 2007: 28; n. 30), these types of thoughts about language were in the air at the time: 'A contemporary linguistic philosopher, Fritz Mauthner, was concurrently working on a theoretical treatise that would endorse Hofmannsthal's insight and later provide the point of departure for Wittgenstein's *Tractatus Logico-Philosophicus*, arguing that all language is inherently metaphorical and all logical thinking psychologically biased and subjective' (Hofmannsthal 2007: 28). Arguably, the idea was not even Mauthner's, since Nietzsche had already developed similar arguments in 'On Truth and Lying in a Non-Moral Sense' (1873; published in 1896).[1] In any case, it is perfectly clear that this topic in various ways became a central issue in the philosophy of the twentieth century. In Banville's fiction, the concept is repeatedly scrutinized from different perspectives.

However, in Banville scholarship the issue has generally been treated as epistemological shortcomings with added ideas about what is salvaged out of the epistemological wreckage.[2] It is certainly the case that this pattern exists, but it does not really explain the persistence of the phenomenon as a creative force. Since Banville keeps returning to the matter, it must have some artistic and/or philosophical energy and significance that goes deeper than the most obvious surface level. Hofmannsthal clearly felt the force of non-linguistic revelation and Banville picked up the idea and let it resonate through his authorship. It is the purpose of this chapter to investigate Hofmannsthal's influence on Banville in greater detail. An additional aim is to give an innovative theoretical framework for how the notions about the shortcomings of language are developed and how they function. Therefore, I shall introduce generative anthropology as a backdrop to the thematic of language and revelation in Hofmannsthal and Banville. The intention in this study is to investigate how the language-versus-world problematic, as derived from Hofmannsthal, echoes through Banville's artistic production. I will also highlight the tension between language and mundane revelation in Hofmannsthal's writing and trace how it has been developed and elaborated by Banville. Finally, through the originary hypothesis outlined below and the paradoxicality of language, I shall try to explain the persistence of these phenomena in Banville's writing.

Generative anthropology, as developed by Eric Gans, starts out from a minimal hypothesis about the origin of language. By 'hypothesis' in the context of this chapter I mean a theory that has explanatory power in relation to the fictional topics analysed. The simplicity of the basic postulate is its strength:

> We shall suppose only the scene of representation as such as the minimal state of our hypothesis: the members of a group surrounding an object, attractive for whatever reason, and designating it by means of an abortive gesture of appropriation. ... The constitution of the act of representation is alone sufficient: the recognition by each member of the group that both he and his fellows are in fact designating the object *for the moment* without actively attempting to appropriate it. (Gans 1985: 19)

Thus, by means of this designating gesture the members of the group can – and paradoxically cannot – have the object, which constitutes the phenomenon that defers conflict. It should be noted here that generative anthropology considers the ostensive the more primordial form of language use: 'It is justifiable to follow past practice in calling this originary form of representation "designation" and the utterance that performs it an "ostensive", with its connotation of pointing' (Gans 1997: 28). Language in turn gives birth to imagination, fiction and even the sacred: 'The source of the sacred in the originary event is the *significance* of the designated object' (Gans 1985: 41). For theologically inclined thinkers this moment could potentially indicate the birth of God as the Word.[3] According to Gans, the sign is inherently and unavoidably paradoxical since it is 'both real and ideal, dualist and monist, "vertical" and "horizontal"' (1997: 13). Hofmannsthal's and Banville's fictional cognitions clearly revolve in large part around this paradoxicality. As shall be argued below, in both authors' writing the tension between ostensive and declarative aspects of language is highlighted. What is at stake in this phenomenological sphere is more than the question of the possibility or impossibility of science. What Hofmannsthal draws attention to in his 'Lord Chandos Letter' is not only the power of the appearance of ordinary things, but also the power of language in its paradoxicality.

In Gans's explanation of language as paradoxical, the topic needs to be understood and treated in terms of faith:

> In this revised understanding and performance of the gesture as a sign representing the central object, renunciation of its appropriative aim becomes not a turning away from the object but a new form of turning toward it. The object that had been the occasion of pragmatic paradox has been removed from the terrain of the participants to an – as yet provisionally – transcendental

realm accessible only through the act of signification. 'Truth' is our name for the guarantee of this accessibility as mediated by the sign. The sign is adequate to designate its referent because, as we have observed, the referent is uniquely adequate to call forth its designation. This is not 'correspondence-truth' but its originary source: the truth of faith in the significance of the designatum. (1997: 54)

In relation to the fiction examined here, the above means that by pushing the literary text in the direction of the ostensive (mundane revelation), both Hofmannsthal and Banville philosophize the roots of art and the sacred within the paradoxicality of language, since this move indicates 'faith in the significance of the designatum'. The whole subject matter goes well beyond the epistemological: 'The originary sign is both the name of God and the primordial work of art' (1997: 136). When exploring this area it becomes clear how much the Austrian *fin de siècle* and proto-modernist author – despite a relatively sparse output – seems to have affected Banville's literary imagination.

In his introduction to Hofmannsthal's *The Lord Chandos Letter and Other Writings*, Banville states:

[Hofmannsthal's] project was the melding of the self with the objects of reality. In this he followed the scientist-philosopher Ernst Mach, whose university lectures he attended; Mach preached a kind of scientific phenomenology whereby the world is conceived as a congeries of our sensations, the duty of both the scientist and the poet being to present and synthesize these sense data into a meaningful union, the scientist by means of mathematics, the poet through linguistic means. (2005: viii)

Here we see the embryo of a philosophical subject and dilemma that will appear and reappear in various thematized versions throughout Banville's oeuvre. The Irish author quite often stages this 'duty' as an endeavour of his protagonists, whether they are scientists/mathematicians (for instance Copernicus, Kepler or Gabriel in *Mefisto*) or artists (for instance Alexander Cleave and Oliver Orme). The seemingly impossible task of synthesizing 'sense data' into unified and lasting scientific theories or artworks is not only presented as a thematized repetition of failures in the novels, but is also part of Banville's own literary project as an author. In an interview in *The Paris Review* he states: 'I loathe my fiction. I have a fantasy when I'm passing a bookstore that I could click my fingers and all my books would go blank, so that I could start again and get them right' (2009b). To some extent Banville sets out to do what his work explicitly, on a thematic level, tells the reader is an impossibility. As the painter Oliver Orme in *The Blue Guitar* concludes, 'So it was the world, the world in its entirety I had to tackle. But world is resistant, it lives turned away from us, in blithe communion with itself' (2015: 58). The repeated failures to capture the world, or even a slim sliver of it, are due to the shortcomings of language, mathematics or any other metalanguage. However, in its entirety the issue is far more complex than a simple representation of a series of epistemological disappointments.

The most obvious starting point in an examination of Hofmannsthal's influence on Banville would be the Austrian prodigy's short story 'A Letter' [*Ein Brief*] (also known as 'The Lord Chandos Letter' mentioned above). A passage from it is used almost verbatim in Banville's novella *The Newton Letter* (1999d: 51). However, in his introduction to the 2005 Hofmannsthal selection Banville quotes another segment, which provides us with a richer array of themes and motifs to pursue. Here is a slightly longer version to add more context:

> It will not be easy for me to convey the substance of these good moments to you; words fail me once again. For what makes its presence felt to me at such times, filling any mundane object around me with a swelling tide of higher life as if it were a vessel, in fact has no name and is no doubt hardly nameable. I cannot expect you to understand me without an illustration, and I must ask you to forgive the silliness of my examples. A watering can, a harrow left in a field, a dog in the sun, a shabby churchyard, a cripple, a small farmhouse – any of these can become the vessel of my revelation. Any of these things and the thousand similar ones past which the eye ordinarily glides with natural indifference can at any moment – which I am completely unable to elicit – suddenly take on for me a sublime and moving aura which words seem too weak to describe. Even an absent object, clearly imagined, can inexplicably be chosen to be filled to the brim with this smoothly but steeply rising tide of heavenly feeling. (Hofmannsthal 2005: 123)

First of all, we are presented with the theme of the inadequacies of language, 'words fail me' and 'words seem too weak to describe', which might be the most easily recognizable Banvillean concern. An identical verbal formation reverberates in the very first sentence of *The Newton Letter*: 'Words fail me, Clio' (Banville 1999d: 1). This dimension can for brevity's sake be connected to the often quoted lines from *Doctor Copernicus*:

> Tree. That was its name. And also: the linden. They were nice words. He had known them a long time before he knew what they meant. They did not mean themselves, they were nothing in themselves, they meant the dancing singing thing outside. … Everything had a name, but although every name was nothing

without the thing named, the thing cared nothing for its name, had no need of a name, and was itself only. (1999a: 3)

This seemingly unmendable fissure between language and world contains a double arbitrariness, both within the sign in terms of the relation between signifier and signified, but also as a consequence thereof, between sign and referent (the vertical and the horizontal in Gans's terminology). The signifier might be either 'tree' or 'linden' and the signified (the meaning content) is similar, but these would make up distinct signs that would point to the same referent, albeit on different levels in terms of the signs' position in a hierarchy of genericity ('tree' generic, 'linden' specific). Thus, language has the unfortunate potential to complicate the simplest natural phenomenon. In all, this illustrates how the world remains for itself and seems to withdraw from language and thereby from the human realm, which it also does in Hofmannsthal's short story. Analysis of the quote from *Doctor Copernicus* in a historical context serves to connect it to Hofmannsthal.

First, we have Saussurean structuralist language theory that demarcates the epistemological theme (interestingly pre-figured in von Hofmannsthal's short story). On this level, language is arbitrary and does not have any 'natural' connection to the world, but the world still seems to be potentially accessible and a scientist might be able to 'synthesize … sense data into a meaningful union' (Hofmannsthal 2005: viii). For instance, John Kenny suggests that it is this more hopeful side of Hofmannsthal's deconstruction of language – the potentially 'regenerating power of external surroundings' – that Banville consistently pursues (2009: 98). But secondly, we cannot avoid confronting an outline of a post-structuralist view on language embedded here too. Since the world may be seen as something in and for itself ('the thing cared nothing for its name'), the realm of language becomes something in and for itself as well, that is a purely semantic world of signifiers in inexorable play. These two ontologies (structuralist and post-structuralist) co-exist in Banville's writing and an oscillation between them is a central fictional component.

In addition, another distinction needs to be made. Within the literary tradition there is arguably still a difference between modernist and postmodernist fiction, even though more sceptical conceptualizations of language start to appear in the late nineteenth century and after the turn of the century. This distinction is of importance when analysing the theme of language and revelation in Banville. In the terminology of Brian McHale, 'the dominant of modernist fiction is *epistemological*', while 'the dominant of postmodernist fiction is *ontological*'

(2001a: 9, 10). Epistemology in any form of empirical framework would indicate something more modernist within literary history, that is declarative sentences reaching out for patterns of facts (psychological or worldly-material). The question is: what can the subject possibly know about the object (or the world)? The possibility of raising that question, and the prospect of answering it, was obviously still Ernst Mach's hope. In contrast, language and fiction as making up a world of its own in relentless play and deferral (*différance*) would denote the postmodern dominant (instability on both the subject and object side, not even a hope of a connection to reality).[4] The repeated retention of the modernist dominant in Banville's writing is one of the things that would make it feel awkward for critics to dub him a clear-cut 'postmodern author'. Banville is anchored in literary modernism (Kenny 2009: 16–18), but also in the post-romantic nineteenth century, as can be seen in the influences of Hofmannsthal. In Banville's fiction it is often as if protagonists who expect a modernist world instead enter a world that functions according to the postmodern dominant, since the attempts at creating or finding order consistently encounter resistance from an unyielding and chaotic world. This aspect provokes enquiries about how the world is constituted, that is ontological questions in McHale's sense: who am I and in what world? (2001a: 10).[5] Banville tends to set up such tensions between the modernist and postmodernist dominants.

The other phenomenon that demands deliberation in the Hofmannsthal passage above is the suddenly appearing sublime aura that the mundane acquires, which fills the speaker with euphoria and makes him sense the power of the ineffable: 'A watering can, a harrow left in a field, a dog in the sun, a shabby churchyard, a cripple, a small farmhouse – any of these can become the vessel of my revelation' (Hofmannsthal 2005: 123). Banville's prose fiction is full of similar quotidian disclosures. For instance Johannes Kepler in *Kepler* has the following experience:

> Johannes, oblivious of the other's anger, idly noted a flock of sheep upon the common, their lugubriously noble heads, their calm eyes, how they champed the grass with such fastidiousness, as if they were not merely feeding but performing a delicate and onerous labour: God's mute meaningless creatures, so many and various. Sometimes like this the world bore in upon him suddenly, all that which is without apparent pattern or shape, but is simply *there*. The wind tossed a handful of rooks out of the great trees. (1999b: 31)

Analogous to how the speaker in 'A Letter' claims that he is 'completely unable to elicit' the mundane revelation (Hofmannsthal 2005: 123), Kepler here states that on this and comparable occasions the 'world bore in upon him'. Unstoppable in both cases, the coming to givenness of these everyday entities shows some form of power inherent to the world itself. For Kepler they do not have 'apparent pattern or shape' but they are 'simply *there*'. As in the case of Hofmannsthal, the world presses on and seems to have the strength to surpass the mediating step in which the subject tries to reach the world through language, science or artistic activity. If both Hofmannsthal and Banville lament the chasm between self and world, the phenomenon of mundane revelation seems to be what has sufficient force to momentarily bridge it. Both authors present the phenomenon in terms of pure *thereness* or *thisness* – fully compatible with Heideggerian *aletheia* – which means that it is more akin to the ostensive than the declarative.[6] Since one cannot articulate exactly what the momentary *lichtung* is, the predication typical of the declarative mode becomes useless. As we know, the owl of Minerva flies at dusk.

Moreover, if we look closely at the two authors' language we may observe another significant detail. Banville here uses personification to create a vivid image: 'The wind tossed a handful of rooks out of the great trees.' This in itself shows convincingly what language actually can do, which speaks against the whole theme of the powerlessness of language (artistic or otherwise). This paradoxicality is of extreme importance. Similarly, in 'A Letter', the speaker beautifully describes the phenomenon of mundane revelation in another passage: '[A] water beetle sculling on the surface of the water from one dark shore to the other, this confluence of trivialities shoots through me from the roots of my hair to the marrow of my toes with such a presence of the infinite that I want to bring out words' (2005: 124). In the midst of complaints about the insufficiency of language the speaker continues to express the phenomenon of mundane revelation in aesthetically appealing prose. As Davies remarks, 'Chandos's farewell to literature in so far as he is his creator's spokesman is of course rhetorical, and his use of imagistic language points the way to its renewal. Hofmannsthal continued to write and to be infinitely fascinated by language' (Hofmannsthal 2007: 29).

This phenomenon addresses several aspects of Banville's writing, both in terms of the content and as regards his own craft. As seen in the quote from *The Paris Review* interview above, Banville has commented on the impossibility of perfection, but also on the obsession with having better success next time. This steadfast hopefulness goes for the protagonists too in certain cases. For instance in *Mefisto*, just before the end of section one, it is written: 'Cancel, yes, cancel, and begin again' (Banville 1999c: 120). In terms of the scientists, artists and writers in Banville's fiction, this shows that the modernist dominant persists in terms of trying to reach an understanding of the world. One might object that Banville's sought perfection remains in the realm of language and fiction. The riposte to that remark is that fictional writing is a different type of knowledge and it cannot exist without some kind of referent such as 'world', 'reality' or 'experience-of-world'. This originary referentiality would be what Gans describes as 'the truth of faith in the significance of the designatum' (1997: 54). As concerns craft and Banville's own writing, disbelief in language displays a linguistic paradox that introduces itself when an author writes about the impossibility of writing. The paradox plays on the self-referential capacity of language, similar to the paradox in 'This sentence is false'. The importance of the designatum and linguistic paradoxicality are emphatically underscored phenomena Banville adopts from Hofmannsthal. Exactly where the demarcation line between 'reality' and 'fiction' goes we will never know. We are destined to live through the mutual haunting of these two realms. As indicated in *Ghosts*: 'Worlds within worlds. They bleed into each other' (Banville 1993: 55). But the Irish author's oeuvre puts forth that mere despair is not a viable option. This is demonstrated by the intimation of regeneration and newness towards the end of many of Banville's novels; for instance, spring in *The Book of Evidence* and *Eclipse*, and pregnancy in *The Newton Letter* and *The Infinities* (c.f. Kenny 2009: 96).

Another aspect to pursue is what Banville himself points out in the introduction to Hofmannsthal when stating that the Austrian's 'project was the melding of the self with the objects of reality' (2005: viii). If the chasm between self and world cannot be bridged by science or artistic writing, then the metaphysical desire to achieve this bridging itself creates another possibility. First Hofmannsthal, who again exhibits the desire for meaning without language:

> These mute and sometimes inanimate beings rise up before me with such a plenitude, such a presence of love that my joyful eye finds nothing dead anywhere. Everything seems to mean something, everything that exists, everything I can remember, everything in the most muddled of my thoughts. Even my own heaviness, the usual dullness of my brain, seems to mean something: I feel a blissful and utterly eternal interplay in me and around me, and amid the to-and-fro there is nothing into which I cannot merge. Then it is as if my body consisted entirely of coded messages revealing everything to me. Or as if we could enter into a new, momentous relationship with all of existence if we began to think with our hearts. But when this strange bewitchment stops, I am unable to say anything about it; I can no more express in rational language what made up this harmony permeating me and the entire world, or how it made itself perceptible

to me, than I can describe with any precision the inner movements of my intestines or the engorgement of my veins. (2005: 125)

The urge is to become one with the world itself, to 'merge' with it, to be in a 'momentous relationship with all of existence'. Thus, the gap is bridged and language cannot interfere and contaminate this sense of 'truth'. The passage also seems to contain a cancellation of *logos* altogether, which constitutes a longing the reader clearly can sense in for instance *Doctor Copernicus* and *Kepler*. Even though there is no explicit pining for a physical amalgamation in the excerpt from *Kepler* above, there is still a yearning for simple *thereness*, to be in experience itself to the hither side of scientifically discernible patterns, that is to experience the ostensive rather than making use of declarative language. To empirically apply mathematics or language to a part of reality requires a distance and some form of translation in which a great deal, maybe everything, runs the risk of being lost. Since the declarative operates with predication it remains on a level of correspondence truth. On this ontological plane paradox needs to be eradicated. In contrast, the ostensive can cope with primordial linguistic paradox, since it reverts to the mode of pointing. Chandos articulates that he cannot say anything about the phenomenon – which paradoxically he has already done – in 'rational language', where rational is synonymous with the declarative. Both in Hofmannsthal and in Banville we witness a desire for truth without any intermediate steps of mediation. In addition, there is a clearly articulated anti-*logos* sentiment, since there is a wish to be able to 'think with our hearts'.

The phenomenon of merging appears in *The Newton Letter* too, when Newton refers to his encounters with ordinary people: '*They would seem to have something to tell me; not of their trades, nor even of how they conduct their lives; nothing, I believe, in words. They are, if you will understand it, themselves the things they might tell. They are all a form of saying*' (1999d: 50–1; emphasis original). By avoiding language something true of the thing itself seems to be preservable. The intriguing question is why this phenomenon keeps reappearing in Banville's prose fiction. One could perhaps see it as merely yet another reinforcement of the fictional argument that empirical science is next to impossible, but that answer does not seem satisfactory. Why does Banville really need to repeat this point? Within the framework of the hypothesis of the originary scene, the phenomenon expresses a desire to inhabit the centre, that is to become the objects themselves and therefore cancel signification altogether. The sacred resides at the centre, but it dissolves as soon as one attempts to seize it. Moreover, the sign reintroduces itself, since the revelation of the workmen themselves is described as 'a form of saying'. The non-linguistic cannot escape the shape of the linguistic and vice versa. The originary sign means that we are always already in mediation (language). The protagonists cannot flee signification. So here again we witness an exploration of the paradoxicality intrinsic to language. The impulse to become one with the object would exterminate language and thereby imagination and art. Both authors investigate the paradoxicality of this desire. Therefore, the *aletheic* immediacy here functions as a reminder of the indispensable centrality of the sacred.

If we move on to Banville's own fiction we notice that he tends to complicate the potentiality of the recurring mundane revelations by sometimes denying them any specific meaning. Nevertheless, he lets the scene balance on the tightrope of ambiguity, as for instance in *The Book of Evidence*:

> I stopped outside the station and watched a flock of birds wheeling and tumbling at an immense height, and, the strangest thing, a gust of euphoria, or something like euphoria, swept through me, making me tremble, and bringing tears to my eyes. It was from lack of sleep, I suppose, and the effect of the high, thin air. Why, I wonder, do I remember so clearly standing there, the colour of the sky, those birds, that shiver of fevered optimism? ... It is just that I do not believe such moments mean anything – or any other moments, for that matter. They have significance, apparently. They may even have value of some sort. But they do not mean anything. (2001b: 23–4)

It is obviously a question of how to define 'meaning', but Freddie's epiphany (or whatever it is) does not have the same unconditional elation that these phenomena seem to have in 'A Letter'. Still, the reader cannot escape the fact that something happens. The insistence of the repetition throughout Banville's oeuvre indicates that something happens or is about to happen, even though the characters do not show any signs of having gone through some kind of conversion. This is the source of philosophical suspense, and we shall try to tease out the conundrum.

First we need to bring in a comparable moment from *Ghosts*. The aesthetic dimensions of such instants in themselves seem to indicate a momentary glimpse of phenomena that are more clearly marked in Hofmannsthal. We are exposed to the manifestation of light as imprisoned among the branches 'like bright water':

> There is a tree at the corner of the garden, I am not sure what it is, a beech, I believe, I shall call it a beech – who is to know the difference? – a wonderful thing, like a great delicate patient animal. It seems to look away, upward, carefully, at

something only it can see. It makes a restless, sibilant sound, and the sunlight trapped like bright water among its branches shivers and sways. I am convinced it is aware of me; more foolishness, I know. Yet I have a sense, however illusory, of living among lives: a sense, that is, of the significance, the ravelled complexity of things. They speak to me, these lives, these things, of matters I do not fully understand. They speak of the past and, more compellingly, of the future. They are urgent at times, at times so weary and faded I can scarcely hear them. (1993: 100–1)

In Banville, as in Hofmannsthal, inanimate objects seem to have the capacity to 'speak' – not in easily translatable human language, but rather in some kind of undecipherable and mysterious sign-system ('coded messages' in Hofmannsthal). Again, we witness the Banvillean oscillation between modernist and postmodernist dominants. This can be seen in the tension between the persevering attempts of the subject to understand the phenomenon in the world (modernist) and the sly self-awareness of the narrator, 'more foolishness, I know' (postmodernist). The critic could easily just conclude that we have a case of animism or personification and stop at that. But a serious philosophical enquiry needs to come up with a more fundamental response. The 'complexity of things' introduces itself in phenomenological ways and perhaps it is only possible to approach it the way Freddie does, that is in terms of descriptive phenomenology. However, against the background of the originary hypothesis, we can get a little further. The withdrawal of language reverses the evolution of the hypothesis from the declarative back to the more primordial ostensive, which is the source of signification and representation. The stark and plain *thereness* of the surrounding world moves us back towards the originary abortive gesture, which gave birth to the horizontal and vertical sign. The sacred that is felt is of course also that which cannot be attained, since that would collapse the whole system. The sacrality in Banville shows its affinity with the one found in Hofmannsthal in that it is ordinary objects that call forth these intimations of the ineffable. It is a sacrality potentially without God. A profane sacrality. Similarly, Davies states of Hofmannsthal's short story that 'Chandos is a mystic without a theology' (Hofmannsthal 2007: 29). But at this point a conspicuous difference between the authors' revelations can also be detected. In Hofmannsthal, mundane revelations are accompanied by language with clear religious connotations – 'heavenly feeling', 'higher life' and 'the infinite' – that evoke a sense of the religious. Banville's counterparts are often given with a postmodern layer of self-awareness or even a more distinctly sardonic tone, as in the quotation from *The Book of Evidence* above.

Another aspect of Hofmannsthal's fictional meditations on language will bring the analysis even further. Lord Chandos writes, 'Even an absent object, clearly imagined, can inexplicably be chosen to be filled to the brim with this smoothly but steeply rising tide of heavenly feeling' (Hofmannsthal 2005: 123). This notion is fleshed out when Chandos tells of an occasion on which he had rat poison spread in the cellar of one of his dairy farms. He goes for a ride in the evening, at first without thinking at all about the rats:

> As I rode at a walk over deep, tilled farmland – nothing more significant in the vicinity than a startled covey of quail, the great setting sun off in the distance above the convex fields – suddenly this cellar unrolled inside me, filled with the death throes of the pack of rats. It was all there. The cool and musty cellar air, full of the sharp, sweetish smell of poison, and the shrilling of the death cries echoing against mildewed walls. Those convulsed clumps of powerlessness, those desperations colliding with one another in confusion. The frantic search for ways out. The cold glares of fury when two meet at a blocked crevice. But why am I searching again for words, which I have sworn off! (Hofmannsthal 2005: 123–4)[7]

A number of things are significant. First of all, words that can appear without the presence of objects paradoxically also have the power of creating the presence of objects. This draws attention to the transcendentality of signification, which in turn highlights the power and transcendental aspects of imagination. The force of imagination is a frequently noted aspect of Banville's fiction, perhaps most thoroughly outlined by Kenny who claims that 'Banville's faith in imagination is absolute' (2009: 99).[8] Another interesting detail is that Hofmannsthal lets Chandos be overtaken by his eagerness to narrate. This again connects to Banville's oscillations between the power and powerlessness of language. Moreover, through the theoretical backdrop of the originary hypothesis, the phenomenon points to the primordial sign, which splits the appetitive object into referent and the object-as-designated-by-the-sign. Here the designated object lives its own life and the referent is pushed into the background.

If we link this to Banville in greater detail, *The Book of Evidence* is a suitable novel. For instance, we may consider the stark contrast between Josie Bell, the real murder victim, and the woman portrayed in the stolen painting. Freddie claims that he could not imagine Josie Bell as real, while the painted woman gets almost three pages of life through his imagination (Banville 2001b: 106–8).

Imagination can be powerful, as in 'A Letter', but it does not always work in the same predictable way. It can make objects present and it can make objects absent (i.e. it can function in relation to a referential context as well as on its own). Banville utilizes both possibilities in the form of prose fiction. The designated object is pulled into the creative imagination and the referent falls into the background. Moreover, in the novel Freddie tells the reader of a party at Charlie French's in great detail, which constitutes a narration that covers six and a half pages (Banville 2001b: 174–80). Then a while later Freddie tells us: 'Look, the fact is I hardly remember that evening at Charlie French's' (Banville 2001b: 182). Imagination can fill in what is missing and it can withdraw. This confirms that the novel has been playing with the reader's belief in 'the truth of faith in the significance of the designatum' (Gans 1997: 54). However, with a complete absence of any notion of a designatum, there could be no novel at all. In our reading through the originary hypothesis, the minimum of designatum would be the centre of the scene and the origin of signification, imagination and art. The whole of *The Book of Evidence* is built on the liar paradox ('I always lie'), which is apt, since the narrative would be next to meaningless without an ounce of truth.

In all, this elucidates why the different types of revelations and the oscillations between referent and designated object may have such a powerful attraction on Hofmannsthal and Banville. In generative anthropology this is the heart of the aesthetic:

> The exploitation of our experience of this paradox, the recuperation of the difference between the object and the object-as-designated-by-the-sign, is the role of the *esthetic*, which I have described as the state of contemplation that oscillates between these two 'versions' of the object. The use of language in situation forecloses the esthetic, which flourishes only when time is allowed for this oscillation. (Gans 1997: 36)

The provocative gap between world and language is fictionally upheld by Banville because he utilizes the aesthetic energy it produces. Mundane revelations (repeated indications of the ostensive) and the imagined amalgamations of subject and objects further nourish the same notion by being impossible, since their realization would smother language, imagination, art and the sacred. The revelatory moments instead function as aesthetic breathing zones, where the oscillation between designation and designatum can take place.

The relevance of the whole argument above may be further highlighted by a comparison to a critic whose work comes close to the thematic pursued here, namely Brendan McNamee in his *The Quest for God in the Novels of John Banville 1973–2005: A Postmodern Spirituality*. In the conclusion he states,

> In Banville's Nietzschean world, God is well and truly dead. Why, then bring religion into the equation at all? Because, I would contend, it is the clearest way of elucidating that ineffable quality that pervades both the lives of the protagonists and the novels themselves as works of art. God may be dead but that for which 'God' is a pseudonym … is not. In a discursive forum such as a critical essay this must have a name, so we may call it the sacred, but essentially it is nameless because it is not any *thing* at all, but, rather, *something that happens*. This mysterious something cannot be grasped by the questing consciousness because it is an event that only happens in the absence of this consciousness. The mystics have best articulated this paradoxical phenomenon. (2006: 257)

If we relate this to the findings in Hofmannsthal and Banville, as seen through generative anthropology, there are a few noteworthy differences. First, the originary hypothesis need not determine if God is dead or not, if he exists or not, since the sacred is concomitant with the birth of the sign. Secondly, within this hypothesis it is not a question of a presence or absence of a particular type of consciousness, but is rather about the fictional moves towards the ostensive and away from the declarative in the mundane revelations. In the analysis above, we see that both Hofmannsthal and Banville probe into the philosophical (and theological) question of the relation between language and concrete reality. In the paradoxicality of language they sense both the power and powerlessness of language. Acknowledging the desire to become one with the centre, they fictionalize its realization, which would cancel language and thereby imagination, art and the sacred. So, paradoxically, the cancellation of language confirms the power of language, since mundane revelations tend to substantiate 'the significance of the designatum' (Gans 1997: 54). More paradox. In the context of this analysis, fictionalized loss of faith in language seems to strengthen the same faith since signification and language are forcefully reintroduced. If God is dead, he seems to have been replaced by philosophical/theological ambiguity and suspense. After all, no one has been able to present evidence of God's existence, but no one has presented proof of his non-existence either.

Notes

1 'What therefore is truth? A mobile army of metaphors, metonymies, and anthropomorphisms: in short a sum of human relations which became poetically

and rhetorically intensified, metamorphosed, adorned, and after long usage seem to a nation fixed, canonic and binding: truths are illusions of which one has forgotten that they are illusions; worn-out metaphors which have become powerless to affect the senses; coins which have their obverse effaced and now are no longer of account as coins but merely as metal' (quoted in Soskice 1987: 78).

2 See for instance Rüdiger Imhof about Kepler and Copernicus: 'The final verdict on [Kepler's] own work thus also involves a kind of redemptive despair, a form of acceptance of one's limitations, as in the case of Canon Koppernigk' (1997: 127). What is left is life itself in its chaotic unfolding. C.f. also Joseph McMinn: 'Kepler smiles at "the mild foolishness of everything" because he realises the ultimate absurdity of trying to explain mystery. His imaginative side laughs at his rational side to see how long it took to recognise what was simply there' (1999: 79). The epistemological failure is turned into mystical wonder.

3 C.f. Gans: 'The originary relation between the sign and its object is not transparent to intuition. It is one that requires thought, that is indeed a defining condition for real thinking, as opposed to models of ratiocination that can be performed by computers. Since it is religion rather than metaphysics that has been concerned with the commemoration of humanity's historical origin, it is not surprising that the best analogy in traditional cultural practice to the operational identity of the originary sign is the name-of-God' (1997: 53).

4 This distinction is summed up in a generalized but lucid way at the very beginning of McHale's study: 'The Cognitive questions (asked by most artists of the 20th century, Platonic or Aristotelian, till around 1958): "How can I interpret this world of which I am a part? And what am I in it?" The Postcognitive questions (asked by most artists since then): "Which world is this? What is to be done in it? Which of my selves is to do it?"' (Dick Higgins, *A Dialectic of Centuries*, 1978; qtd. in McHale 2004: 1).

5 This question is clearly accentuated in *Eclipse*, *Shroud* and *The Untouchable*.

6 C.f. Davies who refers to the same phenomenon in Gerald Manley Hopkins: 'Chandos's account of his epiphanic experiences of humble things like wheelbarrows or basking dogs is an attempt to suggest in words the fact that sensory objects have an intense individuality and presence – what Hopkins termed their *haecitas* – which is not directly communicable in language' (Hofmannsthal 2007: 28). Originally this is a Scholastic concept going back to Duns Scotus (*haecceitas*).

7 Gundula M. Sharman points out that this episode is carried over into *The Newton Letter* (2002: 168). This is the part she quotes: '[A]ll at once I was assailed by an image of catastrophe, stricken things scurrying in circles, the riven pelts, the convulsions, the agonised eyes gazing into the empty sky or through the sky into the endlessness' (Banville 1999d: 8). Sharman's point is that this makes little sense to a reader who does not know the intertext. In the context of this analysis, it shows how meticulously Banville has interwoven Hofmannsthal into his work.

8   The whole subsection 'Making Himself at Home: The Purpose of Imagination' deals with aspects of the imagination (Kenny 2009: 98–103).

References

Banville, J. (1993), *Ghosts*, London: Minerva.
Banville, J. ([1976] 1999a), *Doctor Copernicus*, London: Picador.
Banville, J. ([1981] 1999b), *Kepler*, London: Picador.
Banville, J. ([1986] 1999c), *Mefisto*, London: Picador.
Banville, J. ([1982] 1999d), *The Newton Letter*, Jaffrey, New Hampshire: David R. Godine Publisher.
Banville, J. ([2000] 2001a), *Eclipse*, London: Picador.
Banville, J. ([1989] 2001b), *The Book of Evidence*, New York: Vintage Books.
Banville, J. (2009a), *The Infinities*, London: Picador.
Banville, J. (2009b), 'Interview: With Belinda McKeon', *The Paris Review*, 188 (Spring). Available online: https://www.theparisreview.org/interviews/5907/john-banville-the-art-of-fiction-no-200-john-banville (accessed 25 July 2018).
Banville, J. ([2015] 2016), *The Blue Guitar*, London: Penguin.
Gans, E. (1985), *The End of Culture: Toward a Generative Anthropology*, Berkley and Los Angeles, CA: University of California Press.
Gans, E. (1997), *Signs of Paradox: Irony, Resentment, and Other Mimetic Structures*, Stanford, CA: Stanford University Press.
Hofmannsthal, H. von (2005), *The Lord Chandos Letter and Other Writings*, New York: New York Review of Books.
Hofmannsthal, H. von (2007), *Selected Tales*, London: Angel Books.
Imhof, R. ([1989] 1997), *John Banville: A Critical Introduction*, Dublin: Wolfhound Press.
Kenny, J. (2009), *John Banville*, Dublin: Irish Academic Press.
McHale, B. ([1987] 2004), *Postmodernist Fiction*, London: Routledge.
McMinn, J. (1999), *The Supreme Fictions of John Banville*, Manchester: Manchester University Press.
McNamee, B. (2006), *The Quest for God in the Novels of John Banville: A Postmodern Spirituality*, New York: The Edwin Mellen Press.
Sharman, G. M. (2002), *Twentieth-Century Reworkings of German Literature: An Analysis of Six Fictional Reinterpretations from Goethe to Thomas Mann*, Rochester, NY: Camden House.
Soskice, J. (1987), *Metaphor and Religious Language*, Oxford: Clarendon Press.

Part three

Philosophical, theoretical and artistic forebears

9

A fool's errand: Blanchot, mourning and *The Sea*

Karen McCarthy

Spurred by the death of his wife Anna, Max Morden, the narrator of John Banville's *The Sea*, retreats to the site of his boyhood holidays, where his friends Chloe and Myles Grace walked into the sea one day, to their joined deaths. He rents a room in The Cedars, the house the Graces occupied, and from this attempted return to the past, he proceeds to write. Banville sets his protagonist the impossible task of re-presenting or re-inhabiting the past. In one of Max's more honest moments, he muses, 'and yet, what existence, really, does it have, the past? After all, it is only what the present was, once, the present that is gone, no more than that. And yet' (2005: 40). That the past no longer exists in any inhabitable sense is abundantly clear to him. However, the elliptical repetition of 'and yet', initially indicative of his awareness of the futility of his attempt, and then wilfully appended to the end of his thought, betrays Max's compulsion to attempt the impossible nevertheless. It is his 'fool's hope' with which this chapter engages.

In order to investigate the novel's preoccupation with what lies beyond its scope, I draw on the rich reading of the myth of Orpheus that Maurice Blanchot performs in his essay 'Orpheus' Gaze'. Aside from Max's self-imposed title of 'lyreless Orpheus', the correlations between the two characters are clear (20). Both have lost a wife, and both attempt to retrieve what has been lost by way of their respective art forms. Max registers as a narrative attempt to re-present a past, while Orpheus produces poetry with the musical accompaniment of his iconic lyre. The latter succeeds insofar as he is granted access to the underworld by the gods on the strength of his art; that is, he wins the gods' permission to retrieve Eurydice, his bride, by enchanting them with his music (on condition that he does not look at her amidst the shades). Here, the two stories diverge.

Orpheus is able to descend beyond the realm of the living to where Eurydice is. Max lacks the art that would grant him access to where Anna, or the past, might be found. He is, as he aptly puts it, 'lyreless'.

Blanchot chooses the myth to serve as an analogue for what art, or what he calls 'the work' can do (1955: 177). His essay's opening sentence, fittingly, states that 'art is the power by which night opens' (177). This refers to Orpheus's persuasion of the gods to 'open' 'the night', or the underworld, by the 'power' of his art. Here, Blanchot sets up the distinction between the realms of the living and the dead by applying to them the opposed terms of 'day' and 'night'. This binary proves inadequate when tasked with *placing* Eurydice however, and he resorts to characterizing her as 'the instant when the essence of night approaches as the *other* night' (177). This *other* night or *other* dark is Blanchot's gesture towards Eurydice in her shaded and 'profoundly obscure' state, and an attempt to move beyond the binaries that form part of the systems of order within 'the day' or the realm of the living, of which she no longer forms a part. Max's attempt to enter the past, and to write of something beyond the limits of the present, of life and indeed of the 'day', corresponds with that of Orpheus, whose 'work', Blanchot writes, 'is to bring [Eurydice] back to the light of day and to give [her] form, shape, and reality in the day' (177). Orpheus, like Max, is present, and of the 'day', and yet the object of his desire is entirely without 'form, shape, and reality in the day' (178). Before continuing, I must acknowledge that aside from Max's castaway self-designation of 'lyreless Orpheus', Banville makes no other overt reference to the myth, in this novel, or in his interviews. It is however, as I hope to show, deeply embedded in the text.

An Orphic descent, which Blanchot would argue characterizes all art, is the designation coined to describe the attempt to capture and represent Eurydice, who, metaphorically, is 'the profoundly obscure point towards which art and desire, death and night, seem to tend' (177). All art betrays a desire for something like this instant, which is beyond its reach. Art is therefore, rather aporetically, inspired by what constitutes its own limitation. Orpheus has the 'power' to descend towards the profound obscurity that inspires him and urges him onward, but 'only by turning away from it' (177). If he looks upon it, as he eventually does in the myth, his work will be destroyed. Art and narrative (which I would classify as a form of art), which are inspired by the absolute alterity of something like this 'other night', can be 'the power by which night opens'. Art can trace its movement towards its inspiration (as Max does when he circles the past, death, his wife and the twins in his narrative). However, to render this unrepresentable thing in 'the light of day' proves impossible. Orpheus 'wants to see her not when she is visible, but when she is invisible', which is equivalent to representing the unrepresentable (178).

Orpheus is fated to disobey the gods' orders, and look, and 'by turning towards Eurydice, he ruins the work, which is immediately undone, and [she] returns among the shades' (178). 'When he looks back', Blanchot writes, 'the essence of night is revealed as inessential' (178). Orpheus 'betrays the work, and Eurydice, and the night' (178). However, not to look, Blanchot asserts, would (paradoxically) be 'no less untrue. Not to look would be infidelity to the measureless, imprudent force of his movement' (178). Orpheus's desire (and Max's, for that matter) is for Eurydice, not 'in her daytime truth and her everyday appeal, but ... in her nocturnal obscurity'. He wants 'not to make her live, but to have living in her the plenitude of her death' (178). In other words, art (be it that of Max, Orpheus or any other) is inspired by excess, that is to say, by that which exceeds its grasp. It desires to move beyond itself and in effect wills its own failure as a condition of possibility.

When addressing *his* wife in her analogous obscurity, Max writes, 'why have you not come back to haunt me? ... Send back your ghost. Torment me, if you like. Rattle your chains, drag your cerements across the floor, keen like a Banshee, anything. I would have a ghost' (Banville 2005: 137). Max's desire is for the past, which he states 'is only what the present was, once, the present that is gone, no more than that' (40). His desire is for what he himself describes as inessential, or ghostly. When he addresses his wife, he requests a visitation from her revenant, which is the embodiment of death in life. Blanchot might say that Max wants her 'not as the intimacy of a familiar life, but as the foreignness of what excludes all intimacy' (178). Intimacy requires presence, and it is Max's most profound desire not to be present.

Blanchot states that when a writer attempts to represent that which is of 'the night', what is required is 'fidelity to the norms of clarity' of the world, which, ironically, is 'for the sake of what is without form and without law' (cited in Critchley 2007: 39). Banville draws attention to the fact that *his* work, which is a thing in the world whose fitful concern exists beyond it, must, as a result, remain incomplete. His work begins with Anna's death and circles back to end with it, which is a testament to its (obligatory) state of incompletion. As though to illustrate this, Max's narrative makes one final mention of his wife near the end of the novel, which, as I've intimated, does not have the resources to go anywhere beyond where it began. 'Anna died before dawn', he states, simply

(Banville 2005: 145). The final use of her name places her, permanently, 'before dawn', and thus bound to the shades of night, which is precisely where she was at the inception of the novel.

The issue of circling back is on Max's mind when he directly refers to himself as Orpheus:

> I have just noticed today's date. It is a year exactly since that first visit Anna and I were forced to pay to Mr Todd in his rooms. What a coincidence. Or not, perhaps; are there coincidences in Pluto's realm, amidst the trackless wastes of which I wander lost, a lyreless Orpheus? Twelve months, though! I should have kept a diary. My journal of the plague year. (20)

The repetition of a date accomplishes two (apparently contradictory) things. First, this 'coincidence' marks the second occurrence of that fateful date since it became fateful, and is therefore a kind of re-occurrence, at least in name. Max's entire project hinges on the hope of a re-occurrence, and yet, of course, the second thing an anniversary marks is a year's removal from the fateful day. This perennial bind, in which a date refers to that which it is ever more removed from, is precisely what renders Max's attempt impossible. He is bound to 'the day', and to its 'norms of clarity'. 'Pluto's realm', wherein his desired is now shaded, is one of 'trackless wastes', where tracks, signs and 'coincidences' no longer have any ability to signify, or show him the way. Nevertheless, he regrets not having written a 'journal of the plague year', as though such a thing would have rendered him less bereft than he is now. It is as though he feels the journal would have retained more of Anna's presence were she present for some of its construction. He is now left with only the inessential as inspiration.

Elsewhere in the novel, Max muses over a similar exercise that the artist Pierre Bonnard undertook when *his* wife Marthe died:

> In the *Nude in the Bath, with Dog*, begun in 1941, a year before Marthe's death and not completed until 1946, she lies there, pink and mauve and gold, a goddess of the floating world, attenuated, ageless, as much dead as alive. ... Her right hand rests on her thigh, stilled in the act of supination, and I think of Anna's hands on the table that first day when we came back from seeing Mr Todd, her helpless hands with palms upturned as if to beg something from someone opposite her who was not there. (87)

This painting, begun when Marthe was alive and completed after she died, is the artistic equivalent of Max's hypothesized 'journal of the plague year'. What Bonnard achieved, in Max's opinion, is a vivid representation of Marthe in which she is 'as much dead as alive'. He believes that what Bonnard managed was to somehow pause her deterioration, to suspend her and render her 'ageless', and further to transform her into 'a goddess of the floating world'. Max admires Bonnard because of what he believes is the painter's superior ability to '[catch] texture exactly' (30) and by implication to capture reality with great accuracy – greater than that of Max for example, who refers to his own representations, or writing efforts, as those of a 'second-rater' (59) or 'middling [man]' (29). Bonnard's 'goddess' and her resting hands stand in stark contrast to Anna and her 'helpless hands with palms upturned as if to beg from someone opposite her who was not there'. Orpheus, Bonnard and Max are all bereft of a wife. Max alludes to the other two because of what he considers their superior powers of representation. While Orpheus's art grants him an interview with the gods, and Bonnard's elevates and suspends his 'ageless' 'goddess', Max's is reduced to recording his wife's bootless appeal to 'someone opposite her who was not there', which needless to say mirrors his own inability to access the divine, due to his station of 'lyreless Orpheus'.

Max later qualifies his admiration of Bonnard, whose story has not yet achieved mythic proportions, and writes:

> Anyway, where are the paragons of authenticity against whom my concocted self might be measured? In those final bathroom paintings that Bonnard did of the septuagenarian Marthe he was still depicting her as the teenager he had thought she was when he first met her. Why should I demand more veracity of vision of myself than of a great and tragic artist? (121)

Marthe, it is now known, lied to Bonnard about her age when they first met. The 'teenager he had thought she was when he met her' was in fact 'in her middle twenties' (86). The 'agelessness' of Bonnard's goddess suddenly assumes an irony, given that the 'original' it attempts to depict, which by the power of Bonnard's art is frozen in time, was never the true Marthe. Bonnard never in fact knew the 'teenager', because that teenager had receded into the past (had become inessential) to be replaced by an older, less-than-honest Marthe. To render her ageless, at an age at which he did not know her, illustrates Bonnard's own 'Maxian', or indeed Orphic grasping for what was always already beyond his art's reach.

As Max perspicaciously observes, there are no 'paragons of authenticity', and even the 'self' with which he experiences the present, or illusion of *original* experience, is itself, according to him, a concoction. This suspicion of the present (for my purposes, the 'origin' of the past, or the originary moment) pervades the novel, and I revisit this shortly. For now, it is important to note that, despite his determination to write (an act which must trace an Orphic descent towards what exists beyond the terms of 'the day'), Max's work evinces an awareness that the essence of night is inessentiality. He grasps for the past, the original of which he distrusts.

Being in the present has become strange for Max after his brush with death. He concedes that to 'live amongst the living' is something he must practice or rehearse (108). 'To be' requires that he play a role. 'Among the more or less harrowing consequences of bereavement', he notes, 'is the sheepish sense I have of being an imposter' (113). He writes here of the sense he has of not being present to himself, of not being authentic. He recoils from the tenderness with which he is treated by mourners at Anna's funeral, stating, 'I did not deserve their reverence. ... I had been merely a bystander, a bit-player, while Anna did the dying' (114). Max refers to his 'survival' and Anna's dying, and he apportions all the authenticity to the role she played. It is astride a grave that his inauthenticity becomes apparent.

Banville once stated in an interview, 'I don't believe there is a kind of private self that we call soul ... that we have any single coherence. ... There's never a point of rest ... until the last moment arrives' (Izarra 2003: 244). Similarly, Max writes 'but then, at what moment, of all our moments, is life not utterly, utterly changed, until the final, most momentous change of all?' (Banville 2005: 25). Banville undercuts the very notion of an authentic self, a 'single coherence' or a 'point of rest'. Life's very 'changefulness' makes impostors of us all. Anna and the twins have died and thus undergone 'the final, most momentous change'. They are not impostors. After the 'last moment arrives', however, inauthenticity is not replaced with authenticity. Rather, the binary itself ceases to signify.

When Max returns to The Cedars, his inauthenticity is contrasted with what he imagines to be the house's original inhabitant, 'an old seafarer dozing by the fire' (11). Physical idiosyncrasies of the setting 'sound a nautical note', he thinks, and so the seafarer belongs in a way that Max does not. Indeed, the seafarer would belong in the *past* that the house comes to *represent* in a way that Max cannot. Max's longing phrases 'Oh, to be him. To have been him', sum up his project to occupy a past (11). They are perfectly within the range of what language can express, however the tense shifts and temporal gymnastics they perform with the verb that famously preoccupied Hamlet demand careful analysis. When the lasso of the infinitive form 'to be' tethers Max to 'him' (the seafarer), there is an uncomfortable disjuncture. The impassable chasm that separates the verb, along with Max, its inescapably present subject, from the 'him' that he would rather be, is the very chasm that Max and his narrative attempt to traverse.

The second sentence, with the past perfect 'to have been', acknowledges the impossibility of Max's desire. 'To *have been*' describes a completed action with an end, or more specifically, a lived life with the completion to that life that death entails. For Max to insert himself into the past to the extent that he would 'have been' the seafarer requires a dissolution of his present, or even further, for this, his present, to *never* 'have been'. He encounters here, rather abruptly, the limit of his reach as a writer and a creature of the 'day'. If he were able to achieve his desire to traverse the divide of past time and of death, and to 'have been', it would destroy his ability 'to be', which is the condition of possibility for him *to write* at all.

Yet, reliving the past is the thing he is compelled to do, even though this is beyond the limit of what his writing can achieve. At one stage he calls what he is 'compiling' a 'Book of the Dead' (131). The 'Book of the Dead' is the accumulation of Egyptian funerary texts with spells to assist the deceased's journey to the next life (Assman 2005: xi). Such a text, were its effects verifiable, would narrate from beyond the threshold of death. To return to Max's phrase 'Oh, to be him', the existence of the sentence proves that the expression of the desire is within the range of what language and narrative can accomplish. 'To have been him', however, comes up against its own impossibility. 'To have been him', and to narrate from beyond death, which is what the phrase implies, requires that Max write a 'Book of the Dead' from beyond the threshold of death. Only such a text, were it possible, would accommodate such ambitious phrasing without drawing attention to its unfeasibility.

To further illustrate this, early in the novel he writes, 'last night in a dream, it has just come back to me, I was trying to write my will on a [typewriter] that was lacking the word *I*. The letter *I*, that is, small and large' (Banville 2005: 45). A will is a document which purports to contain the voice and agency of its writer, even after he is absent in the most profound sense. While all writing can continue to exist in the absence of its writer, the will is a form of writing in which the presence of the writer supposedly retains its potency, even when he is no longer alive. His wishes are voiced from beyond the grave, and the will's executors are legally obliged to carry those wishes out with the respect they would afford its writer were he in fact present. The will allows its writer to traverse the divide between the living and the dead. Interestingly, however, Max's typewriter lacks the letter and the word 'I', and therefore inhibits his ability as an 'I' or a present self to express that presence, and assert its implied agency, even at the moment of writing. His compulsion to insert himself into the past and absent himself from the present is precisely what inhibits him from inserting the mark of his presence into this document. The 'I' that he is looking for is not the 'I' that signals present presence ('to be'), but rather the one that signals past presence ('to have been'), the 'I' from the will of a dead man, which is simply not available to him, given his cumbersome continuance in the present and his obligation 'to be'. This 'obligation' or even inertia is referred to when he later writes, 'I too could go and be as though I had not been, except that the long habit of living indisposeth me for dying, as Doctor Browne has it' (80).

The divide between life and death is explored with care by Banville again when he considers the trope of death by drowning. In *Eclipse*, he writes the following:

> And drowning, of course, drowning is strange, I mean for those on shore. It all seems done so discreetly. The onlooker, attention caught by a distant feathery cry, peers out intently but sees nothing of the struggle, the helpless silencing, the awful slow motion thrashing, the last, long fall into the bottomless and ever blackening blue. No. All that is to be seen is a moment of white water, and a hand, languidly sinking. (68)

The 'strange[ness]' of drowning is preserved by its remoteness. It is an experience that Max, who has never drowned, is incapable of knowing, since his position in relation to the ones drowning mimics that of this 'onlooker' in *Eclipse*. Instead of being able to write or narrate the twins' end, he is reduced to being a reader of signs diluted by distance. In the passage reproduced here, the signs available to the distant reader of 'a moment of white water' and 'a hand, languidly sinking' do not accurately portray the event, in that they do not impress upon that reader or 'the onlooker' the severity of 'the struggle' and 'the helpless silencing'. I would argue that, in the novel of the same name, the sea (or rather the surface of the sea) comes to mark the point at which signification loses its ability to channel meaning adequately. It is also suggestive of the juncture between life and death. Very simply, the person who is able to break the surface of the sea with even the weakening signification of a bit of white water and a sinking hand is not yet dead, and a person relegated to 'the bottomless and ever blackening blue' beyond the surface is dead. It is possible to live above the surface, and it is not possible to live beneath it. A person who sinks beneath the surface is also beyond signification – he or she is beyond both the ability to signify his or her existence, and beyond the capability of someone else to represent him or her with absolute accuracy. Language has no capacity to signify beyond death, and so 'drowning' or dying must remain 'strange'.

Chloe's and Myles's drownings are described from a similarly distanced perspective. Max recalls that 'it was all over very quickly, I mean what we could see of it. A splash, a little white water, whiter than that all around, then nothing, the indifferent world closing' (135). The notion of an 'indifferent world' features again at the end of the novel, when Max remembers being carried along by an unusual 'rolling swell' of the sea as a child. He recalls being 'set down on [his] feet as before, as if nothing had happened. And indeed nothing had happened', he continues, 'a momentous nothing, just another of the great world's shrugs of indifference' (145). The 'indifference' Max describes is double-edged. Of course, the relentless continuation of the world, which feels to him as though it is utterly imperceptive of his loss, forms an unmistakable part of this 'indifference'. However 'indifference', with its prefix of negation 'in-', can also mean 'no difference'. Difference is the condition of possibility for signification because meaning is generated by the play of difference. A place of 'no difference' would be one impenetrable to signification, one of 'trackless wastes' (20). Such a place, where Max's difference-dependent narrative cannot follow, is of the kind to which the twins have been relegated. The phrase 'the indifferent world closing', which is Max's description of the surface of the sea returning to a state unperturbed by the drowning children, can refer to what is both above and beneath that surface. The indifferent world that Max is obliged to continue within closes to the children; they are lost to it. Conversely, the world beneath the surface, the world of 'no difference' also closes, and leaves Max outside. As the survivor, he cannot follow, and neither can his narrative. What lies beneath the surface is that 'momentous nothing' the swell of which he felt as a child. 'Nothing', which he refers to again when describing the twins drowning, is the only word he has to signify imperfectly what is beyond signification. The word 'nothing' contains within it an implicit acknowledgement that it does not designate anything absolutely, but rather performs the relatively unique function of standing in as something of a placeholder for what exists beyond signification. At the surface, just before the children sink into 'nothing', they manage 'a splash, a little white water, whiter than that all around'. The last bit of difference that enables the last bit of narrative that describes them alive is between 'a little white water' and that which surrounds it, which is not as white. Already, difference has faded to the faint alteration of hue between water that is disturbed and water that is not.

Anna, once she is dead, belongs to this indifferent world. But even before that, as she is dying, she seems more at home where Max cannot follow. She acts pre-emptively when dying, and Max recollects her final days as follows: 'Mostly ... she kept herself quiet ... half in a doze, half in a daze, indifferent equally, it seemed, to the prospect of survival or extinction' (60). Her own retreat from the indifferent world and entry into that of 'no difference' is marked by her refusal to use language and her preference for silence (although her silence is certainly not to be equated with the absence of signification – not yet anyway). He describes her as 'half in a doze, half in a daze'. The words 'doze' and 'daze', with only the 'difference' of one letter between them, signify much the same thing, regardless of this difference. Anna's last splash on the surface is also marked by fading difference, and Max's ability to generate a description of her is therefore fading too. While it is not yet gone, as is apparent in the traces of her that remain in his narrative, it is fading.

How might one end a work that cannot ever be completed? In the final sentence of the novel, Max recalls being outside the place where his wife dies, and writes, '[a] nurse came out then to fetch me, and I turned and followed her inside, and it was as if I were walking into the sea' (145). This final sentence marks the work's inevitable and necessary limitation. It is no coincidence that the novel ends with the two words that also title and thus begin it. This repetitive gesture is again present in the plot structure, since, as I mentioned before, Banville both begins and ends his novel with the death of Anna. A narrative like Max's, which is inspired by what is beyond its scope, while capable of gesturing towards it, is bound to the realm of 'the day' and is thus bound, in turn, to an end that mimics its beginning. The beginning inevitably has much to do with the work's inspiration (an inspiration leads to a beginning, after all) and the end marks the point beyond which the work cannot go, or in other words, a limitation. Banville's repetitive gesture (it is ultimately Banville's, after all) appears to perform a bracketing function, which encapsulates both his protagonist's attempt and his failure. By encapsulating this failure, Banville illustrates an awareness of what *his* work can only mark an absence of. A circular plot line, as opposed to a linear one, virtually draws a line around that to which it cannot adequately correspond. At the centre of Banville's 'circle' is death.

In the novel, the closest that language comes to filling this void is with Banville's use of the metaphor of the sea. A large, fluid, shifting and seemingly unknowable entity provides as accurate an approximation as possible from within the world for something that lies decidedly beyond it. Banville's use of the term to both begin and end his novel, and thus frame it, is yet another indicator though that metaphor, which is the most powerful tool at his disposal, is unable to 'fill' the void, however fluid it might be. There is, however, the compulsion to try, nevertheless, to fitfully, restlessly circle that which is beyond narrative with narrative. (A circle is a movement without end and therefore without respite.) Recall the fool's hope Banville infuses Max with when the protagonist writes, 'And yet, what existence, really, does it have, the past? After all, it is only what the present was, once, the present that is gone, no more than that. And yet' (40). Once again, Banville frames what has no 'existence' or what is beyond his ability to represent, with a repetitive gesture. The first 'and yet' signifies his limitation (the inspiration and the limitation are essentially interchangeable and it therefore matters little that, in this case, the limitation comes first). He goes on to explicate why 'the past' is beyond what he can experience and consequently replicate in his narrative. The final 'and yet' signifies his obstinate resolution (or compulsion) to try nevertheless.

To return one last time to 'Orpheus' Gaze', one of Blanchot's many designations for the absolute alterity which is beyond signification is 'the deep' (1955: 177), which corresponds with what I believe Banville intends for the sea to signify. 'The deep does not reveal itself directly; it is only disclosed hidden in the work', Blanchot writes (177). Now, inescapably, the designation of 'the deep' generates its meaning in opposition to our understanding of 'shallow'. However, it has the connotation of having an unknown limit, of being 'bottomless' like Banville's 'ever blackening blue'. 'The deep', like 'nothing', is a term that reaches out, blindly, in the dark. 'Shallow' implies something that is easily within our grasp. Within the context of *The Sea*, the shallow parts are the safe ones, whereas the deep parts are those from which we may not return. Indeed, they are those which may accommodate our death. When Max walks with the nurse towards his dead wife, he feels '*as if* [he] were walking into the sea' (emphasis added). The 'as if' inserts the mark of distance (or of metaphor) between what he is describing, and an actual approach of Anna. The actual depths into which she has descended are beyond the reach of metaphor. They are too deep, and not shallow enough. *And yet.*

References

Assman, J. (2005), *Death and Salvation in Ancient Egypt*, trans. D. Lorton, New York: Cornell University Press.
Banville, J. (2005), *The Sea*, London: Picador.

Blanchot, M. ([1955] 1982), 'Orpheus' Gaze', in G. Josipovici (ed.), *The Sirens' Song: Selected Essays by Maurice Blanchot*, trans. S. Rabinovitch, 177–81, Brighton: Harvester.

Critchley, S. (2007), *Very Little ... Almost Nothing: Death, Philosophy, Literature*, London: Routledge.

Izarra, L. P. Z. (2003), 'Interviewing John Banville', in M. H. Mutran and L. P. Z. Izarra (eds), *Kaleidoscopic Views of Ireland*, 227–47, Sao Paulo: Editora Humanitas.

10

Reading Banville with Lacan: Hysteric aesthetics in *The Book of Evidence*

Mehdi Ghassemi

In *The Book of Evidence,* Banville stages his narrator as an existentialist in turmoil, cleft between his self-aggrandizing perceptions and a sense of self marked by alienation. The narrator, Freddie Montgomery, begins his narrative on an island where he is staying with his wife Daphne and his son. After failing to blackmail a drug dealer he finds himself indebted to a local gangster. In an attempt to raise the debt money, he leaves his family, held hostage by his creditor, with no sign of remorse or fear for their lives and returns to Ireland. On his arrival at his maternal home, he learns that his mother has sold off the valuable paintings he had hoped to sell to acquire the money. He then visits the Big House, which bought the collection, and steals a painting he was captivated by, murdering the servant who interrupts the act of theft before being eventually captured by the police.

Freddie rejoices in his 'elegant pose' (Banville 1989: 5)[1] while he bemoans the fact that 'other people' possess 'a density, a thereness, which I lacked' (16). What alienates him from others, says Freddie, is the fact that 'they understood matters. … They knew what they thought about things, they had opinions' (16–17). What he lacks is, on the one hand, linked to his inability to belong to a community that shares an epistemological paradigm based on knowing and understanding. On the other hand, what separates him from them is related to his lack of opinion – a relatively stable source of intentionality from which he can articulate his authentic thoughts and desires. Freddie's element is doubt: 'I stood uneasily, with a hand to my mouth, silent, envious, uncertain' (16). He feels 'unhoused' (16), that is to say, not contained within the framework that includes other people; he is an outsider. Yet, he is an outsider with style: he sees himself as an 'exiled king' (10). His alienation seems self-imposed, stemming from his megalomaniacal self-perception constantly adorned by such self-characterizing words and phrases as 'interesting figure' (4) and 'a sort of celebrity' (56). The combination of Freddie's self-alienation and self-aggrandizement hints at a hysteric constellation of subjectivity in *The Book of Evidence*. In addition, from the opening pages of the novel, the reader comes across the narrator-outlaw's problematic relationship with the law – a hallmark of the hysteric structure.

The advantage of the Lacanian understanding of hysteria lies in the fact that the latter is not regarded merely as a set of symptoms, but as a psychic configuration. In fact, in Lacan's psychoanalysis the etiological processes of hysteria as an illness and the different symptoms associated with the hysteric 'patient' are considered only as a subset of the structural subjective position. In this sense, as Cormac Gallagher points out, hysteria is primarily 'a discourse aimed at creating a particular social bond, one based on a display of frustration and dissatisfaction about one's place in the social order, whether that order be the family or a wider social grouping' (1995: 112). Along with the psychotic and the perverse structures, the neurotic structure is one of the three basic ways in which the subject relates to the signifier. Therefore, far from any attempt at vulgar nosology, the Lacanian understanding of hysteria (as a variation of the neurotic structure) allows us to explore the literary elements Banville manipulates in this narrative in order to explore a subjective constellation. Pure narratological theory would help us to identify a kind of unreliable narrator, but a Lacanian reading of *The Book of Evidence* as a hysterical testimony of unstable identity will enable us to look more deeply into the narrator's tactics. As I trace the narrator's relation to the signifiers I hope to reveal a psychic structure characterized by (in-) authenticity, unreliable narration, and the aestheticization of reality. These are fundamental issues at the heart of Banville's work, but we will argue that in, the Frames trilogy, they are given a hysteric twist.

The hysteric subject

One can distinguish between pathological hysteria and something that can be called 'healthy' hysteria. Since my aim here is not to attempt a pathological study of character, I will delimit the discussion to the latter.[2] According to the Lacanian model, the hysteric structure is the name for the way in which the subject situates herself with regards to castration. Lacan uses the term metaphorically and develops it into a concept. Castration, in fact, is Lacan's name for the subject's acceptance of the paternal Law as a result of which the subject ends her dyadic relationship with the primary caregiver and realizes that she is not the mother's sole object of desire. By doing so, she accepts the (Symbolic) identity as male, female, daughter or son, that is, the Symbolic space given to her by the Law, a space that guarantees her existence as a subject. Subjectivity is first and foremost the (by)product of the individual's interaction with the Other, the result of the articulation of signifiers by a speaker. Every time one speaks, one is forced to choose from a set of signifiers that lie in the 'treasure trove of signifiers' (Lacan 2006: 682). Unlike the psychotic, the hysteric does not reject castration but she does not completely accept it either. The hysteric never abandons the position of being the object of the mother's desire. Her desire is thus primordially linked with the other's desire, resulting in her 'subjective alienation' (Dor 1999: 76). In order to exist as a desiring subject, she is in constant need of identifying with others whom she *imagines* to be desiring subjects. The hysteric is eternally doomed to mistake others' desires for her own. Her predicament thus lies in her inability to single out her authentic desire in the plethora of other desires. The other, for the hysteric, functions 'as a privileged support for identificatory processes' (Dor 1999: 76). Indeed, such identifications are doomed to fail since they cannot yield a satisfactory result. Instead, says Joel Dor, they only fuel her 'neurotic ploy' (1999: 77), leading to a vicious circle of identification and failure. For the hysteric, Dor observes, identification with the phallus is 'an attempt to evade the question of having' since the latter foregrounds 'the inevitable confrontation with lack' (1999: 81) This results in her constant urge to identify 'with the ideal object of the other's desire' (1999: 80). She is deeply attracted to situations 'in which this imaginary identification can be brought onstage' (1999: 81). The hysteric's element is phallic narcissism and all of her acts are directed towards staging a performance, since her 'primary goal is to offer [herself] to the other's gaze as the embodiment of the ideal object of desire … to appear as a brilliant object that will fascinate the other' (1999: 81).

 A defining aspect of the hysteric's self-perception is his uneasy relation with the Symbolic order. This malaise stems from an ambiguous relation with castration. Lacan defines hysteria as a subjective configuration in which the subject is primordially concerned with the question of sexual position (1993: 170–5). What is crucial here is that sexuality as a Symbolic function is predetermined, always already situated. In other words, insofar as sexuality is subjected to the Symbolic law of castration, the sexes are but two aspects of subjectivity. One is *a priori* pushed to the feminine or masculine position within the dual structure (nowadays, thanks to echography, even before birth). In this sense, adopting an identity as such entails the adoption of an already sexualized identity: one becomes a subject only if one chooses the masculine or feminine side. Consequently, Symbolic castration produces a rupture between one's immediate uncastrated being (jouissance) and the Symbolic capacity in which one speaks or exercises power. To quote Slavoj Žižek, 'Because of this gap, the subject cannot ever fully and immediately identify with his symbolic mask or title; the subject's questioning of his [S]ymbolic title is what hysteria is about: "Why am I what you are saying that I am?"' (2007: 34–5). As a result of this split, there is always an irreducible sense of incongruity between one's title, on the one hand, and the way one immediately perceives oneself. What is specific with regard to a person with a hysterical structure is that s/he is immersed in this malaise, constantly dwelling on the 'discomfort in his or her [S]ymbolic identity' (2007: 34). This is why the Lacanian understanding of hysteria challenges the traditional view of hysteria as an inherently feminine phenomenon and argues, instead, that it presents the same set of 'problematics' for both sexes (Dor 1999: 81). As a result of the lack that the hysteric constantly faces in the Symbolic, the Imaginary takes the predominant role in the psyche. Paul Verhaeghe sees the origin of hysteria as rooted 'at the junction between the Real and the Symbolic' (1997: 41). The Symbolic cannot completely overwrite the Real, and consequently, the Symbolic is always lacking. The hysteric attempts to make up for this lack by relying on the Imaginary. However, Verhaeghe adds, since the Imaginary is itself 'subjected' to the Symbolic, 'a solution in terms of the Imaginary is doomed to failure' (1997: 42).

Discomfort in Symbolic identity

Given the aforementioned outline of hysteria, Freddie's relationship with his parents is unsurprisingly uneasy. He abandons his mother and visits her after ten years only to ask for money. He later finds out that he has been disinherited by her (170); that is, he is literally ruled out of his Symbolic capacity as the heir. He demonstrates an equally troubled and ambiguous relation with his father. Freddie's overall attitude towards his father is characterized by a combination of mockery and disgust: 'He was so laughably earnest. He made the mistake of imagining that his possessions were a measure of his own worth, and strutted and crowed, parading his things like a schoolboy with a champion catapult.

Indeed, there was something of the eternal boy about him, something tentative and pubertal' (28). The words 'laughably' and 'mistake' evoke a sense in which Freddie finds his father not as someone who offers a successful Symbolic model, someone who can be taken seriously in his role as the agent that represents law. Instead, he is 'tentative', that is, hesitant and provisional, lacking a plausible (Symbolic) conviction. Moreover, the word 'pubertal', as well as depicting the father as immature, ties in with Freddie's disgust at his father's moustache, which he describes as 'indecent, like a bit of body fur, soft and downy, that had found its way inadvertently on to his face from some other, secret part of his person' (28). His disgust for his father's moustache leads to his neurotic squeamishness about moustaches in general: 'There is something lewd about them that repels me' (84). Not only does the father appear as ridiculous and repugnant, but Freddie's descriptions of him at times display a reversal of roles between the father and the son. In the passage cited above the father is remembered as behaving like a 'schoolboy'. Furthermore, he remembers his father 'as impossibly young and me already grown-up, weary, embittered' (28). This suggests a role reversal in the father–son relationship as a result of which the narrator conceives of himself as a father in relation to his own immature father. At the same time, Freddie fails at fulfilling his actual fatherly role with regard to his son. In this sense, being a father only interests Freddie as a *would-be* function, as a performance and not as an actual (i.e. Symbolic) role.

Insofar as the father traditionally embodies the rules, mocking the father allows Freddie to challenge the very source of familial law. By doing so, he attains the freedom to slip from one role to another. Symbolically regulated *rules*, then, are bent so as to give way to Imaginary *roles*. As succinctly put by Schwall, 'a hysteric does not like a general law; he only accepts self-imposed rules' (1998: 284). This is why Freddie looks to set up his own version of familial relations, ones not bound to the Symbolic in which he constantly finds himself alienated. In contrast to his depictions of his father, Freddie's depictions of Charlie French, the 'old family friend', reveal a deep admiration: 'He gave an impression of equilibrium … he had presence, it was almost an air of imperium' (34). The fact that Charlie is an art dealer arguably plays a crucial role in his being admired by Freddie in that the figure of Charlie appeals to the aestheticist in Freddie. Moreover, the word 'imperium', in a sense, fills Freddie's narcissistic need for magnificence. In fact, it is in relation to Charlie that he comfortably refers to himself as a son: 'We might indeed have been a father and son – not *my* father, of course, and certainly not *this* son' (37). The modal 'might' is crucial in Freddie's hysteric reconfiguration of the paternal role: Charlie is accepted as a father figure only because he could hypothetically fulfil the paternal role. In other words, Freddie only accepts Charlie as a virtual (as well as unlikely) father figure in relation to whom he can freely set up his imaginary scenario. This suits Freddie's hysteric agenda perfectly: it allows him to defer castration, to indefinitely postpone being assigned a fixed Symbolic role. Not only does Charlie provide an alternative paternal figure for Freddie, but he also incarnates the maternal grace which Freddie finds lacking in his own mother: Charlie 'seemed almost maternal, in his apron and his old felt slippers. He would take care of me' (140). Charlie thus acquires a privileged status in Freddie's hysteric scenario, enabling him to entirely reshuffle the familial relationship. The traditionally triangulated mother–father–child is transformed into a dual relationship between a son and a sexually undecidable figure, who can function as both parents depending on Freddie's hysterical vagaries.

But his relationship with Charlie becomes even more complicated when Freddie stays at Charlie's house. The seagulls outside the window approach Freddie, thinking that he is 'Mammy' (138), that is, Charlie's mother; hence, yet another role reversal of parent and child. When Charlie moves away from Freddie's imaginary version of the perfect parent and approaches being a 'real' person, the role of the son in Freddie's psychic scene is deemed threatening since it introduces the possibility that he might *actually* be assigned the role of the son. Therefore, Freddie immediately strives to liberate himself from this role and adopts another, in an attempt to maintain the all-important freedom from imposed rules. He is comfortable in his identity only if he is the author of the psychic script. As soon as a rule is deemed imposed, his unconscious spares no effort in undermining the entire psychic scenario. This is also why, while he fails to be a fulfilling husband to his actual wife, he is assigned the imagined role of the husband in relation to the maid: 'We were shouting at each other now, like a married couple having a fight' (113). He accepts being a husband so long as the role is not fully actualized, enabling him to maintain the possibility of opting out of castration.

The other father figure in *The Book of Evidence* is Helmut Behrens, who figures relatively briefly in the novel (within the space of two pages) in comparison to Charlie French whom Freddie periodically refers to throughout his narrative. In contrast to Charlie's depiction as extremely benign, that of Behrens reveals a certain maleficence: 'He took my hand and squeezed it slowly in his strangler's grip, looking deep into my eyes as if he were trying to catch a glimpse of someone else in there. Frederick, he said, in his breathy voice' (84). The paternal grip is immediately threatening. Behrens's 'strangler's grip' transforms the handshake into a suffocating experience. In contrast to Behrens's firm grip, Freddie's grip is insecure, wobbly and awkward: 'My hands were trembling' (69); 'I am not mechanically minded, or handed' (111). What is more, this is the only instance in the entire narrative in which Freddie is addressed by another character as Frederick, that is, his Christian (Symbolic) name. In a sense, Behrens's overwhelming figure both literally and metaphorically fixes him, that is, castrates him at the Symbolic level. This is why Behrens is perceived as a threatening figure in whose 'raptor's gaze' (85) Freddie sees himself as prey.

Hysteric speech

Freddie's discomfort with regard to the Symbolic is also discernible in the way he relates to language: 'What I said was never exactly what I felt, what I felt was never what it seemed I should feel, though the feelings were what felt genuine, and right, and inescapable' (124). There is a fundamental gap that separates his feelings from his speech. Speaking as such bifurcates him between his immediate, 'genuine' mode of being and the Symbolic locus from which he enunciates. This rupture is most visible when he is confronted by a woman on the road while fleeing with the maid's half-dead body lying at the back of his car: 'Madam! I said sternly (she would later describe my voice as *cultured* and *authoritative*), will you please get on about your business! She stepped back, staring in shock. I confess I was myself impressed, I would not have thought I could muster such a commanding tone' (117). The adjectives introduced in between brackets bring to the fore the split in Freddie's discourse. Insofar as both adjectives are signifiers that represent his subjectivity, they do not seem to follow naturally with the rest of the enunciation. By bracketing them, thus, he demonstrates his inability to recognize himself in what his 'tone' conveys.

Freddie's narrative is often punctuated by an address to the Other (of Law) such as 'Your honour' (06) and 'my lord' (11). His very status as a defendant hystericizes his position, requiring him to endlessly engage in articulate self-explication: 'Please, do not imagine, my lord, I hasten to say it, do not imagine that you detect here the insinuation of an apologia, or even of a defence' (16). But the articulate explications soon reveal a troubled relation with speech: 'I was at a turning point, you will tell me, just there the future forked for me, and I took the wrong path without noticing – that's what you'll tell me, isn't it, you, who must have meaning in everything, who lust after meaning, your palms sticky and your faces on fire! ... Forgive me this outburst, your honour' (23–4). What is clear from the passage is Freddie's excessive preoccupation with how his speech is perceived by the other, taking on both the enunciator and the interpreter of his enunciation. His speech moves from self-explication to an obsession to demonstrate the faulty nature of (Symbolic) language. Insofar as language is based on conveying (constructing) meaning, Freddie deems it an inadequate means of representing his subjectivity. This can be clearly seen when interpellated by the officer to explain why he killed the maid. Faced with the interpellation, he stares at the officer while 'startled, and at a loss', and then vomits (196). After vomiting, he says, 'I wanted to talk and talk, to confide in him, to pour out all my poor secrets. But what could I say?' (197). Unable to produce an adequate, verbal (Symbolic) response, he musters up an answer from the Real. He literally pours out what cannot be expressed in words.

Freddie's uneasy relation with language seems, for the most part, to stem from the words' failure to correspond to what he wants to convey: 'I took up the study of science in order to find certainty. No, that's not it. Better say, I took up science in order to make the lack of certainty more manageable' (18). He is never satisfied by his speech since there is always a 'better' way to 'say'. Consequently, he continually paraphrases his utterances with an additional statement. Even when words do seem to correspond to what he wants to say, the correspondence is not straightforward: 'I fled before them, and dived into Wally's pub. Dived is the word' (30). His very attempt to affirm the correspondence between language and thought doubles his statement via a repetition. More than anything, the repetition evokes the sense in which he is not comfortable in his utterance since, if he were, he would not need the complementary statement ('Dived is the word') in the first place. The latter's inclusion, if anything, produces a discontinuity in his discourse and is, thus, counter-productive. Freddie's apparent discomfort in speech is in fact verbal (or linguistic) self-sabotage in the sense that his hysteric jouissance[3] causes him to be not fully at home in his speech. This allows him precisely to prolong his desire in speech, since by prolonging speech he ensures his subjective existence as a desiring being. Remarkably, in parallel to his discomfort in speech, Freddie emphasizes 'how easily one slips into the lingo!' (129). The verb 'slip' describes his relation with language perfectly since it designates a temporary sliding into an Imaginary aspect of language. In other words, he is comfortable with that aspect of language that entails identification with an Imaginary role rather than a Symbolic capacity that fixes him in a structural position as the speaker of a language.

Freddie's hysteric narcissism as well as his constant reformulation of his initial positions can be elaborated further by consideration of the instances in which he uses the verb 'to mean.' He often paraphrases his previous statements using the phrase 'I mean': 'I fancied it was me, I mean I thought this smell was mine' (4); 'The American, for instance, seemed no worse than I myself – I mean, than I imagined myself to be, for this, of course, was before I discovered what things I was capable of' (12); 'I can't believe that she's gone, I mean the fact of it has not sunk in yet' (101). His linguistic predicament lies in the fact that while he mocks the Other for his obsession with meaning, he is obliged to articulate his speech using the very system that alienates him, namely, Symbolic signification. As Jeanne Lorraine Shroeder puts it, the hysteric 'is hyper articulate because she is fixated in the [S]ymbolic order that partially excludes her' (2008: 152). Nevertheless, at times, the paraphrasing statement is not even available for Freddie, resulting in the statement's open-endedness: 'I thought how odd it was to be there, I mean just there and not somewhere else. Not that being somewhere else would have seemed any less odd. I mean – oh, I don't know what I mean' (24). Far from providing an alternative verbal solution to his linguistic predicament, the phrase 'I mean' disrupts the very train of thought and introduces a momentary loss in Freddie's enunciation. His constant attempt at paraphrasing is another hysteric strategy he devises to maintain an evasive stance in relation to Symbolic speech. However, his fixation on using such evasive strategies results in a split psyche which is directly imported into the fabric of the text: 'When I say *I did it*, I am not sure I know what I mean' (150). The statement on the one hand highlights how, as a hysteric, Freddie never commits fully. On the other hand, it is as if the italicized phrase, again, represents a locus of enunciation different from the one related to the non-italicized phrase. Faced with his discombobulated sense of self, he is 'not sure' where his true agency lies. The rupture between 'I say' and 'I did' results in the incompatibility between 'I say' and 'I mean', between what he says and what he *wants* to say. Lacan speaks of the 'incompatibility between desire and speech' (2006: 275) in order to highlight the fundamental limit of the articulability of desire. Since desire is animated by the unconscious, there is a limit to the degree speech can express desire. The unconscious is only available in bits, therefore, it can neither be known nor expressed completely. Rather, 'there is always a leftover, a surplus, which exceeds speech' (Evans 1996: 37). In Freddie's case, his speech produces an unintended excess when he inadvertently makes a joke: 'It was just nervousness and surprise that made me say it, I had not meant to attempt a joke. No one laughed' (199). This is why he is constantly worried about how his utterances may be interpreted: 'Clerk, strike that last sentence, it will seem to mean too much' (8).

In addition to signifying something, the verb 'to mean' figures in Freddie's narrative in its other usage as 'to intend': 'I killed her, I admit it freely. ... Nor can I say I did not mean to kill her – only, I am not clear as to when I began to mean it' (150). Though he openly admits to having carried out the murder, his problem lies in determining the source of intentionality behind it. In addition to the rupture between 'I say' and 'I did', therefore, there is a schism between 'I did' and 'I want'. He is plighted to a fundamental incertitude regarding the nature of his 'true' desire. He is inhibited by a foreign desire the origin of which he is unable to find; yet it is a desire that animates what he does. This results in a shaky sense of intentionality that can provoke a permeable sense of self. Freddie complains that when he reads 'an argument' he finds himself 'agreeing with it enthusiastically' but then he 'discover[s]' that he 'had misunderstood [it] entirely', that, 'in fact', he 'got the whole thing arse-ways' (17). The fluctuation between drastically different opinions 'show[s]', according to Freddie, 'an open mind' that enables him 'to switch back and forth between opinions without even noticing it' (17). This is contrary to the way he marvels at other people's ability in understanding and having opinions, as we saw at the beginning of this chapter (16–17). His interiority is not self-contained, but permeable, always prone to other influences. At certain moments even his memories seem foreign to him: 'It seemed to be not my own past I was remembering' (141).

Preponderance of the imaginary: Play

What underlies Freddie's hysteric universe is the incompatibility between the Symbolic and the Real. This is due to the fact that the Symbolic is unable to provide adequate signification for the Real. Consequently, different forms of lack figure in the Symbolic (e.g. in speech as we saw above). According to Verhaeghe, 'The hysteric appeals to the Imaginary in order to deal with the Real ... to work out that aspect of the Real where the Symbolic lacks a definite signifier' (1997: 41). For Freddie, reality is a locus in which the lack at the heart of the Symbolic order comes to the fore. In turn, he aims at patching these lacks with his overactive imagination. This results in the transformation of his narrative into an extended episode of daydreaming. In effect, many scenes in the novel are marked with phrases such as 'I picture'. For instance, in his prison cell, says Freddie, 'I pictured myself a sort of celebrity' (5) and he 'picture[s]' his father 'on those Sunday afternoons with his mistress' (29). Not only does his imagination provide a parallel scenario that supplements reality via picturing, reality itself becomes a locus in which he can stage his imagination. This goes to such extent that his perceptions become supplemented, or even replaced, by imaginary enactments. The American, for instance, is initially seen as 'quite a young man' (12). However, he is then reminded by Daphne of the man's old hands (12).[4] In fact, as Freddie admits, this character is referred to as 'the American' 'because I did not know, or cannot remember, his name, but I am not sure that he was American at all' (12). He is not so much a real person to Freddie as he is a prop by means of which Freddie can enact his imaginary version of reality. Freddie's imagination actively overrides reality, altering it and blinding him to *facts* (for instance, the American's old hands). The man 'spoke with a twang that might have been learned from the pictures' and reminds Freddie 'of some film star' (12). Freddie's insistence on the use of the word 'picturing' with regard to his imagination is related to *the pictures,* that is, cinema. He uses the latter as an artistic metaphor for staging his imagination, a means with which he can transform reality into a dramatic performance. His recourse to such imaginary processes is rooted in his inability to deal with the Real on a Symbolic level. Therefore, he fails to grasp the gravity of the Symbolic repercussions of his murderous act and, instead, conceives of his 'fix' as 'one of those mad dreams that some ineffectual fat little man might turn into a third-rate film. I would dismiss it for long periods, as one dismisses a dream, no matter how awful' (20). He literally uses the adjective 'unreal' to refer to his situation (20). By the same token, the officer who has come to arrest him is depicted as 'a keen student of the cinema' (189). And, finally, in a bout of narcissism, he perceives himself as a film star while stealing the painting: 'I see myself, like the villain in an old three-reeler, all twitches and scowls and wriggling eyebrows' (110). There is a systematic attempt on Freddie's part to delve into the realm of the fictive whenever he faces the imperative to sort out Symbolic inconsistencies. As Verhaeghe points out, for the hysteric, the 'lack of a symbolic answer results in an ever-increasing series of Imaginary as-if answers' (1997: 43). Indeed, one of the phrases that occurs most frequently is 'as if', that is to say, not reality *as it is*, but reality *as it would be*, or *could be,* constantly creating virtual scenarios in parallel to actual situations.[5]

In addition to 'as if' and 'picturing', the reader encounters many occasions during which Freddie uses the word 'play' in order to depict his relationship with the other characters. At times *playing* is used to signify *pretending to be*, that is, playing a role: in relation to the American, he is 'playing at being a blackmailer' (14), to Daphne and Anna, he is 'playing at being relaxed' (64), and back in his hometown, he is 'playing the returned expatriate' (76). At other times, *playing* is used in the sense of taking part in an amusing activity. For instance, meeting Anna back in Whitewater, Freddie is given a drink by Anna: 'I felt excited and bemused, and ridiculously pleased, like a child who has been given something precious to play with. I said it to myself again – I loved her! – trying it out for the sound of it. The thought, lofty, grand, and slightly mad, fitted well with the surroundings' (82). The enunciation of 'I loved her' preceded by 'I told myself' points to the performative aspect of his amorous confession. This is further emphasized if one considers the fact that 'the thought' of Freddie's love for Anna 'fitted well' with the background, resulting in an image in which the entire episode is perceived as a staged performance. At the same time, there is an observable tension between the authenticity of a playing child and his inability to have first-hand, authentic relationships as an adult. In this sense, the word 'play', insofar as it can be used in both cases, provides Freddie with a linguistic tool with which to bridge the gap between authenticity and the lack thereof. This is why he also evokes the figure of the child in his depiction of his troilism with Daphne and Anna. During the sexual performance children are 'at play' outside (70) and the entire ménage à trois is described as a 'children's not quite permissible game' (69). Freddie's conception of the affair in terms of an impermissible 'game' illustrates his attempt at redefining his (hysteric) problematic relation with the law. The make-believe scenario of play allows him to tease the boundaries of what is permissible and what is not and enables him to provide a playful, alternative version in order to momentarily forget about the boundaries that delineate the lawfully acceptable and unacceptable. His work, too, is 'hardly work at all' but 'a form of play' (135). It is as if by perceiving actual encounters in terms of different forms of child-play he is simultaneously afforded both the minimal leeway by means of which he can define reality as a game, that is, to maintain his preferred mode of make-believe, and the possibility of staging the idealized form of authenticity he lacks. In an episode in which he stalks unknown people in the street, Freddie is 'puzzled and happy, like a child who has been allowed to join in an adult's game' (167). His *flânerie* enables him to observe the crowd, the people in relation to whom he has always felt an outsider: he wonders how he was never 'a part' of 'the community of men' (193). The word 'part' illustrates the problem of belonging at the heart of Freddie's narrative. On the one hand, he is unable to *be* part of the community defined by Symbolic interactions – even his money is 'mostly foreign' (128). On the other hand, he can *play* a part in an imagined world based on Imaginary semblance.

Considered alongside his adamant self-referential and metafictional gestures[6] throughout the novel, Freddie's insistent use of 'play' indicates Banville's attempt to render explicit the relation between reality and play in *The Book of Evidence*. According to Patricia Waugh in *Metafiction*, metafictional narratives aim at demonstrating 'that play is a relatively autonomous activity but has a definite value in the real world. Play is facilitated by rules and roles, and metafiction operates by exploring fictional rules to discover the role of fictions in life. It aims to discover how we each "play" our own realities' (2001: 35). Fiction, says Waugh, is similar to play in that both construct 'an alternative reality' via the manipulation of 'the relation' between 'a set of signs' (2001: 35). Since literary fiction deals primarily with language, and since language 'does not have to refer to objects and situations immediately present at the act of utterance', it provides an excellent field in which the metafictional writer can introduce his vision of an alternative world (2001: 35–6). Following Gregory Bateson, Waugh argues that play provides a tool by means of which the writer explores 'new communicative possibilities' since any form of play requires a '"meta" level', a level that transcends the immediacy of the play. It is a higher level at which the very rules of play are defined (2001: 36). Manipulating rules at this level is precisely what allows the writer to create new forms of 'behavior and contexts' (2001: 36). In Freddie's case, constant supplementation of reality by different forms of play allows him to discover new spatial experiences: 'I found myself in places I had not known were there' (167). His purposeless 'criss-crossing' leads to 'crooked alleyways and sudden, broad, deserted spaces, and dead-end streets under railway bridges where parked cars basked fatly in the evening sun, their toy-colored roofs agleam' (167). It is a world that does not seem to be governed by traditional rules of reason shared by the community, but rather, an alternative world characterized by the 'sudden', unforeseen emergence of objects, objects that are '*toy*-colored', fit for his play-world (167).

The reconstruction of the Symbolic: The hammer

In Lacanian terms, play provides a means of creating a new set of relations that redefines the Symbolic order. This fits Freddie's hysteric agenda perfectly. As

Shroeder points out, the hysteric discourse reveals different forms of knowledge. Initially, 'the hysteric can learn what is *lacking* in the symbolic – to identify its flaws and decide whether to cope or seek to change them' (2008: 150). The next step is the realization 'that the Big Other does not exist' (2008: 150). The hysteric finds out that the reason he is unable to get a satisfactory answer from the Symbolic order is that it 'is not a pre-existing "thing" but a human construct, that it is not whole in itself but "a work in progress"' (2008: 150). This moment of realization is accompanied by discovering that the answer for the subject's desire does not lie in the Symbolic Other. Rather, 'only the subject herself can answer the question of how to follow her own desire and how to change the Big Other better to accomplish this' (2008: 150). There are two possible ways in which the hysteric can respond to this knowledge. On the one hand, since the Other does not exist, and consequently the entire epistemological quest of the hysteric at the level of the Other is doomed to failure, the subject can be extremely disillusioned. On the other hand, this realization 'gives the hysteric the courage to go on' (Shroeder 2008: 151). That is, once she realizes that completely filling the holes in the Symbolic is impossible, that the Symbolic is inherently lacking, never complete, the hysteric can aim at 'building the Other', at creating her version of the Other. She 'can express her creative freedom by furthering its progress' (151).

The second response seems to be precisely the one Freddie adopts. Being uncomfortable in his Symbolic roles as well as rules, unable to express his authentic desire through speech, and feeling excluded from the Symbolic community, he redirects his epistemological quest to the Imaginary level. Constantly faced with the lack at the core of the Symbolic order – even the 'traffic light' is 'faulty' (193) – he sets out to mock the very agencies that represent Symbolic law. For instance, 'The police station' is a 'mock-Renaissance palace' (194). It is only as a criminal, that is, as the obverse side of law, that he literally feels comfortable: 'My fate, I was convinced, awaited me all around, in the open arms of the law. Capture! I nursed the word in my heart. It comforted me' (129).[7] Paradoxically, he can be integrated into 'the law' only by breaking it. It is only by negating the law that his 'true' identity can be 'captured', fixed. He can finally be housed inside the outside of the Law, so to speak. Being a criminal allows him to be free from the law while being defined against it. This is the only way in which he can be both fixed (captured) and satisfied. Being defined as a criminal affords him the added advantage of being the very centre of attention. He wonders how he is perceived as a 'dangerous criminal' (140). 'I saw myself', says Freddie, 'as they would see me, a blurred face floating behind glass, blear-eyed, unshaven, the very picture of a fugitive' (141). He does not mind enduring all the hardship of being a fugitive so long as it allows him to stage the 'picture', the aestheticized image, of a fugitive, hoping to attract the other's gaze, the gaze that inherently bound up with his desire, transforming his every act into an act of display. Still, the image is 'blurred', not completely outlined and defined, not finished, but a work in progress. The word 'blurred' is reiterated immediately afterwards: 'How quaint it all seemed, the white tipped sea, and the white pink houses, and the blurred headland in the distance, quaint and happy' (141). The blurring then also adds to the beauty of the scene. This idea infuses him with happiness, a happiness linked with beauty. The repetition of the word 'quaint' highlights the significance of the aesthetic project he is so adamantly seeking to accomplish. This is why, against his council's advice, he is not at all reluctant to hastily sign the confession written by the clerk, a document that will surely incriminate him. To his council's warning Freddie replies: 'But I'm guilty ... I *am* guilty' (209). The repetition and the italicization of the verb indicate the significance of the role of the criminal in Freddie's aesthetic-hysteric self-reconstruction.

Vexed by 'the poverty of language' (54) Freddie adopts a Nietzschean extra-moral stance:

> I ask myself if perhaps the thing itself – *badness* – does not exist at all, if these strangely vague and imprecise words are only a kind of ruse, a kind of elaborate cover for the fact that nothing is there. Or perhaps the words are an attempt to make it be there? Or, again, perhaps there is something, but the words invented it. (55)

As Eoghan Smith points out, Freddie in this passage seeks the 'the truth of moral codes' from Nietzsche (2013: 90). But it is not only in relation to ethical truth that language is problematic for Freddie. His linguistic predicament lies in the incompatibility of the Real and the signifier, that is, language's (in)ability to name things and people. This is specifically evident in his attitude towards proper names: 'The charm I had felt in Kingstown, I mean Dun Laoghire, did not endure in the city' (30). The 'stable-girl' is referred to by a variety of names: 'Joan', 'Jean' (46), 'Jane' (49) and 'Joanne' (56). His failure to mention her 'real' name stems not from his poor memory, but rather because names do not correspond to the person-thing he has in mind: 'Jane – no, I can't call her that, it doesn't fit' (50). At certain moments, the name does fit: 'I found my way by mistake into Joanne's room. (Joanne: that's it!)' (52). This moment brings about what Lacan called a *point de capiton*, a temporary halt in the slippage of the signifier over the signified. Again, the bracketed phrase is telling. As to why this particular name produces this effect, one can put forward the hypothesis that Jo*anne* contains 'Anne', which links her with Freddie's object of desire, Anna Behrens. Therefore, choosing the name *Joanne* is related to his unconscious discourse momentarily opening up in his conscious speech. In any case, the name Joanne is only satisfactory for a short while. Towards the closing pages of the novel Freddie refers to the girl, again, as the 'stable-girl' (218). His return to the initial form of reference to the girl shows the impossibility of naming: the name and the thing remain forever incongruous. At the same time, one can argue, the circular movement around naming the thing/person, although ending in a non-name (stable-girl), reveals the relationship between Freddie's speech and desire. Freddie's seeming inability to find the girl's actual name is but the play of his unconscious in order for the signifier *Anne* to appear. This is the other aspect of play that is at work in Freddie's narrative. The proliferation and circular movement of names around the thing reveals the way in which Freddie's hysteric (strategic) jouissance wins over functionality, that is to say, over naming as a 'social reference', in order to prolong his unsatisfied desire.

His reliance on the Imaginary is to the extent that he seeks to redefine ethics as such. His (ethical) 'imperative' requires him to give birth to an imaginary version of the real life he murdered. Far from being remorseful, he is 'strangely excited', feeling 'wonderfully serious' at the prospect of being able to finally set things right (216). In other words, he is never rid of the fantasy of wholeness, clinging to the very end to his imaginary prowess that he deems capable of bringing about the solidity he so fervently sought to uncover by knocking down the Symbolic: 'I seem to have taken on a new weight and density' (216). It is not Real solidity, but one that comes as a result of his reconstruction of ethical signification through aesthetics. According to Schwall, the hysteric's 'predilection for all matters aesthetic' together with 'his narcissism' leads him to 'develop a system in which moral values will be tightly linked with an aesthetic sense' (1998: 283).

By staging his narrator as a hysteric daydreamer who considers reality secondary to imagination, Banville self consciously aims at providing a mirror of the real that shows its inconsistencies, inconsistencies that originate from the fundamental lack at the heart of the Real, the Symbolic, and the Imaginary. On the one hand, *The Book of Evidence* is a *mise en scene* for Nietzsche's (another highly creative hysteric)[8] idea that truths are but illusions morphed in such a way that we forget they are illusions, the idea that also informs, and is intricately engaged with, in *Shroud*. On the other hand, Freddie's hysteric narrative is also an elaboration on the idea that there is no metalanguage, no safe position from which one can *see it all*, not even based on as highly creative an imagination as Freddie's. It reveals how signifiers can over-determine the unconscious, trapping the narrator in a vicious circle facing him with the ultimate impasse of desire.

Notes

1   All subsequent references to Banville's *The Book of Evidence* are cited by page number only.
2   Although several of Banville's narrators do demonstrate an array of psychological traits that can be deemed 'pathological' (pathological narcissism as a primary example), focusing on the narrator's pathology is arguably not a terribly useful critical stance when one aims at tracing Banville's creative use of language (signifiers) in his fiction.
3   Jouissance can be roughly equated with the Real aspect of the subject, that part of subjectivity that resists being caught in the network of signifiers (the Symbolic order).
4   'At first I thought he was quite a young man, but Daphne smiled and asked had I looked at his hands' (12).
5   To cite but a few examples: 'The daylight too is strange, … as if something has happened to it' (4); Freddie perceives 'a remote expression in Daphne's eyes, as if she were trying to remember who or what precisely [the boy] was' (8); he finds 'a peculiar pleasure' in treating 'a fool and a liar as if I esteemed him the soul of probity' (13); 'I felt as if I had ascended to some high, fabled plateau' (18).
6   The most striking metafictional statement by Freddie comes near the end of the novel when he literally refers to his narrative as a fiction: 'I thought of trying to publish this, my testimony. But no. I have asked Inspector Haslet to put it into my file, with the other, official fictions' (186).
7   Incidentally, in Freddie's description, it is the word 'Capture!' which touches him, rather than the actual, present act of capture. This is in line with the fact that, as a hysteric, he lives at one remove from life. For him, the present is never as important as a quaint, blurry and beautified version of the past and future.
8   In explaining the link between hysteria and aesthetics, Schwall argues that Nietzsche and Kafka are examples of the sort of the hysteric-creative thinkers who set up 'a philosophical system' that allows them 'to order the hysteric's manifold art-inspired observations of an always intriguing life. Examples from Irish life are to be found in W. B. Yeats, Maud Gonne, Florence Farr, and Lionel Johnson' (1998: 283).

References

Banville, J. (1989), *The Book of Evidence*, New York: Vintage Books.
Dor, J. (1999), *The Clinical Lacan*, New York: Other Press.
Evans, D. (1996), *An Introductory Dictionary of Lacanian Psychoanalysis*, London: Routledge.
Gallagher, C. (1995), 'Hysteria: Does It Exist?', *The Letter: Lacanian Perspectives on Psychoanalysis*, 3: 109–24.
Lacan, J. (1993), *Seminar. Book III: The Psychoses*, ed. Jacques-Alain Miller, trans. Russell Grigg, London: Routledge.
Lacan, J. (2006), *Ecrits. The First Complete Edition in English*, trans. Bruce Fink, New York: Norton.
Schwall, H. (1998), 'Forms of Hysteria in *A Portrait of the Artist as a Young Man* and *Stephen Hero*', *Irish University Review*, 28 (2): 281–93.
Shroeder, J. L. (2008), *The Four Lacanian Discourses: Or Turning Law Inside-Out*, Oxon: Birkbeck Law Press.
Smith, E. (2013), *John Banville: Art and Authenticity*, Oxford: Peter Lang.
Verhaeghe, P. (1997), *Does the Woman Exist?: From Freud's Hysteric to Lacan's Feminine*, trans. Marc du Ry, New York: Other.
Waugh, P. (2001), *Metafiction: The Theory and Practice of Self-Conscious Fiction*, London: Routledge.
Žižek, S. (2007), *How to Read Lacan*, London: Granta Books.

11

Existential precursors and contemporaries in Banville's Alex Cleave trilogy

Stephen Butler

John Banville has never been afraid of courting controversy in literary circles, with a consistent rejection of mainstream literary values causing some element of notoriety when accepting his Booker Prize. The Irish author may have been dabbling in wilful media antics on this particular occasion, but an invariable element of the comments he makes on his own work is that it fails to employ the traditional elements of fiction the average reader would expect upon opening a novel. Banville even went so far as to say: 'I do not think I am a novelist. As a writer I have little to no interest in character, plot, motivation, manners, politics, morality, social issues' (Banville 2012a: 343). This is a fairly exhaustive list of the basic novelistic techniques and devices, so if the notoriously impish novelist is to be taken at his word the question remains as to whether anything remains in Banville's work once all these constituents of the novel are excised. A clue to addressing this question is offered by Joseph McMinn who, in the conclusion to his study of Banville, mentions the 'interdisciplinary passion' that informs Banville's work (1999: 164). Throughout his critical analysis of the Irish author's oeuvre, McMinn identifies four of the pervasive interdisciplinary strands in Banville's novels – namely science, pictorial art, psychology and philosophy.

This chapter's focus will be primarily on the final two elements, including their interrelation, and in particular on the philosophical intertexuality that is so prevalent in Banville's work. In both interviews and in the novels themselves the wealth of references to both Nietzsche and Heidegger (and to a lesser extent Wittgenstein) are significant and illustrate just how important these two thinkers were for Banville's own philosophical musings in his novels. In the Alex Cleave trilogy in particular, which is comprised of the novels *Eclipse*, *Shroud* and, more recently, *Ancient Light*, the existential motifs are most explicit, as these novels often directly employ both Nietzschean and Heideggerian terminology and their chosen themes possess an existential predilection which will be the subject of discussion in these pages. Banville, however, does not blindly accept the tenets of existentialism, and his interest in contemporary philosophers who question and yet expand on the ideas of those existentialist philosophers who preceded them, such as John Gray, Raimond Gaita and Mary Midgley, emphasizes how Banville thoroughly engages with the theories of both modern and contemporary philosophy.

The interest in both Nietzsche and Heidegger has been a constant throughout the Irish novelist's career. Direct quotations from Nietzsche and Kierkegaard pepper the early novel *Doctor Copernicus*, and in a 1980 talk at the Iowa Writer's Centre he explicitly utilizes the key term from Heidegger's *Being and Time* when discussing the function of writing, the purpose of which, he argues, is to express 'the Dasein which is the thereness of the world' (Harmon 1981: 14). In an interview with Rüdiger Imhof from the same period he again invokes Heidegger to explain the formal complexities of his novel *Kepler* which he describes as a 'formal imposition, the means by which I attempt to show forth, in the Heideggerian sense, the intuitive shape of the work of art' (Harmon 1981: 6). Despite the use of the existential terminology in his talks and interviews, it is questionable whether Banville was completely committed to the ideas of the existentialist philosophers, a point he later raises in the essay 'Fiction and the Dream'. Here, Banville questions whether his utilizing of formal and structural principles in his early novels was an endeavour worth pursuing, as he perceived that he was approaching his fiction as a 'scientist-like manipulator' (2012a: 370). The image is apt given the interest in science and scientists in the early novels, an interest that Nietzsche, for one, would have been scornful of, given his view that science's belief in objectivity is misguided. In fact, the supposed dispassionate observation that science prides itself on is actually as much a passion as any of the other human emotions and desires, and just as susceptible to error, in Nietzsche's opinion. Therefore, Nietzsche believed that science is as much a 'possible humanization of things' as any other human endeavour, including art (1977: 62). This is also the conclusion that Andreas Copernicus arrives at in Banville's novel, quoting Kierkegaard on his belief in a 'redemptive despair' at the fact that science will never be able to penetrate to the truth of existence (1999: 208 and 299). It is clear, then, that Banville is viewing the world of science through an existentialist lens in this early work.

Thus, his desire for formal, scientific impositions was being questioned in the work itself, and it is not surprising that, at some point, he would have sought after a different approach. This occurred, according to his admission in the above-mentioned essay, in the mid-1980s while writing *Mefisto* and just before he embarked on the Frames trilogy. The latter trilogy features the 'authentic hero' Freddie Montgomery, so labelled by Gecikli in his illuminating discussion of Heideggerian motifs in *The Book of Evidence* (2011: 5). Given the thoroughness of the discussion of these elements in that paper, and to avoid the risk of repetition, this discussion focuses on the subsequent trilogy starring Alex Cleave. Yet, there is another rationale for focusing on this particular trilogy, and it is to do with another precursor who begins to assume importance for the Irish author. Banville described the change of approach in his fiction thus: 'I began to let things happen on the page which my conscious, my waking, mind could not account for. And this was, I realised, a new way of working' (2012a: 370). He freely admits that the precursor for such an approach to writing is Freud, which may be surprising given his many consistently disparaging comments on psychology, such as his assertion that art should be 'the absolute opposite of psychology', and cites approvingly Kafka's diary entreaty: 'Never again psychology!' (2009: 7).[1] This polemical statement was expressed quite recently in 2009 in *The Paris Review*, and one wonders whether it contradicts an equally fractious statement he made back in the 1970s when being interviewed with Francis Stuart. Then, he had asserted,

> Psychoanalysis has changed our view of human beings. It seems to me that artists haven't caught' up with it at all. People are forever talking about psychological novels. There has never been such a thing as a psychological novel. I don't think any writer has ever really taken full regard of Freud. (I'm not saying he should.) (Deane 1979: 79)

Banville most certainly did take regard of Freud in his later work due to the change of approach that occurred in the mid-1980s, which was as much due to the influence of Nietzsche as of Freud. As Lesley Chamberlain, a writer that Banville has reviewed quite favourably over the years, mentions, there is a clear affinity between the two thinkers, and she describes them both as 'Seelsorger[s]', or people 'who cared for other men's souls' (1999: 81). More importantly, through the 'discovery of the unconscious', to use Henri Ellenberg's phrase, both men replaced the idea of human beings as rational creatures with the much more disturbing notion of the 'tragic irrational' (Chamberlain 1999: 82).

Banville himself labelled his early work the product of a 'rationalist', albeit an 'ecstatic' one (2012a: 369). While he does include characters such as Andreas Copernicus to question a rational approach to human beings, his early work could be liable to the criticism that the character's behaviour is stilted and rather limited due to this overly rational approach to the work. Such an accusation cannot be levelled at the novels that make up the Alex Cleave trilogy, which thoroughly immerse themselves in the tragic and irrational view of human beings. As Axel Vander queries early in the novel *Shroud*, using distinctly Freudian and Nietzschean terminology: 'Was I more than a moving complex of impulses, fears, random fancies?' (2002a: 27). The conclusion to this line of questioning is that he isn't, and that 'there is no self: no ego', a point made earlier in the same novel via a direct quote from Nietzsche's *Will to Power*, the title of which suggests an answer to the question: if there is no self or ego, then what is it that dictates the movement of people's actions? Freud's answer, controversial then and now, was that it is the libido that is the prime mover of people's actions and behaviours. As the following passage from Chamberlain makes clear, Freud's concept of the libido is one that overlaps extensively with a similar term in existential philosophy: 'Sex underlies and belies the sanity and calm of men and women everywhere. To dynamize the metaphor because Freud's system of personality is dynamic, sex – and envy – and this is an overall formidable drive to mastery and pleasure like Schopenhauer's Wille – is always threatening to break through to the surface' (2001: 74). The 'drive to mastery' of Schopenhauer's concept of 'will', which Chamberlain compares to Freud's concept of the libido, is in no way different than Nietzsche's view of the 'will to power' as the existential underpinning of life itself. Axel Vander agrees when he again asks perplexedly: 'Mere being, that insupportable medley of affects, desires, fears, twitches?'[2] (2002a: 286). The importance of sex in Banville's work is little commented on by critics, although Mark O'Connell's recent study *Narcissistic Fictions* explores it in perceptive detail, and the more recent novels *The Infinities*, *Ancient Light* and *Mrs. Osmond* illustrate just how vital a theme it is in his work. In *Eclipse* Alex may state that 'I think I have at last cured myself of sex, certainly the symptoms are clearing up nicely' (2000: 97), but in the later novel *Ancient Light* it is clear that it is a subject still much on his obsessive mind. In this novel, Alex relates his first love affair as a tender teenager, and the act itself is described by him as a 'triumphant climacteric' (2012b: 41). Through this act, and the relationship he has with an older married woman, Alex believes that he is engaged in a process of self-discovery in which 'one discovers oneself through another' (Banville 2012b: 42).

O'Connell is quite right to see the three novels of the trilogy as a treatment of 'a kind of narcissistic blindness toward the lives of others' (2013: 8). He cites

Freud's view of narcissism as a personality type in which people use others merely as love-objects in a relationship in which they are really in love with themselves and would prefer to be their own love-object, if possible. O'Connell quickly goes on to point out that the term 'narcissism' itself is a highly contentious one in psychiatric circles, and why wouldn't it be, given that, at its heart, it is a deeply paradoxical phenomenon? On the one hand, the narcissist is entirely self-involved, yet, on the other hand, it is a personality type that desperately seeks out some kind of relation with another. Or, as Norman Brown has described the paradox: 'The aim for Eros is union with objects outside the self; and at the same time Eros is fundamentally narcissistic, self-loving. How can a fundamentally narcissistic orientation lead to union with objects in the world?' (1985: 45). Vander answers this question by comprehensively embracing his narcissism in the relationship with Cass: 'The object of my true regard was not her, the so-called love one, but myself, the one who loved, so-called. Is it not always thus? Is not love the mirror of burnished gold in which we contemplate our shining selves?' (2002a: 239). While it is clear from a similar passage in *Ghosts* that Banville derives this sense of narcissism from Freud, which O'Connell also amply demonstrates, the passage is notably similar to one from a literary precursor who occupies much of the background of *Shroud*, Fernando Pessoa and, in particular, his modernist masterpiece *The Book of Disquiet*. The quote is as follows: 'We never love anyone. What we love is the idea we have of someone. It's our own concept – our own selves – that we love' (2002a: 234).

That Pessoa's novel was very much in Banville's mind when writing *Shroud* is evident given that at one point Vander quotes directly from the novel: 'If it could think, the heart would stop beating. A great writer whom you have not read wrote that' (2002a: 304). There are other more subtle references to the Portuguese writer's novel in Banville's own, not surprising given the intertextual wealth on display in practically every novel. As Joseph McMinn illustrates, detecting a fond regard on Banville's part for German literature and philosophy in particular (1999: 169). Few critics, however, mention Pessoa when describing influences on Banville, which is understandable given the Irish author's own lack of mention of the author. This is connected with the lack of regard for Pessoa in general, which is only being corrected in recent years through the tireless work of his translator and notable scholar in his own right, Richard Zenith. A mere cursory glance at Pessoa's life and work reveals just how similar in outlook he is with his literary successor. The name Pessoa itself derives from the same source as the English word 'person' which is the Latin word 'persona', an important point to consider when discussing Pessoa's views on human personality and identity, according to Irish poet Paul Muldoon (2007: 223). He cites the OED definition of the word 'persona', the relevance of which for both the Portuguese author's and for Banville's narrators should become clear: 'A character sustained or assumed in a drama or the like, or in actual life; part played; hence function, office, capacity; guise, semblance; one of the characters in a play or story'. The definition seems to imply that characters seen in plays or stories are no different to those in real life, that the self is merely a part that can be assumed or discarded depending on the situation. Alex Cleave, himself an actor in the theatre, voices a similar sentiment in both of the novels in which he features. He sees his roles as 'personae' and he often reflects on how his self is frequently lost amidst empty theatricality: 'What do they see in me? What is there in me to be seen? Maybe it is only the surface that they see? When I was young I was often dismissed as a matinee idol. This was unfair' (2000: 9).

The theatrical nature of the self is one that Pessoa often discusses in his novel and the implications of this idea are far-reaching not just in Pessoa's work, but also in Banville's. As Bernardo Soares, one of Pessoa's heteronyms, reveals:

> I've created various personalities within. I constantly create personalities. Each of my dreams, as soon as I start dreaming it, is immediately incarnated in another person, who is then the one dreaming it, and not I. To create, I've destroyed myself. I've so externalized myself on the inside that I don't exist there except externally. I'm the empty stage where various actors act out various plays. (2002a: 459)

The first point to note in this passage is the lack of a unitary notion of the self. Pessoa himself wrote under many heteronyms, all of which were as valid a part of his personality as any other. This notion of the self as a multiple (in psychology the term is 'multiplex'), pluralistic phenomenon is a leitmotif expressed by every single Banville narrator, without exception. There is Alex's reflection in *Ancient Light* on the 'incoherence and manifold nature of what used to be considered the individual self' (2012b: 114). In *Shroud*, Axel describes Cass as a 'protean dear, thrown together from a legion of selves' (2002a: 240). This is remarkably similar to how Pessoa describes himself in his heteronymous novel. It is also an apt description of Axel's own multiple identities, or 'aliases' as he prefers to label them, not to mention Banville's, given that he is now also the crime writer Benjamin Black who has himself written a pastiche of Raymond Chandler: 'Each of us is several, is many, is a profusion of selves. So that the self who disdains his surroundings is not the same as the self who suffers or takes joy in them. In the vast colony of our being there are many species of people who think and feel in different ways' (2002a: 458). In this, both Banville and Pessoa have the same precursor: Nietzsche, as Richard Zenith has drawn attention to in several articles on the Portuguese novelist (2012: 139–49). Chamberlain is correct to emphasize that both Nietzsche and Freud viewed the human personality in dynamic terms, and Nietzsche makes the point regarding the multiplicity of the self repeatedly throughout his work. In *Will to Power* he speculates that 'the assumption of one single subject is perhaps unnecessary; perhaps it is just as permissible to assume a multiplicity of subjects, whose interaction and struggle is the basis of our thought and our consciousness in general?' (1967: 490).

Nietzsche often employed theatrical terms when discussing the nature of the self or the subject. Roberto Calasso identifies in his later works a 'wild theatricality' when Nietzsche is presenting himself to his readers and to the world, and the Italian author associates this idea with 'the sinister archetype of the simulator' that Nietzsche derides in his former friend and mentor Wagner (2001: 12, 23). The theatrical analogies and their connection with ideas of simulation are also a noticeable feature of Banville's fiction. Alex, as an actor, is constantly meditating on his chosen profession and how his own sense of self is intimately connected with the roles he takes on. As he sees it, his acting is a means to achieve a 'total transformation, a making-over of all I was into a miraculous, bright new being'. He admits, however, that this is a project destined to fail due to the paradoxical nature of the actor's state, summed up elegantly in his admission that 'I learned to act, that was all, which really means I learned to act convincingly the part of an actor seeming not to act' (2000: 37). Calasso discusses how Nietzsche often viewed the actor as a 'coward', because rather than escaping his sense of self by inhabiting roles in the theatre, what the actor is really trying to do is 'return to himself because he has persuaded himself that he has an identity' (2001: 43). Throughout the novel, Alex confirms Nietzsche's suspicions on this matter as he persistently yearns for the 'unmasked self itself' (2000: 102), again a superbly contorted phrase. Similarly, Axel Vander pines for 'my real self at last' and an 'enduring core of selfhood' but is courageous enough to admit that he is, in fact, the archetypal simulator that Nietzsche accuses the actor of being. He refers to himself as an actor, or 'fabulist', and unlike Alex, he is more than happy to simply assume various roles as he believes, as did Nietzsche, that 'Man and mask are one' (2002a: 287).

Nietzsche goes further with the theatrical analogy and applies it not just to the nature of the subject or self, but to the process of knowledge as well. Calasso argues that Nietzsche viewed knowledge as 'ineradicable theatricality' (26), and therefore as illusory as the sense of self. This inevitably means that, for Nietzsche, the quest for self-knowledge was doubly misguided as an enterprise. Again, this is an aspect of Nietzsche that shares many similarities with Freud's thinking, despite the common misconception that the latter's psychoanalytic project is concerned with plumbing the depths of the self. This misconception of Freud's endeavour may explain the aforementioned dismissal of psychology in Banville's own work, or, more particularly, of 'cheap' or 'even expensive psychologizing' in most contemporary fiction (McKeon 2009: 7). That Banville was aware that Freud's thinking is actually akin to Nietzsche's regarding the notion of self-knowledge is clear from many of his articles in *The Irish Times* in which he references the German psychiatrist. In one article Banville quotes his novelistic predecessor, and own frequent inspiration, Thomas Mann's remarks on Freud: 'The analytic revelation is a revolutionary force. With it a blithe scepticism has come into the world, a mistrust that masks all the schemes and subterfuges of our own souls. Once roused and on the alert, it cannot be put to sleep again. It infiltrates life, undermines its raw naiveté, takes from it the strain of its own ignorance' (2006: 10). The tendency is to attribute contemporary Western society's self-help obsession to Freudian psychoanalysis, or depth psychology's desire to penetrate the abysses of the psyche, but Mann's description counters this by claiming that, actually, psychoanalysis is more to do with living in ignorance of such depths, or subterfuges. Rather than self-knowledge, it is ignorance of the self that Mann promotes in Freud's thinking, thus emphasizing, once again, the affinity of the Austrian psychiatrist with the German philosopher. As Nietzsche had claimed, in true Freudian fashion, 'we are unknown to ourselves, we men of knowledge' (Nietzsche 1969: 33). This is an idea often echoed in the sentiments of many of Banville's narrators, not to mention the novelist himself in various interviews. As he frequently states: 'I think that art has nothing to do with personal, or, if you like, *intimate* self-expression' (Deane 1979: 12–13). And, to quote Axel Vander in *Shroud*: 'I am going to explain myself, to myself, and to you. … I shall speak only of what I know, of what I can vouch for. At once the polyp doubt rears its blunt and ugly head: what do I know? For what can I vouch?' (2002a: 5–6).

Both Banville and Mann, then, perceive in the two thinkers a 'passion for ignorance' in their view of human psychology due to the individual's unwillingness to face certain truths about reality and themselves. Specifically, what people are afraid to confront, according to Banville in the article on Freud, are his controversial concepts of eros and thanatos. Banville perceived, as did Norman Brown in his *Life after Death*, that Freud had a fundamentally dualistic view of the human subject, and that rather than a single, unitary self, Freud posited that in each individual, not to mention in the metaphysics of existence itself, there are two warring instincts forever in strife with each other; namely, eros, or the will to further life, and thanatos, the 'drive towards death' as Banville glossed it in his article on Freud (2006: 10). Because of this eternal strife in the individual's psyche, the self is seen in Freudian terms as a site of eternal 'civil war', as Norman Brown described it (1985: 5). This sense of a split or divided consciousness is a staple feature of the majority of Banville's narrators, Alex lamenting, for one, his desire for 'the union of self with sundered self? I am weary of division, of being always torn' (2000: 70). Here, Alex is on the side of eros, given that this drive is concerned with 'the aim of eros as unification or seeking union', in Norman Brown's words (1985: 44). Vander, on the other hand, provides possibly the most succinct association of the subject with the Freudian death drive: 'What I wondered ... was whether a half of the self itself might be an anarch, bent on the destruction of the whole' (2002a: 393–4). This dualistic framework to Freud's thought may indicate a difference between his scheme of the self and Nietzsche's. The German thinker mentions both 'interaction and struggle' as the relationship between the multiple subjects in a single being. Later in the same work he mentions the exact nature of this relationship: 'Organization and co-operation – just as a human community is a unity – as opposed to an atomistic anarchy, as a pattern of domination that signifies a unity but is not a unity' (1967: sect. 490). While Nietzsche here believes that it is possible for there to be a unity of subject despite the multiple elements that constitute it, Freud's view of the warring subject seems to have more in common with the oppositional view of 'atomistic anarchy' described by Nietzsche.

This distinction between the positions of Freud and Nietzsche, however, fails to do justice to the complexity, not to mention the complementary aspect, of thought in both men. In Nietzsche's case, he may talk of unity and organization, and he uses the biological analogy of cells in the body to illustrate his point, but he also makes clear what he perceives as the driving force that propels the cells to seek organization in the first place, and it is his controversial notion of the will to power that he provides as the answer: 'The only force that exists is of the same kind as that of the will: a commanding of other subjects, which thereupon change' (1967: sect. 490). As mentioned earlier, Nietzsche's controversial notion of the will to power is remarkably similar to Freud's no less controversial concept of the libido, described by Chamberlain as a 'drive to mastery and pleasure' (2001: 13). The link between sex and a domineering attitude towards others is a dark seam that runs through Banville's novels – including in his latest in the character of Gilbert Osmond: 'Of course, once he saw how it was with her, he saw too how to turn the thing to his advantage. Her passion was the question, and it would be his power' (2017: 273–4). This equation between sex and power is an issue that concerns many of the Germanic thinkers and writers that Banville is influenced by. Rollo May (1993), for example, illustrates this conjunction in Goethe's work, where he argues that sex is 'largely … an expression of power' (242).³ Alex freely admits to a 'nascent streak of erotic cruelty' in his personality in *Ancient Light* (2012b: 69). This is unsurprising given the number of revelations as to his sexual conduct in both *Eclipse* and the later novel, and he often uses striking images of violence when discussing the erotic such as in the following disturbing, if not downright Sadeian, analogy: 'The erotic intimacy that binds the torturer to his victim' (2000: 110). While reading in the biography of Axel Vander about the scholar's relationship with Alex's daughter Cass, a fact unbeknownst to the father at this point, he refers to their 'savage love', a description with which Vander would undoubtedly concur. He himself believes that the purpose of love is to 'isolate and be in total possession of another human being' (2002a: 368), a rather lopsided view of human relations that may contribute as much as anything to Cass's eventual suicide. In Vander's case, this view of personal relations seeps into his political convictions also, and Banville purposefully used Paul de Man as the template for Vander to explore the caliginous relationship between the intellectual and their endorsement of totalitarian political systems. Unlike the quietist figure of Pessoa, Vander assumes different identities for many reasons: 'I lied to be loved, I lied for placement and power' (2002a: 12). As a way of dealing with the multiplicity of the subject one of his suggestions is to sublimate it in 'the totalitarian ethic' (2002a: 214).

While *Shroud* deals with Vander's 'murky accommodations with power', to use John Gray's phrase, it is also a critique of certain aspects of existentialist thought (2003: 87). Philosophers such as Mary Midgley and Raimond Gaita, not to mention Gray himself, have been astute at revealing the limitations of existentialist thought, particularly regarding human relationships. Gaita, for example, would take strong exception to Vander's notion that love is about isolating and possessing people. He would counter that

> love must be responsive to the independent reality of the beloved – must be so in order actually to count as real love. That means one must respect her faculty of free consent, that one must try to understand how she sees things, and more

besides. But the character of such efforts is conditioned through and through by a response to her as to someone who is unique and irreplaceable. (2004: 79)

Given the narcissistic proclivities of the narrators in Banville's fiction, is it possible for them to feel true love, as defined here by Gaita? The numerous statements of both Alex and Vander that they are only seeking for themselves in their relations with others would suggest that they are incapable of genuine feelings of love. However, most critics of Banville at some point have drawn attention to the key quote in *The Book of Evidence* that Freddie Montgomery murdered a woman due to a 'failure of imagination'. By not attending to his victim as a unique individual, he is able to commit the act of removing her from existence. Yet, it is Freddie himself who realizes what his mistake was, and he seeks to rectify it by producing the novel itself. In other words, he seeks redemption through the act of narration, and hopes that he will be able to attend fully to his victim in the retrospective act of informing the reader about her. This coincides with Gaita's notion that remorse may be a valuable tool in helping people to understand what it means to wrong another human being. Or, as Alex describes it: 'The harm *of* others, that is; the harm to others' (2000: 14). The insight to be gleaned is that 'every human being, whatever their distinctive characteristics or lack of them, is precious and irreplaceable, that informs our sense of what it means to wrong them' (2000: 165). By the very act of writing their narratives, both Alex and Axel reveal their remorse, and elucidate their failings to properly love another: in both their cases this refers to Cass. Gaita discusses the moral implications of parenthood, and by his criteria Alex would probably fail to fulfil his role as loving father to Cass. Alex often muses on his daughter with 'an angry buzzing of emotions' but after her suicide it is clear that the prevailing emotion is one of grief and deep loss. Yet, even when alive and a source of deep exasperation to her father, it is clear that what Alex struggles with most in relation to Cass is her unique individuality. As he admits, 'There was no keeping track of her moods, I never knew when she might veer aside and turn and confront me with a new version of her self ... perhaps that is her secret, that she does not act, but variously is' (2000: 72). On the one hand, Cass is the antagonist to all the theatrical existential men and their precursors who dominate her life: her father, Vander, Banville and his predecessor Nietzsche. Yet, she is also the embodiment of their notions of the self as she 'variously is' and her mental illness is a confirmation of the multiplicity of selves that can occupy one solitary individual.

Gaita's discussion of love and how it connects with the treatment of others does have an existential precursor, not in Nietzsche's or Freud's dark musings on sex and power, but in Heidegger's philosophy of being. While Axel Vander frequently admits to his narcissistic cruelty and blindness, he is also apt to engage in metaphysical musings on the nature of his narcissistic self that are also closer in spirit to Heidegger's metaphysics of being than to either Freud's or Nietzsche's. He states,

> I am, as is surely apparent by now, a thing made up wholly of poses. ... There is not a sincere bone in the entire body of my text. I have manufactured a reputation, from material filched from others. The accent you hear is not mine, for I have no accent. I cannot believe a word out of my own mouth. I used Cass Cleave as a test of my authentic being. No, no, more than that. I seized on her to be my authenticity itself. That was what I was rooting in her for, not pleasure or youth or the last few crumbs of life's grand feast, nothing so frivolous; she was my last chance to be me. (2002a: 329–30)

Throughout the novel Axel has been on a quest to discover (or should it be uncover? Or recover? Translating Heidegger's term *aletheia* is a tricky undertaking) his 'real self', and believes that he may be able to do so through his relationship with Cass. Rather than a narcissistic cleavage (pun intended on Banville's part) of the self and other that is a feature of Freud's thought, Axel is desperately seeking the existential approach of Heidegger in which the concept of the self and other are seen as mutually interdependent rather than oppositional. As Heidegger postulates, 'By "Others" we do not mean everyone else but me – those over against whom the "I" stands out. They are rather those for whom, for the most part, one does not distinguish oneself – those among whom one is too'[4] (1967: 162). One has to realize that 'being' is 'being-with', and that therefore one's relationships with others are characterized by 'care' and 'concern' – defining characteristics of an 'authentic sense of being' (1967: 173). The tragedy of Banville's novel is that Vander only really begins to feel care and concern for Cass once she takes her own life, but at the end of the novel there is a sense in which he has realized how much his self is now 'bound together' with Cass's, as his attention to pronouns emphasizes: 'Why should I have life and she have none? She. She' (2002a: 405).[5]

As Gaita draws attention to, one of the crucial questions regarding the concept of love is whether it is genuine or not, whether it is truly love for another human being or just another of the 'unsavoury forms of self-love' (2004: 80). This is an issue that preoccupies Vander throughout the novel, as he is desperate for his relationship with Cass to provide him with some form of 'authenticity', a word that Axel obsessively returns to in his thoughts. Banville has acknowledged that this is a central theme in his work and extends it beyond the confines of his own thematic preoccupations: 'The problem of authenticity is at the very centre of the human predicament, and perhaps never more centrally located than in our, now closing, century' (2012a: 351). Heidegger's philosophy is an attempt to make a distinction between an authentic and inauthentic way of being, a distinction later taken up by Sartre with his idea of 'bad faith'. In *Being and Nothingness* Sartre discusses this as a form of 'self-deception', thus highlighting the concordance between his thought and Freud's discussions of repression and projection (2003: 68). Banville makes explicit reference to Sartre's idea in *Ghosts*, and tellingly connects the concept to the artist when he remarks on the uniqueness of Beckett's work as a 'rare and exemplary instance of artistic good faith' (2012a: 375). Banville's reasoning is that artists, and particularly novelists, are so preoccupied with the theme of (in)authenticity due to the inherent insincerity of the artist's enterprise. Axel in *Shroud* is preoccupied with the 'existential predicament' of identity and authenticity for the same reason as Banville; he is also an artist, practically indistinguishable from Banville himself, yet he is aware that, unlike Beckett, he has lived his career in a state of bad faith. He yearns to be an 'alchemist of word and image' but he knows he is simply a writer of 'poses' and that his 'mature style' is simply an accumulation of other people's characteristics and forms of expression, which is possibly Banville's commentary on his own work and its 'interdisciplinary' nature. His conclusion to this line of thinking is a lament at the 'thought of all I might have done had I been simply – if such a thing may be said to be simple – myself' (2002a: 62). Sartre made a similar point that an 'authentic' life is one in which the individual accepts the responsibility for both their consciousness and subjectivity while acknowledging that others have those qualities as well. Abdicating that responsibility is to live in 'bad faith' and to reduce both the self and others to the level of an object or thing, a dehumanization that allows for the awful treatment of others that is a hallmark of Banville's ethically and morally compromised characters (Charlesworth 1976: 98).

Here, a possible paradox at the root of existentialist thought could be seen to manifest itself. While Nietzsche and Freud took a 'hammer to the illusion' that there is a self or subject, Sartre is implying that an authentic existence is one in which the individual takes responsibility for the fact that they are a 'conscious subject' (2003: 74). This may explain the paradox at the heart of Banville's narrators also. While they often declare that there is no coherent, authentic self, it is an idea they can't seem to free themselves of. At least, such is the case with Vander, who seems unable to relinquish his almost mystical (certainly esoteric) view of an authentic 'enduring core of selfhood'. That he is leading a life of bad faith is clear from the following assertion: 'I desired to escape my own individuality, the hereness of myself, not the thereness of my world' (2002: 285). The supposition of individuality will be duly attended to but it is worth commenting here that while Axel is employing Heidegger's terminology concerning the self he is doing so incorrectly, as it was precisely Heidegger's view that an authentic self is one that does not distinguish between the self and world any more than it does between the self and other, or between 'here' and 'there' (as everything is 'already-there'). According to Heidegger, the self does not reside 'in the world', but rather 'alongside' the world, so that being 'absorbed in the world' is seen as an authentic way of being (2003: 79–80). Banville sees such an idea as an aesthetically beautiful one, quoting approvingly a passage from Heidegger that poetically illustrates how to be absorbed in a pair of peasant shoes lying in a field that 'vibrates the silent call of the earth, its quiet gift of the ripening grain and its unexplained self-refusal in the fallow desolation of the wintry field' (2002b: 34). Unfortunately for Axel, he is living an inauthentic existence and is thus oblivious to the 'silent call of the earth', as he himself admits at one point by claiming 'I am a bad fit with the world, an awkward fit' (2002: 37). His choice of preposition is interesting from a Heideggerian perspective as he at least knows he is a bad fit *with*, not *in* the world. Yet, Banville's own description of the world seems to suggest that he shares with Axel an inauthentic existence, described as a 'dark hopelessness before the phenomenon of a world that is always *out there*' (Harmon 1981: 14).

It could be argued that this sense of hopelessness is conceptually akin to Kierkegaard's notion of 'despair', a term used by many critics when placing Banville as a writer of the 'modern condition' (Hand 2002: 1). In Vander's case there is a definite Kierkegaardian, as well as Heideggerian and Sartrean,[6] element to his existential plight, given that he desires to 'escape [his] own individuality' (2002: 113). This is a desire born of despair, according to the Danish philosopher, who describes it thus: 'Despair is veritably a self-consuming, but an impotent self-consuming that cannot do what it wants to do. What it wants to do is to consume itself, something it cannot do, and this impotence is a new form of self-consuming, in which despair is once again unable to do what it wants to do' (2000: 355). Kierkegaard's argument is that this is not a psychological or emotional state that can affect certain individuals but, rather, an existential prerequisite of existence, and is, thus, something that everyone possesses. This is not an entirely disheartening idea in the philosopher's scheme of things, as he believes that it is through despair, or 'disquietude' that the individual is able to achieve 'spirit' in a heroic 'venture to wholly be oneself, as an individual man' (Kierkegaard 1941: xi).

Mary Midgley is one contemporary philosopher critical of this aspect of existentialist thought as she views it as both an endorsement of 'unrealistic, icy individualism' (2002a: 340) and an example of 'intellectualist machismo' (2002b: 192), two labels that could easily be applied to any Banville narrator. Banville's comments on the art of the novel often espouse a similar championing of individuality, as he has stated that it deals 'almost exclusively with the individual soul, with the individual consciousness' (Ní Anluain 2000: 24–5). This is both an existential imperative, displaying Banville's affinity with his existential precursors, and a moral one, illustrating his affinity with contemporary philosophers such as Raimond Gaita. For Gaita, it is precisely due to the fact of 'human individuality' that murder is such a reprehensible act, as it dismisses this view of the other person as a distinct and autonomous individual (2004: 149–50).

Kierkegaard argued that consciousness is the defining characteristic of the individual, the 'decisive criterion of the self', and went on to associate the notion of consciousness with that of the will, thus displaying an affinity with Nietzsche's and Schopenhauer's thinking (1941: 46). Both Alex and Vander spend much of their novels wrestling with this aspect of their selves, and it is due to an extreme bout of 'crippling self-consciousness' on the stage that Alex is forced to take a hiatus from his acting career. He defines this as an essential element of his personality: 'This hideous awareness, this insupportable excess of self' (2000: 88). That both Alex and Axel refer to their self-consciousness almost always in negative terms would suggest that Banville is offering a critique of the existential philosophy with which his novels are engaged. In this, the influence of more contemporary philosophers is evident. John Gray roundly dismisses 'our ingrained belief that consciousness, selfhood and free will are what define us as human beings' (38). In its place, Gray proposes that 'action preserves a sense of self-identity that reflection dispels' (194). Alex longs for such a way of living in the world, free of his burdens of self-consciousness. He believes he glimpses such an authentic way of being while observing a naked young girl who is unaware that she is being observed. Due to this lack of knowing she is being watched she is able to act in a completely uninhibited fashion, a 'purity of gesture' that reflects her 'perfect self-absorption'. As Alex makes clear, this is the opposite of self-consciousness or awareness: 'All was dependent precisely on there being no thought attached to what she was doing, no awareness' (2000: 101). He refers to this as a 'state of being that is beyond, or behind, what we think of as the human' (2000: 102), thus illustrating that Banville has thoroughly engaged with the ideas of Gray. Gray contends that the human sense of identity is deluded and that we should live in a way closer to the existence of animals who do not possess the faculty of self-consciousness or awareness. In this, he is agreeing with a similar point made by both Chamberlain and Gaita. Both writers stress the need to embrace the 'creaturely nature we have in common' (Gaita 2004: 194) with animals, although Gaita does admit that the element of reflection on our deportment is the characteristic that separates us from the animal world. Chamberlain makes this point in reference to Nietzsche, arguing that he in fact makes the same case regarding how we conduct ourselves, and the iconic action of Nietzsche embracing a horse in the street and shedding tears at the conduct of its human owner speaks volumes as to how literally Nietzsche endorsed the rapport that the human and animal spheres of existence possess. As mentioned, it was Nietzsche who also labelled the actor (as well as the scientist, the other figure Banville likes to use in his fiction) a 'coward', and it may be due to the inherent self-consciousness that this profession demands. As Gray mentions, Stanislavsky, a theatre theorist that Alex informs us he has read thoroughly, was aware of the limitations of the acting profession which 'reaches a limit beyond which human consciousness cannot extend … only nature can perform the miracle' (2003: 134). Alex lives with the burden of this throughout the novel.

In conclusion, it has hopefully been illustrated just how thoroughly immersed Banville's novels are in philosophical and psychological frames of thought, rather than the purely literary. Both the author and his narrators are self-confessed autodidacts who wear their learning on their sleeve and choose to ignore Seamus Heaney's prescription: 'Don't have the veins bulging in your Biro' (1998: 159). Every novel is teeming with references to the philosophical influences that inform Banville's work, drawing as he admits from a 'European tradition' rather than simply an Irish context, a point that George Steiner discerns as a defining characteristic of the Irish novelist (McMinn 1999: 163). That Banville often turns to the existentialists for inspiration is a testimony to the importance of these thinkers in defining the hybrid form of the philosophical novel, a point Áine Mahon raised in a recent *The Irish Times* article. She also suggests that such an approach to literature is still a rare one in contemporary Irish writing and offers a suggestion as to why this is the case: 'If we think of philosophy as an attempt to understand the universal human condition, we might say that Irish literature misses the universal in its insistence on the local' (Humphreys 2014: 11). This is not an accusation that could be made of Banville, as his locales are notoriously fictional, with no research on them to provide a sense of authenticity of place, so whether a novel is set in Dublin or Kraków is of no real interest to the Wexford author. In fact, he would seem to confirm Mahon's point when he labelled his own upbringing as 'boring and provincial' (McKeon 2009: 6). However, this repudiation of the local and provincial suggests the influence of the Irish precursors of Joyce and Beckett who may protest at the constricting 'nets' of Ireland but do not seem to be able to engage with any other subject in their work. In Banville's later novels there is a redolence of local details that belies their fictional nature. The tension in all three Irish writers is that they employ the local even as they aspire towards a transnational body of work focusing on 'the universal human condition', a theme that seeks to transcend both the boundaries of place and of discipline. As the author has stated, 'The writing of fiction is far more than the telling of stories' (2012a: 372).

Notes

1 Banville may have adopted his scorn of psychology from Nietzsche who was equally scathing of 'English psychologists' (1969: 34), but Chamberlain and others have pointed out that Nietzsche's philosophy (like Kierkegaard's) is often psychological in its interests and pronouncements. The confusion of the stances of both Banville and Nietzsche on this matter may well stem from the lack of a clinical definition of what they mean by the term.
2 *Shroud*, 286.
3 Joseph McMinn (1999) was the first scholar to draw attention to the influence of Goethe on Banville's work.
4 This is not to say that Heidegger's thought does not coincide with Freud's on occasion. His remarks on the 'projection' of the self on to another show he is more than aware of the dangers of a narcissistic personality in his thinking (1967: 162).
5 One can't help but see this as an inversion of a similar situation in Beckett's *Not I* where the 'she' is also violently affirmed.
6 And from a literary perspective it is also Eliotic: 'Of course, only those who have personality and emotions know what it means to want to escape from these things' (1980: 48).

References

Banville, J. (1999), *Doctor Copernicus*, London: Picador.
Banville, J. (2000), *Eclipse*, London: Picador.
Banville, J. (2002a), *Shroud*, London: Picador.
Banville, J. (2002b), 'A Curious Chorus in Favour of Tyranny', *The Irish Times*, 11 May.
Banville, J. (2006), 'Freud's Turn on the Couch'. *The Irish Times*, 4 March.
Banville, J. (2012a), *Possessed of a Past: A John Banville Reader*, ed. Raymond Bell, London: Picador.
Banville, J. (2012b), *Ancient Light*, London: Viking.
Brown, N. O. (1985), *Life against Death: The Psychoanalytic Meaning of History*, Middletown, CT: Wesleyan University Press.
Calasso, R. (2001), *The Forty-Nine Steps*, Minneapolis: University of Minnesota Press.
Chamberlain, L. (1999), *Nietzsche in Turin*, New York: Picador.
Chamberlain, L. (2001), *The Secret Artist: a Close Reading of Sigmund Freud*, London: Seven Stories Press.
Charlesworth, M. (1976), *The Existentialists and Jean-Paul Sartre*, London: George Prior.
Deane, S. (ed.) (1979), 'Novelists on the Novel: Ronan Sheehan Talks to John Banville and Francis Stuart', *The Crane Bag*, 3 (1): 76–84.
Eliot, T. S. (1980), *The Sacred Wood*, London: Methuen.
Gecikli, K. (2011), 'Authentic Hero in the Book of Evidence by John Banville', *International Journal of Humanities and Social Sciences*, 1 (5): 282–6.
Gaita, R. (2004), *The Philosopher's Dog*, London: Routledge.
Gray, J. (2003), *Straw Dogs: Thoughts on Humans and Other Animals*, London: Granta.
Hand, D. (2002), *John Banville: Exploring Fictions*, Dublin: The Liffey Press.
Harmon, M. (ed.) (1981), *Irish University Review*, John Banville Special Issue, 11 (1) [incls. Rüdiger Imhof, An interview with John Banville', pp. 5–12; John Banville, 'A Talk', pp. 13–17].
Heaney, S. (1998), *Opened Ground*, London: Faber & Faber.
Heidegger, M. (1967), *Being and Time*, trans. John Macquarrie and Edward Robinson, Oxford: Basil Blackwell.
Humphreys, J. (2014), 'Is Irish Literature too Local to Have Philosophical Heft?', *The Irish Times*, 23 May. Available online: http://www.irishtimes.com/culture/is-iri sh-literature-too-local-to-have-philosophical-heft-1.1805600?page=2 (accessed 7 February 2015).
Kierkegaard, S. (1941), *The Sickness unto Death*, Princeton, NJ: Princeton University Press.
Kierkegaard, S. (2000), *The Essential Kierkegaard*, ed. Edna Hong and Howard Hong, Princeton, NJ: Princeton University Press.
May, R. (1993), *The Cry for Myth*, London: Souvenir Press.

McKeon, B. (2009), 'John Banville: The Art of Fiction No.200', *Paris Review*. Available online: http://www.theparisreview.org/interviews/5907/the-art-of-fiction-no-200-john-banville (accessed 15 January 2015).

McMinn, J. (1999), *The Supreme Fictions of John Banville*, Manchester: Manchester University Press.

Midgley, M. (2002a), *Beast and Man: The Roots of Human Nature*, London: Routledge.

Midgley, M. (2002b), *Evolution as Religion*, London: Routledge.

Muldoon, P. (2007), *The End of the Poem*, New York: Farrar, Straus & Giroux.

Ní Anluain, C. (ed.) (2000), *Reading the Future: Irish Writers in Conversation with Mike Murphy*, Dublin: Lilliput Press.

Nietzsche, F. (1967), *The Will to Power*, trans. Walter Kauffmann and R. J. Hollingdale, New York: Vintage.

Nietzsche, F. (1969), *On the Genealogy of Morals and Ecce Homo*, trans. Walter Kauffmann, New York: Vintage.

Nietzsche, F. (1977), *A Nietzsche Reader*, trans. R. J. Hollingdale, London: Penguin.

O'Connell, M. (2013), *John Banville's Narcissistic Fictions: The Spectral Self*, London: Palgrave MacMillan.

Pessoa, F. (2002), *The Book of Disquiet*, ed. and trans. Robert Zenith, London: Penguin Classics, 139–49.

Sartre, J.-P. (2003), *Being and Nothingness*, trans. Hazel E. Barnes, London: Routledge.

Zenith, R. (2012), 'Nietzsche and Pessoa's Heteronyms', *Partial Answers: Journal of Literature and the History of Ideas*, 10 (1): 139–49.

12

'An *earthly* glow': Heidegger and the uncanny in *Eclipse* and *The Sea*

Michael Springer

The uncanny occupies a prominent place in John Banville's work: the lexeme appears at important junctures in his fictional and non-fictional writing, and he has notably claimed that he considers the role of art itself to be connected to the eliciting of the sensation associated with the phenomenon (Haughton 2012). While the author is hardly averse to the broad claim, there appears to be much to be gained from heeding this point when approaching his writing. Novels such as *Eclipse* and *The Sea* are centrally concerned with haunting, doubling, subjective fragmentation – in short, the uncanny – and the treatment of the phenomenon is animated by a profound and searching exploration of the nature and basis of, to lapse rather precipitously into earnestness, Being.

This is an aspect that has been commented on before, by, most prominently, Hugh Haughton, Hedwig Schwall and Romain Nguyen Van. All three (save for an intriguing footnote from Schwall's paper) approach the matter from the Freudian direction. This in some respects takes Banville on his own terms: certain of his discursive treatments of the uncanny directly invoke Freud's discussion of it (Banville 1995), and there is obvious interpretative mileage to be made from a Freudian reading of the novels. However, what this approach misses, I argue, is an interesting way of accounting for the significance of Heidegger's thinking for Banville's work, and through this an important resource for understanding the author's attitude to the nature and aims of his own art, if not art more generally. It seems to me that Heidegger's understanding of the uncanny involves an existential and ethical dimension that corresponds exactly to that explored in novels such as *Eclipse* and *The Sea*, and that the place of the uncanny in Heidegger's work and the response to it that is proposed as being appropriate correlates with that which Banville seeks to elicit through his own writing. In this chapter, I begin with a discussion of the prior treatments of the uncanny in Banville's work identified above. I then consider Banville's explicit references to Heidegger and his work to establish the philosopher's importance to him, before looking at the treatment of the uncanny in *Eclipse* and *The Sea* and comparing this with Heidegger's statements on the phenomenon in *Being and Time*, drawing out the analogies between the two and moving towards a statement of the significance of this for Banville's work. The analysis of the place of the uncanny in Banville's work takes two approaches. First, I consider how *Eclipse* (and where it relevantly intersects with it, *Shroud*), *The Sea* and other novels may be said to take the uncanny and its effects as object – to explore the uncanny as topic and subject. Then, I turn to the ways in which the works may themselves be said to instantiate the uncanny through form, structure and other means. This latter allows me to turn to the aesthetic effects achieved by Banville's work, and the extent to which the uncanny is central to them. I conclude by discussing certain of Banville's statements on art and literature, and their relation to the uncanny, in order to establish the extent to which his conception of these coincides with Heidegger's own. I choose these two novels as a methodological convenience, because they thematize the vision of the uncanny I am seeking to elucidate more explicitly than any of Banville's others. I argue, however, that this version of the uncanny informs the entire oeuvre in a number of ways.

It is not my intention to establish the validity of the Heideggerian formulation of the uncanny over the Freudian, to 'refute' Freud's account, or some such. The two appear to me to run parallel, so to speak, rather than athwart one another, and both to be products of the vision of subjectivity and awareness from whence they proceed. Freud's depends centrally on the psychodynamic picture of the operation of the mind and hence selfhood, with its metaphors of force and contestation, such as drive, repression and discharge (Lear 1990); Heidegger's on the idea of existential *geworfenheit* ('throwness'), and the shock and angst of the encounter with unmediated, untheorized being. The difference hinges on the question of the role of knowledge in the emergence of the uncanny. For Freud, the uncanny occurs as a result of a recognition of one's knowledge of a thing known that one had forgotten one knew, the return of a thing known that should have remained forgotten, precisely because of what is known about it. For Heidegger, in contrast, it consists in the submersion in a state of being that is otherwise kept at bay by habitual systems of thought and perception – what one might call knowledge. For Freud, the uncanny is made possible by knowing; for Heidegger, it's precisely knowledge – or a certain type of knowledge, or a certain relation to knowledge – that occludes it.

An important corollary of this difference is the concomitant picture each version provides of the role of knowing in the constitution of our subjectivity. The Freudian account posits interpretation, and with it an ever clearer understanding of the thing being interpreted (ourselves), as a solution. In Heidegger's version, this ceaseless interpretation is precisely the problem: we are given to – we have no choice but to – attempt to make sense of ourselves, our world, and our place in it, but have no way of establishing the validity of this sense-making itself (Withy 2015: 71). We are therefore constituted by this sense-making, and our sense-making shapes and edits ourselves and our world. Knowledge, the sum product of this activity, is therefore an overlay on the face of thrown being, an arbitrary closure of our radical openness out of instrumental necessity – a subsumption of the present-at-hand into the ready-to-hand. This being the case, interruptions of knowledge represent certain benefits, and means of achieving such interruptions are to be understood as having ethical, epistemological and existential value. Where the Freudian scheme would imply the need to domesticate the otherness of the uncanny to the same of interpretative reason (Lear 1990), in the Heideggerian picture, the uncanny calls for preservation in precisely its otherness. As I'll demonstrate in what follows, Banville's depictions cleave more closely to the latter.

'At length – how else?': Banville on Heidegger

In terms of allusions and direct references, there is much evidence for Banville's reading of and interest in Heidegger's work. The most extensive of Banville's engagements with Heidegger's work or person is the radio play *Todtnauberg*, aired on the BBC in 2006, which deals with the meeting between the philosopher and Paul Celan (Banville 2006). While far less speculative than a novel like *Shroud*, for example – perhaps due the greater historical pressure of the material dealt with and the concomitant requirement for sensitivity in its treatment – the date of the airing of the piece does point to an extensive interest in Heidegger at the time of the writing of the novels that most clearly demonstrate the preoccupations I explore in this chapter. And indeed, in the play the character of Heidegger himself has much in common with figures such as Alexander Cleave, Axel Vander and Max Morden: what appears to interest Banville about the philosopher here is his myopia, his blindness to certain aspects of his life and personality that leads to his isolation and estrangement from the basis of any value existence may once have had for him. He is, like Vander, a monument to arrogance and self-will, and a cautionary tale for that.

There are also sporadic comments on the philosopher in interviews and reviews, which are generally characterized by a self-deprecatory, jocular tone. For example, in 2006, describing his attempt to produce a 'Great European novel of ideas' in the science tetralogy, Banville told Hedda Friberg, 'I had an image of myself – there is this series, Fontana Modern Masters, with perhaps Frank Kermode on Proust, or George Steiner on Heidegger, or whatever – and I could see my name on the spine of one of these: Steiner on Banville. I could see myself as one of the European modern masters' (Friberg 2006). Rather more recently, in the review of a translation of Rilke's *Letters to a Young Poet* in the *New York Review of Books*, there is the wonderful aside, 'Heidegger dwells at length – how else? – on the central function of boredom as a spur to human action' (Banville 2013a). Both comments are dismissive. In the first, I read the self-deprecatory note with an ear attuned to his frequent references to his own autodidacticism, to my mind most memorably in *Ancient Light* (80–1). This invocation of canonical figures is intended to achieve bathetic contrast with himself, and to describe his sense of being an interloper, and the interloping autodidact's accession to the community of ideas. In the second, the deprecation is perhaps of the politics of the constitution of this community: the earnestness, self-importance, narcissism it can be based on. The nearness in time of the first of these to the airing of *Todtnauberg* would also suggest, however, that the levity may be disguising a deeper involvement. Another comment from the latter review appears to work to a similar end, in a less light-hearted manner: 'Heidegger once remarked that he was only trying to do in philosophy what Rilke had already achieved in poetry.' Given that the review in which this statement appears is one of a translation of Rilke's work, the placing of the emphasis on the poet would seem only natural. Nevertheless, considering the importance of Rilke's work to Banville, it does provide a glimpse into the way in which he conceives of Heidegger's significance: as having, like Rilke's work, to do with the broad question of – in Banville's own words – 'why we persist in our humanness', and what role art is to play in this persistence (Banville 2013b).[1]

Banville's uncanny: The thoughts thus far

To turn to those who have considered the matter of the uncanny in Banville's work, Hugh Haughton (2000) claims that '*Eclipse* is, among other things, a study of haunting, a portrait of a modern consciousness riven by the Freudian uncanny. … Freud's reflections on the relation of the unheimlich to the *heimlich* go to the heart of this story of the enigmatic and multiple hauntings undergone by its aptly named narrator' (105). There is clearly something to this, yet the glibness of Cleave's wife Lydia's 'What would Doctor Freud say?' in response to one of his dreams suggests that a Freudian construal might ultimately be too simple. Cleave has described to her a dream of his, about a plastic chicken into which one can insert eggs that the chicken then 'lays':

> 'How do you get the egg back into the chicken', she said, 'for it to come out again? In this dream.'
> 'I don't know. It just ... pushes back in, I suppose.'
> Now she did laugh, sharply.
> 'Well, what would Doctor Freud say.'
> I sighed angrily. 'Not everything is ...' Sigh. 'Not everything ...' I gave it up.
> (Banville 2001: 7)

This loss of words with which the encounter concludes is significant: prior to it, Cleave claims, 'Lately I had been finding it hard to understand the simplest things people said to me, as if what they were speaking in were a form of language I did not recognise; I would know the words but could not assemble them into sense' (7), echoing similar descriptions from throughout the novel. This is linked, though, to symbols of fertility that similarly appear frequently: 'In the dream it was Easter morning ... and the already blossoming cherry trees shivered in vernal anticipation' (6), and the image of the egg re-appears in close connection to a meditation on the uncanny and the *heimlich* later in the novel ('I shut my eyes and in a sort of rapture see myself stepping backward into the cloven shell, and the two halves of it, still moist with glair, closing around me' (70)). This suggests that the aspects of inexpressibility and incomprehension aroused by the events and phenomena described by the novel, and the acute sense of the uncanny that these events and phenomena give rise to on Cleave's part, are connected to certain creative possibilities or potential for renewal.

And in this conjunction, Banville's vision follows Heidegger's very closely. In its interruption of everyday familiarity, the uncanny allows the subject to view her assumptions, projects and habituations as it were from the outside, and thus to get a perspective on their accidental character and, therefore, their limitations. Such interruption forces one to reconfigure schemes of thought and modes of relation that, taken for granted, may have begun to occlude the world and the other, rather than enable access to them – forces one to remake oneself to better engage with the indeterminacy that one lives within. Jonathan Lear's (2011) idea of the 'ironic uncanny' captures this aspect of ethical self-fashioning especially well: the ironic uncanny occurs when, for example, in the pursuit of an ideal, one experiences the insufficiency of the social modes available to one for the expression of that ideal. This experience interrupts the association between the ideal and the social forms whereby it is expressed, thus allowing – or forcing – one to rethink the social configurations, and the assumptions that underpin them. This analysis makes clear the ways in which the uncanny can therefore have an ethical dimension. Heidegger's treatment does too, whether or not one subscribes to the broader existentialist frame in which it is couched: anyone willing to admit that normative claims and assumptions can benefit from being interrogated is a large part of the way to this conclusion (Crowell 2013). Beyond this, though, the uncanny has the ability to make us aware of the extent to which normativity shapes us – of quite how much of what we take to be given is in fact chosen, shaped, crafted, made.

Romain Nguyen Van (2012) catalogues aspects of *The Sea* that betoken qualities claimed by Freud to be uncanny, enumerating a great many. He does, however, also note Banville's 'compound of reluctance and reliance with regard to psychoanalytical theory and its use by academics for coping with these phenomena' (60), which seems to me a crucial aspect of the fiction's explicit and self-conscious engagement with the uncanny. While *Eclipse* and *The Sea* are both about repressed or forgotten memories, they are also about the inexplicable and the inexpressible and our relation to it, often figured in elemental terms. There is more than a hint in such instances that the voracious interpretative apparatus of the psychoanalytic approach necessarily rides roughshod over something of potentially great value and meaning – the inability to mean, the failure of meaning in the face of experience figured in *Eclipse*, as discussed above. Where the Freudian treatment of the uncanny details various situations that fit the description and offers some explanations of its basis, Heidegger's account ties it fundamentally to our basic existential and ethical comportment, which hence allows for a broader and more general elaboration of its significance for literature, art and subjectivity.

This is illustrated by the discussion of superstition in Nguyen Van's article. He notes Morden's sardonic remarking of the 'joke in bad taste on the part of a polyglot fate' (13) whereby the consultant who delivers his wife her diagnosis of terminal cancer is named 'Mr Todd' (*der Tod*, death), and argues that this signals 'a propensity … to believe in … a language that puns of its own accord' (35). This is linked in turn to Freud's sense of the capacity of the uncanny to give rise to animistic-type perceptions ('an almost occult feel' (97); Freud (2003: 147)), with the boundary between the inanimate and animate being blurred (as Rebecca Downes's chapter in this volume also explores). If anything, though, in *Eclipse* – as elsewhere in Banville's work – language and the world of objects are presented as being insufficiently human (and our own humanness, at least as we habitually conceive of it, as hence anomalous). Morden notes how, on arriving back home from the consultant's rooms, 'I marvelled, not for the first time, at the cruel complacency of ordinary things. But no, not cruel, not complacent, only indifferent, as how could they be otherwise?' Where the animistic perception is of a world uncannily human, a consistent emphasis in Banville's work is the utter alienness of our mode of being to our surroundings. Similarly, while language is on occasion personified, the highly mannered, self-conscious style of the writing would seem to encourage a reading of such figures as explicitly figural, rather than half-consciously animistic revenants – and indeed, the dense working of the language itself points to a similar conclusion. In addition, the object-like intransigence and inertia of language, as well as its opacity, is also frequently emphasized: 'Take off your coat, at least,' Max Morden says to wife in *The Sea*, then reflects, bemusedly, 'But why at least? What a business it is, the human discourse' (21). Morden's almost compulsive noting of synonyms does not indicate an apprehension of an occult order or significance glimpsed through the veil of language, but rather a sense of the chaotic equation of disparate things in a medium that warps the weft of the everyday world. Further, as Monica Facchinello notes, all the novels from *The Newton Letter* on posit a connection between verbal invention and chronic inauthenticity (Facchinello 2010: 34). A central aspect, it appears, of all Banville's writing is this inadequation between subjectivity and the means available for its expression, which is performed in the highly wrought writing itself – the foregrounding of the means of expression diminishing the possibility of its being considered 'natural' or immediate. Such is a problematic that chimes very neatly with a general existential scheme encompassing concerns with the potential for authentic modes of being.

Hedwig Schwall (2006) similarly follows the Freudian lead, drawing on the analysis of Hoffman's *The Sandman* to discern three sources of the uncanny in literature generally and Banville's specifically: '"[T]he belief in the omnipotence of thoughts and the technique of magic based on that belief", whereby the psychic reality overrules the material one; ... childhood events which instilled in the subject a repeatedly repressed castration fear; ... [and] a lack of distinction between inner and outer world, between self and o/Other' (117). As with Nguyen Van, the first and last of these three thus emphasize an animistic, gothic mode, which is rather different to the dimension of the phenomenon that interests me. In an intriguing footnote, however, discussing parallels between Banville and the artist Edward Hopper, Schwall delineates certain connections between the uncanny, the inaccessibility of 'the ordinary' as discussed by Wittgenstein, and Heidegger's notion of 'everydayness' and associated concepts (footnote 19). My own strongest sense of the valence of the uncanny in Banville's work falls very much in line with this construction. But I suspect it would not be possible to draw a connection between it and the Freudian version through the idea of the 'subliminal' that Schwall proposes.

Schwall draws on the idea of the subliminal in accounting for the way in which the narrative engages with supernatural material. Distinguishing it from the 'sublimating' (such as fairy tales, wherein 'all is homogenously marvellous'), and the 'ordinary' ('where strange things are explained ... by [for e.g.] a certain intake of drink or by psychic disorders'), in the subliminal 'the normal, and supernatural are mixed in rather plausible terms, so that the status of reality remains unfathomable to the reader' (2006: 117). The initial point of contestation would be the extent to which Banville in any of his work, and certainly in his later novels, in fact relies on the supernatural. While there are effects such as doubling and other similar as identified by Schwall, nothing from *The Untouchable* on appears to rely on supernatural means to evoke or convey these. In *Eclipse*, the novel Schwall focuses on most extensively, what Cleave had taken to be ghosts turn out to be squatters,[2] and his identification of them as supernatural comes in hindsight to seem a means of avoiding engaging with the all-too-real concerns represented by his daughter and wife. In such a reading, supernatural explanations are fictions that enable the narrator/protagonist to evade the ordinary itself, and he thus comes to miss what was staring him in the face all along. Banville's work hence deconstructs the opposition: the ordinary is figured as precisely extraordinary, while the supernatural is a banality that prevents this from being acknowledged.[3] In Heidegger's work, the uncanny is linked to the experience of immediate thrownness, to which one accedes when the 'they-self' – a mode of being-by-consensus, according to inherited scripts and explanations – is overcome (or escaped from, or collapses – much hinges on the verb one chooses, and to what one attributes the agency in it). In *Eclipse*, and other of Banville's fiction, returns to the 'ordinary' are similarly depicted as consisting in the dismantling of fictions that obtrude into subjectivity and warp it. These are returns to an 'ordinary' because they consist in disillusionments and divestments of delusions, and the ordinary to which the characters return is uncanny because, as in Heidegger's characterization, it is a reality habitually mediated that is suddenly experienced directly.

Importantly, all three of these critics, Haughton, Nguyen Van and Schwall, also appear to elide the difference between the thematic exploration of the idea of the uncanny and the attempt to elicit its affective dimension. Freud's discussion – or the part of it concerned with the uncanny in literature rather than art – focuses on works that produce a feeling of the uncanny on the part of the reader, and his analysis of these focuses on the techniques used to do this. These seem to me fundamentally different ends than those of novels such as *Eclipse* or *The Sea*. Alex Cleave is certainly subject to forces that produce a sensation of the uncanny in him, but the style and structure of the novel in no way implies that Banville is seeking to produce the same in us (at least in the Freudian sense). The hauntings he experiences are ultimately explained by very quotidian factors, and there is no real hint of the gothic in its conception or execution. In contrast, numerous of his statements coincide neatly with effects one would associate with the uncanny as understood in Heidegger's account of it.

'so emphatically not our medium': The uncanny in *Eclipse*, *The Sea* and elsewhere

A crucial statement of the uncanny is that in *The Sea*, where Max Morden muses, 'How is it that in childhood everything new that caught my interest had an aura of the uncanny, since according to all the authorities the uncanny is not some new thing but a thing known returning in a different form?' (8). By 'all the authorities' is presumably intended primarily Freud, whose account of the phenomenon has become the most influential, and the statement is of interest in thus raising a certain dissatisfaction or query with it.[4] The specific query also points to what I take to be the crux of the alternative, Heideggerian formulation of the phenomenon, one that traces it to the shock and angst of *geworfenheit*. The treatment of childhood in *The Sea* emphasizes the immediacy of it, the way in which it is not yet dulled by memory and habit (e.g. p. 12), which are presented, in the adult Max's mourning and remembering, as such a profound impediment to authentic engagement with oneself and one's world. Alex Cleave's profession as an actor, as well as the more tawdry, quotidian pretence that he has in common with Max Morden, Axel Vander, Anthony Blunt, Oliver Orme, *et alia* similarly work to underscore their inauthenticity in contrast to the unmediated state of being that childhood is presented as consisting in.

Heidegger states in *Being and Time*, 'as Dasein falls, anxiety brings it back from its absorption in the "world". Everyday familiarity collapses. Dasein has been individualized, but individualized *as* Being-in-the-world. Being-in enters into the existential "mode" of the "*not-at-home*". Nothing else is meant by our talk about "uncanniness"' (Heidegger 1962: 233). Given that this immediately follows the first use of the idea of the uncanny in the book, the final statement is interesting insofar as it suggests that Heidegger is himself trying, somewhat emphatically, to distance his understanding of the term from Freud's.[5] This impression is further bolstered by the word-play of the passage that emphasizes the relative literalness of his use of the German term: elsewhere in the passage he states, 'But here "uncanniness" [*unheimlicheit*] also means "not-being-at-home" [*das Nicht-zuhause-sein*]' (233). We dwell in poiesis; the uncanny pulls us outside of our projects and self-fashioning, to show these to us as the constructions they are (Withy 2015: 55). This implies that the experience of the uncanny represents some sort of ultimate good faith: given that angst is characterized as the inevitable mood of authentic engagement with being, freed from convention, habit and everyday familiarity, the encounter with the uncanny would thus be one in which such angst is undergone in a clear consciousness of it, rather than an attempt to escape from it. This brings this view of the uncanny in line with the depiction of childhood in *The Sea*, and helps illuminate the contrast that is implied in the novel between adult and childhood experience.

Another revealing passage in Banville's work on his view of the uncanny, and one with extensive implications for an understanding of the projects of *Eclipse* and *The Sea*, is the following from the former novel:

> Why do I find the thought of the sea so alarming? … is it that it is so emphatically not our medium? I think of that world beneath the ocean, the obverse of ours, the negative of ours, with its sandy plains and silent valleys and great sunken mountain ranges, and something fails me in myself, something that is mine draws away from me in horror. Water is uncanny in the way, single-minded and uncontrollable, it keeps seeking its own level, like nothing else in the world that we inhabit. (Banville 2001: 67)

In light of this, the topological organization of the two books (as well as the very title *The Sea*), with both protagonists being driven by some obscure and inexplicable compulsion to return to a seaside abode of their childhood, appears to demonstrate the protagonists' sense of the need to put themselves into proximity with this particular source of the uncanny. Such a reading is borne out by their own sense of the purpose of their actions.

Alex Cleave, in describing his return to his childhood house that constitutes the initiating action of the events described in the novel, states, 'To be watchful and attentive of everything, to be vigilant against complacency, to resist habituation, these were my aims in coming here. I would catch myself, red-handed, in the act of living; alone, without an audience of any kind, I would cease from performing and simply *be*' (Banville 2001: 46). This would suggest that Cleave is actively seeking out the interruption of conventional structures of engagement with the world that Heidegger identifies as characteristic of the uncanny. He does so because he has come to understand himself to have lost any essential self through his too consistent inhabitation of theatrical roles; having played a part for too long, he finds that what he has taken to be his self is nothing but a series of masks:

> I thought that by coming here I would find a perspective on things, a standpoint from which to survey my life, but when I look back now to what I have left behind me I am afflicted by a disabling wonderment: how did I manage to accumulate so much of life's clutter, apparently without effort, or even full consciousness? – so much, that under the weight of it I cannot begin to locate that singular essential self, the one I came here to find, that must be in hiding, somewhere, under the jumble of discarded masks.

Heidegger characterizes the form of inauthenticity most obviously in contrast to such an experience of nothingness as 'Being-with-one-another'. Like Sartre's being-for-others, as contrasted with being-for-self, Heidegger characterizes it as a construction of 'the they' that arise 'through idle talk and the way things have been publicly interpreted' (Heidegger 1962: 221). The effect of such Being-with-one-another is as follows:

> Idle talk and ambiguity, having seen everything, having understood everything, develop the supposition that Dasein's disclosedness, which is so available and so prevalent, can guarantee to Dasein that all the possibilities of its Being will be secure, genuine, and full. Through the self-certainty of the 'they', it gets spread abroad increasingly that there is no need of authentic understanding or the state-of-mind that goes with it. (Heidegger 1962: 222)

As elaborated at the very beginning of this chapter, Heidegger sees knowledge as an impediment to 'authentic understanding or the state of mind that goes with it'. Or rather, one should say that he sees the assumption that one knows as the impediment, one's belief that the knowledge one has is in fact some sort of guarantee of the security, authenticity and fullness of being. It is this assumption, the 'self-certainty' that one has 'seen everything … understood everything', that gives rise to the complacent relation to being that obscures the incommensurability of such knowledge to Dasein and its consequent inapplicability. Bad faith as a consoling fiction, or role.

An important point in regard to the mode of 'being-with-one-another' is Cleave's vocation as an actor and the motivations that appear to be provided for his taking up of it. Describing his first love affair, with Dora, his partner in the amateur theatrical society, he claims,

> It was for Dora, offstage, that I gave my first real performances, filled my first authentic roles. How I posed and preened in the mirror of her sceptical regard. Onstage, too, I saw my talent reflected in her. One night I turned in the midst of my curtain speech … and caught the flash of her specs in the wings from where she was watching me narrowly, and under the heat of her sullen envy something opened in me like a hand and I stepped at last into the part as if it were my own skin. Never looked back, after that. (Banville 2001: 87)

The passage highlights the extent to which Cleave is in thrall to the gaze of others, and through it and other hints the novel suggests that his choice of occupation and way of life have been premised on the need to be watched, to find his identity in the validation of the other's consideration. The description of Dora's 'sceptical regard' as a 'mirror' suggests that he sees – or, given the vantage point of the narration of the novel, saw – himself only as seen by others, and has operated entirely in this mode of being-for-others. This attitude is fundamentally narcissistic: Cleave finds his calling in response to another's 'hot sullen envy', and his interactions with his wife, daughter and others are frequently characterized as involving some form of intersubjective violence.[6] If this holds, the implication is that such a mode of being-for-others precludes the possibility – in Cleave's case, at least – of a fully ethical human relationship.

His relationship with his daughter Cass – Cassandra – bears this out. Cass suffers from a debilitating schizo-affective disorder named Mandelbaum's Syndrome, which causes visual, aural and olfactory hallucinations and distorts her grasp on and engagement with objective reality. Cass's story is related in detail in *Shroud*, the events of which take place over more or less the same period covered by *Eclipse*, and some of which are seen from both respective perspectives of the characters in the two novels. Cass is researching the fate of the abandoned children of Rousseau when she comes across a clue to the identity of a famous academic, Axel Vander (some of the details of whose life correlate with those of Paul de Man). She tracks him down, reveals what she knows, and begins a relationship with him in part motivated, the novel gives us to infer, by a need to assuage a paternal absence – opposite Vander's need to nullify a threat. Cleave's breakdown gives him some insight into Cass's condition, and through this he comes to take on the paternal responsibilities he has failed to, if in surrogate, through his intervention to help Lily at the circus.

The event that initiates the action of the novel, Cleave's corpsing mid-performance, is described as a sudden perception of the schism between himself and the role he is performing and a resulting alienation from it. The very term 'corpsing' points to the uncanny experience of the body as body, rather than the obedient and transparent medium for the expression of agency it 'ought' to be – an experience further explored in the detailed dwelling on the physical consequences of ageing in *The Sea* ('grog blossoms' etc.). As at other important junctures such as described above, the event of the corpsing is described primarily as a failure of words, and inability to respond. I take this to indicate the collapse of such a form of bad faith and the accession to some essential nothingness it occludes. Cleave is thrown by this event into an apprehension of the uncanniness of his self and the world around him, which he describes as 'a dizzying sensation, as when a word or object will break free from the mind's grasp and drift out into the empty space of its own utter separateness. Everything is strange now. The most humdrum phenomena fill me with slow astonishment' (Banville 2001: 52). As discussed above, in Heidegger's scheme the uncanny, like poetry in his later work, is prized precisely for its capacity to induce strangeness and break down habitual modes of thought and comportment. Significantly, Cleave is depicted as seeing this estrangement and disorientation as a potentially positive and creative state of being, and as seeking specifically to sustain and prolong it:

> *Making strange*, people hereabouts say when a child wails at the sudden appearance of a visitor; how was I to make strange now, and not stop making strange? How was I to fight the deadening force of custom? In a month, in a week, I told myself, the old delusion of belonging would have re-established itself irremediably. (Banville 2001: 46)

The significance of Cleave's conscious attempts to bring about an uncanny disruption of his identity is made clear by Heidegger's association of the uncanny with the call of conscience. '*What if this Dasein, which finds itself in the very depths of its uncanniness, should be the caller of the call of conscience?*' (Heidegger 1962: 321). In describing the call of conscience, he states, 'it calls without uttering anything. The call discourses in the uncanny mode of *keeping silent*. And it does this only because, in calling the one to whom the appeal is made, it does not call him into the public idle talk of the "they", but *calls* him back from this into the reticence of his existent potentiality-for-Being' (Heidegger 1962: 322). Here, Heidegger emphasizes the way the call of conscience, in an uncanny way, calls the subject 'back from' social discursive formations to some prior, unformed immediacy. The emphasis on the 'silence' and 'reticence' of this call, of the way it calls one out of speech and discourse, chimes with the representations of the failure of language in *Eclipse* and *The Sea*.

In terms of what this unformed immediacy that precedes the subject's entry into language consists in, Heidegger appears to identify the uncanny as a crucial component:

> Uncanniness is the basic kind of Being-in-the-world, even though in an everyday way it has been covered up. Out of the depths of this kind of Being, Dasein itself, as conscience, calls. ... The call of conscience, existentially understood, makes known for the first time what we have hitherto merely contended: that uncanniness pursues Dasein and is a threat to the lostness in which it has forgotten itself. (Heidegger 1962: 322)

The point made explicitly here, and as discussed above, is that '[u]ncanniness is the basic kind of Being-in-the-world'. The primary state occurring in response to our thrown condition, the uncanny can hence be seen as the most fundamental, most authentic mode of human awareness. It is, however, 'covered up' through the exigencies of 'everyday' living. But 'Dasein itself' calls, with a call equivalent to a 'call of conscience', to bring the subject back from the 'lostness' of this everyday mode of being. The call of the uncanny hence has an ethical dimension, analogous to that of 'conscience', and its interruption of habitual modes of being is tinged, in Heidegger, with a redemptive valence. In a markedly similar manner, Alex Cleave's and Max Morden's respective returns to their childhood homes are both inspired by some such silent appeal from beyond the horizon of their current schemes of intelligibility and understanding. Cleave describes how he screeches to a stop before an animal ('some wild unknown thing' he cannot identify (5)). 'I wanted to turn the car around and drive back the way I had come, but something would not let me go. Something.' It is this that leads him to realize that he has driven to within sight of the seaside town in which he grew up, and he freewheels down the hill towards it. Cleave's encounter with the animal, described as profound and freighted with numinousness ('Such fierceness in that stare, the electric eyes an unreal neon-red' (4)), is not incidental to the decision he takes, and it is significant that the nonhuman is represented as interpellating him in this way:

> The incident with the animal on the road in the wintry gloaming was definitive, though what it was that was being defined I could not tell. ... So came the April day when I drove with Lydia down those familiar roads and found the keys, left under a stone beside the doorstep by an unknown hand. Such seeming absence of human agency was proper also; it was as if ...
> 'As if what?' my wife said.
> I turned from her with a shrug.
> 'I don't know.'

In this event, again, the relation to the indefinable and inarticulable is emphasized, and indeed apparently linked to the compulsions that engender the attempted transformations of the self. The failed simile ('As if ... I don't know') in a work so richly imbued with the figure is potently suggestive, and the fact that it concerns a 'seeming absence of human agency' reiterates the concern with a discarding of masks and interruption of subjectivity by an uncanny force.

Withy (2015) demonstrates the extent to which, in Heidegger, the force of the uncanny rests on the interruption of sense-making. She defines Dasein as sense-making itself, the condition of being the thing that needs to make sense of its existence. Ordinarily taken for granted as simply the nature of being, the uncanny shows this up as the activity it in fact is, enabling us to see our sense-making procedures, rather than merely to see through them. I read the repeated failures of characters such as Cleave to make sense as emphasizing this lapse: their awareness of the constitutive disjuncture that makes such uncanny events possible, and the dawning realization of the ethical implications they pose. We ourselves are frequently caught up in the irresistible momentum of an apparatus that, in fitting the new into pre-existing schemata, collapses distance, tramples difference and precludes actual knowledge. This clarifies why Banville sees the relation between art and knowledge the way he does:

> Far from allowing us to know things with any immediacy, art, I believe, *makes things strange*. This it does by illuminating things, literally: the making of art is a process in which the artist concentrates on the object with such force ... that the object takes on an unearthly – no, an *earthly* glow. ... its result is a different order of understanding, which allows the thing its thereness, its outsideness, its absolute otherness. (Banville 1990: 78)

It would be of interest to trace the ways this conception of the work of art develops and changes in Banville's career. This version was propounded at the time of the writing of the Art trilogy. However, aspects of the novels themselves having a bearing on this question appear to change subsequent to this, and there would certainly be value in comparing equivalent statements from later. The claim does nevertheless make abundantly clear the extent to which the concerns explored in the fiction similarly inform the processes of its making, the way the works themselves are conceived of as objects having the capacity to effect uncanny disruptions and thus reinvigorate our relations with ourselves, others, and the world. In the following, final, section of the chapter, I therefore consider how the novels can be seen to do this via formal, stylistic and other means.

'art … *makes things strange*'

The claim, quoted above, that 'the making of art is a process in which the artist concentrates on the object with such force' that it begins to 'glow' provides a useful entry into a discussion of the formal and stylistic devices whereby Banville's work achieves effects he associates with the uncanny. His novels are marked by a dearth of plot and event. While vexing to numerous reviewers (Kakutani 2005; Lesser 1993), this slightness of exterior content allows for a close focus on states of mind, processes of memory and self-analysis, the permutations of intersubjective negotiation, and other similar components. In our habitual, objective-driven activity, these remain out of sight, or at least in the background. Through their close observation of the interior, and the underpinning of the exterior by the interior, novels such as *Eclipse* pull back from this everyday instrumental mode, in a bewildered tabulation of the strangeness of the means we have of making our way in the world.

The structural conceit of *Eclipse* is central to the achievement of this pulling back, or zooming in. Indeed, one can discern the same structuring device in *The Sea*, *Ancient Light* and *The Blue Guitar*: an instigating trauma in the narrative present forces the narrator-protagonist to engage in a task of mourning for some past loss that was never properly carried out. The narrative then comprises two strands, in which the work of mourning is enacted via the relation of the events of the past, in parallel to the narrator's working through the complications as they manifest in the narrative present. The novels in this way are able to enact the process of self-scrutiny and -analysis whereby the narrator comes to perceive himself as other – to see that he is not, and others are not, as he had assumed, and, as often as not, to see that his life has not been as he has thought that he knew it.

The achievement of such dramatic irony within the theatre of a single mind is a sophisticated technical accomplishment, and among the most obvious ways in which the works themselves can be identified as achieving uncanny effects. By enacting subjective displacements thus, the novels achieve the equivalent of the shift in perspective whereby the framework with which one made sense comes to be seen as the means of making sense itself. Like Heidegger's idea of the uncanny, this slippage is that of the apparently given being discovered to be made, and the consequent shifting in the paradigms that have been based on such assumptions. The bifurcation in the self links this aspect to what one might call the sense of the uncanny as extraordinary, such as embodied in absurdist and gothic treatments. But in affective terms, while in Banville's work such events may initially induce vertiginous self-estrangement, in the longer run they are more likely to effect forgiveness, acceptance, reconciliation. *The Sea* and *Ancient Light* demonstrate this trend, with the relevant interruption allowing the respective protagonists a renewed vision on the past that allows them to complete a task of mourning. There are equivalent effects in *Eclipse*, with the tragedy being that they come too late to prevent the occurrence they otherwise might have.

The wrought phrasing, idiosyncratic lexicon, and mannered style similarly intrude into the instrumental function of the language. This micro-stylistic quality, manifest at the level of word choice, phrasing and sentence structure, is perhaps the most distinctive characteristic of the writer's work – one would be unlikely to mistake an isolated paragraph of Banville's for anyone else's. Following the general reading of the work offered above, this can be seen to be intimately imbricated with the aesthetic conceptions informing his writing. Wallace Stevens claims, in 'Notes toward a Supreme Fiction', that 'description is revelation', and the poetic transmutation of the ordinary effected through Banville's use of the figural resources of language enacts this, bringing about the glow he, in the passage quoted above, defines as characteristic of art. An associated aspect that works in a slightly different direction is the way the first-person narration enables him to enact the narrator-protagonists' displacement in language: the way it intrudes between them and their own aims and meanings; the way it obscures, rather than enlightening.

The broader significance of such a reading of the place and mode of the uncanny in Banville's work is the light it casts on the aims of his own work. As noted at the beginning of this chapter, he states in an interview that he considers the goal of 'all art' to be that of evoking the uncanny (Haughton 2012). His style, and his avowed desire to produce works with 'the kind of denseness and thickness poetry has' (Schwartz 2010), can thus be seen as linked to an attempt to create works that interrupt habitual modes of apprehension and thought and in doing so produce creative possibility. These novels demonstrate the moral dimension of imagination and vision, bringing about, through the force of their engagement with the perceived world, an altering of that world, and an altering of our inhabitation of it. As Heidegger argues poetry is able to, Banville's work seeks to re-enchant the world, not through the creation of a supernatural realm through which to escape from it, but through the uncovering of the extraordinary quotidian so easily occluded by habit and convention. This sense of a moral dimension to the aesthetic falls squarely in line with the Heideggerian attitude, and via this to a broader Romantic valorization of the imagination and creative vision.

Notes

1 I discuss Banville's attitude to Rilke in Chapter 7 in this volume. As will be clear from that, I see the Heideggerian uncanny elucidated here as contrary to the valences Banville identifies as most significant in Rilke's work.

2 I read *all* the ghosts in the novel to be implied to be reducible to such, almost wilful, miscomprehension on Cleave's part. (With the possible exception of the one he claims to have seen in childhood.) They are figures he conjures, in various ways, out of his own immediate circumstances: sometimes relatively directly, as in this example with the squatters; and sometimes in more oblique means. In this I appear to differ with Rebecca Downes's view in her chapter in this volume. Detailed exploration of this difference must unfortunately be postponed to some later date.

3 A further interesting implication of the differences between Downes's and my readings hinges on my view of the deconstruction at work here. Where Downes sees the realms of the ordinary and extraordinary as interacting, my argument is that the novels show the extraordinary to be a function of a wilful misrecognition of the ordinary. This too, though, is beyond the scope of the present discussion.

4 Nguyen Van argues that this disavowal of the Freudian explanation is in fact an unconscious affirmation of it, in that the speaker supresses the idea of repression that is so crucial an aspect of it (7). Morden is however not recalling a specific incident or memory (in which case such a reading might hold), but rather a general mood that permeated childhood itself ('*everything* new').

5 Hayi Carel's (2006) *Life and Death in Freud and Heidegger* is an excellent treatment of Heidegger's many, often rancorous, differences with Freud.

6   Mark O'Connell details Banville's engagement with narcissism in detail in his 2013 book, *John Banville's Narcissistic Fictions: The Spectral Self.*

References

Banville, J. (1990), 'Survivors of Joyce', in Augustine Martin (ed.), *James Joyce: The Artist and the Labyrinth*, 73–81, London: Ryan Publications.

Banville, J. (1995), 'The Un-Heimlich Maneuvre', *The New York Review of Books*, 2 February. Available online: http://www.nybooks.com/articles/1995/02/02/the-un-heimlich-maneuver/ (accessed 27 January 2019).

Banville, J. (2001), *Eclipse*, London: Picador.

Banville, J. (2006), *The Sea*, New York: Alfred A. Knopf.

Banville, J. (2013a), 'Study the Panther!' *New York Review of Books*, 10 January. Available online: http://www.nybooks.com/articles/2013/01/10/study-panther/ (accessed 30 July 2018).

Banville, J. (2013b), *Ancient Light*, London: Vintage.

Crowell, S. (2013), *Normativity and Phenomenology in Husserl and Heidegger*, Cambridge: Cambridge University Press.

Facchinello, M. (2010), '"The old illusion of belonging": Distinctive Style, Bad Faith and John Banville's *The Sea*', *Estudios Irlandeses*, 5: 33–44.

Freud, S. (2003), *The Uncanny*, London: Penguin.

Friberg, H. (2006), 'John Banville and Derek Hand in Conversation', *Irish University Review*, 36 (1): 200–15.

Haughton, H. (2000) 'The Ruinous House of Identity', *The Dublin Review*, 1 (Winter): 105–13.

Haughton, H. (2012), 'The Uncanny', *BBC Radio 4*, 28 June.

Heidegger, M. (1962), *Being and Time*, trans. J. Macquarrie, Oxford: Basil Blackwell.

Kakutani, M. (2005), 'A Wordy Widower with a Past', *The New York Times*, 1 November. Available online: https://www.nytimes.com/2005/11/01/books/a-wordy-widower-with-a-past.html (accessed 30 July 2018).

Lear, J. (1990), *Love and Its Place in Nature: A Philosophical Interpretation of Freudian Psychoanalysis*, New Haven, CT: Yale University Press.

Lear, J. (2011), *A Case for Irony*, Cambridge, MA: Harvard University Press.

Lesser, W. (1993), 'Violently Obsessed by Art', *New York Times*, 28 November. Available online: http://www.nytimes.com/1993/11/28/books/violently-obsessed-with-art.html (accessed 30 July 2018).

O'Connell, M. (2013), *John Banville's Narcissistic Fictions: The Spectral Self*, New York: Springer.

Schwall, H. (2006), '"Mirror on mirror mirrored is all the show": Aspects of the Uncanny in Banville's Work with a Focus on *Eclipse*', *Irish University Review*, 36 (1): 116–33.

Schwartz, M. (2010), 'Banville Creates a Parallel Universe in *The Infinities*', *The Harvard Crimson*, 23 March. Available online: https://www.thecrimson.com/article/2010/3/23/john-banville-the-infinities/ (accessed 17 March 2018).

Van, R. N. (2012), '"According to all the authorities": The Uncanny in John Banville's *The Sea*', *Études anglaises*, 65 (4): 480–99.

Withy, K. (2015), *Heidegger on Being Uncanny*, Cambridge, MA: Harvard University Press.

13

John Banville's ekphrastic experiments

Neil Murphy

John Banville's use of ekphrasis as a complex aesthetic device has long been acknowledged as a characteristic feature of his narrative fictions,[1] and in all of his novels from *The Book of Evidence* onwards one can discern traces of the ekphrastic – depending on what definition of ekphrasis one accepts. In its European origins ekphrasis was generally deployed as a temporary reprieve from the sequential energy of narration, as with Homer's celebrated ekphrastic description of Achilles's shield in *The Iliad*. However, the manner in which ekphrasis was used in the lyric poem, particularly from the romantic poets onwards, shifted the emphasis away from providing temporary hiatus to a full emphasis on the image, or visual representation, as the central focus. This represents a crucial distinction in the evolution of the device. As James Heffernan argues, 'When the representation of a work of art is no longer surrounded by a larger narrative that subsumes it, when the work of art becomes the poet's chief or only subject, the struggle for mastery between word and image intensifies' (2004: 134). This is evident in such diverse poems as Browning's 'Eurydice to Orpheus' (responding to Frederic Leighton's *Orpheus and Eurydice*, 1864), Keats's 'Ode to a Grecian Urn', and Derek Mahon's 'Courtyards in Delft' (responding to Pieter de Hooch's *Courtyards in Delft*, 1658), in which the various visual representations (specific or, in the case of Keats, general) occupy the poets' full attention. As we shall see, this distinction is pertinent to Banville's prose-fiction ekphrases in which the various paintings, or images – real or imaginary – that he uses, are folded into larger narrative forms, closer, in a sense, to a Homeric detour than a romantic celebratory engagement. And yet, Banville also extends the use of ekphrasis far beyond the description of a shield or any image in a painting and, as this chapter will illustrate, frequently constructs elaborate narrative structures that integrate visual images into their aesthetic forms in a manner that marks Banville's work as exemplary of the contemporary innovative novel form.

From the outset, it is important to both acknowledge the contested nature of the term 'ekphrasis' and to illustrate the degree to which Banville's work in turn forces one to consider some of the assumptions inherent to the debate, particularly given his own self-reflexive critical interventions in the novels. Initially, Murray Krieger's influential *Ekphrasis: The Illusion of the Natural Sign* argues for a largely unrestricted understanding of the term in line with what he argues was the original meaning assigned to it by the Greeks, 'a verbal description of something, almost anything, in life or art' (1992: 7):

> Backed by historical precedent, then, I want also to summon this original, more universal sense of ekphrasis ... I will broaden the range of possible ekphrastic objects by re-connecting ekphrasis to all 'word-painting'. I want to trace the ekphrastic as it is seen occurring all along the spectrum of spatial and visual emulation in words. (1992: 9)

Krieger's open definition has been resisted by many more recent critics, including James Heffernan, who alternatively claims that '*ekphrasis is the verbal representation of visual representation*' (2004: 3; emphasis original). Heffernan's position rests on the view that Krieger's 'word-paintings' are actually distinct from ekphrasis and insists instead that there is a difference between pictorialism and iconicity – which are ways of mingling literature and the visual arts – and ekphrasis: 'What distinguishes these two things from ekphrasis is that both of them aim chiefly to represent natural objects and artifacts rather than works of representational art' (2004: 3), but 'ekphrasis differs from both iconicity and pictorialism because it explicitly represents representation itself. What ekphrasis represents in words, therefore, must itself be *representational*.' Heffernan's view in part rests on the desire that ekphrasis is a 'distinguishable mode' that 'binds together all ekphrastic literature from the age of Homer' onwards (2004: 4). This echoes Elizabeth Bergmann Loizeaux's more recent definition of ekphrasis as 'the poem that addresses a work of art' (2008: 1), of which she claims that 'writing on a work of art differs from writing on a natural object in that the work of art constitutes a statement already made about/in the world. As the staging of the relation between words and images, poet and artist, ekphrasis is inherently dialogic' (2008: 5). These distinctions rest largely on a few key issues: the desire to declare a clearly distinguishable aesthetic form; and the view that there is a fundamental distinction between the representation of a representation, and the representation of a 'natural sign', to borrow Krieger's term for an object that already exists in the world. Loizeaux's insistence on the essentially dialogic nature of true ekphrasis is persuasive but one could make the same statement about a verbal response to a complex imaginary painting, as is often the case in Banville's work, particularly in the invented paintings that feature in *Athena*, as well as in the fusion of several Watteau paintings in *Ghosts*, which are attributed to the imaginary painter Jean Vaublin[2].

Furthermore, the aesthetic response to any object, even one that contains a statement already made about the world, may not always be dialogic in nature. Many works of art do not even contain *explicit* statements about the world to begin with – and Banville's own work can be said to occupy this aesthetic ground, as he has repeatedly insisted.[3] In addition, there are poems that might fit Loizeaux's or Heffernan's definitions of ekphrasis, like Wallace Stevens's 'Man with the Blue Guitar' (1937), but yet have only tangential relations to the paintings to which they are connected, in this instance Picasso's *The Old Guitarist* (1903–4), not to mention Banville's own ekphrastic reaction to the same poem and painting in his novel, *The Blue Guitar*, which has little to do with a direct representational response. Essentially, the theoretical confines identified by many critics are themselves challenged and critiqued by literary responses, especially those of a writer like Banville who has always absorbed influences into the texture of his own art works, to be refined and enlarged within his self-conscious critical context rather than simply submit to technical limits. Strictly speaking, in the views of many critics of ekphrasis after Krieger a significant amount of Banville's engagement with the visual arts does not amount to ekphrasis but this chapter will consider several ways in which the author effectively demonstrates the benefits of a more expansive understanding of the term.

With particular reference to Banville's 'Art trilogy' (*The Book of Evidence*, *Ghosts*, *Athena*), *The Sea* and *The Blue Guitar*, this chapter will demonstrate some of the ways that particular artistic influences have been absorbed and reinvented to such a degree that they become constituent parts of Banville's own fictional storyworlds. This is not simply a matter of identifying allusions to specific paintings, although it is clear that the work of certain painters – Watteau, Drost, Vermeer, Bonnard, Picasso, Manet, Klimt, Van Gogh, Tintoretto, El Greco and Fragonard – are repeatedly referenced throughout both Banville's (and Benjamin Black's[4]) work. In many cases, Banville alludes to writers and painters in order to engage in critical discourse with their philosophical and aesthetic positions, as with his deployment (and eventual rejection) of Nietzsche's moral philosophy in *The Book of Evidence*. This chapter seeks instead, however, to trace the manner in which Banville's work occupies a shared aesthetic relationship with a few of these painters, particularly Watteau, Bonnard and Picasso, or as

David Lloyd puts it with respect to his interest in Beckett's relationship with the visual arts, to consider 'how Beckett forged his own literary aesthetic through his observations of the tendencies of contemporary painting' (2016: 4). This is achieved in Banville by virtue of his overt self-conscious engagement with a range of aesthetic positions throughout his career, many of which are derived from, or linked to, particular paintings or theories of art. Furthermore, the embedding of ekphrastic moments in literary fictions inevitably includes elements of both representation, in verbal form, and critical commentary on the representation itself. So, in Murray Krieger's sense, ekphrasis is both an example of 'the creative act itself – through the Greek mimesis, imitating, copying – and of the secondary critical act of commentary, description, revelation' (1992: 185) The former tendency is frequently evident in the descriptions of paintings, real or otherwise, that we discover in Banville's work, while the latter, critical commentaries, are everywhere present in the overt discursive mode deployed by many of his aesthetically obsessive first-person narrators.

Several critics of Banville have considered his deployment of ekphrasis, particularly Joseph McMinn, Françoise Canon-Roger, Anja Müller and Joakim Wrethed, in diverse and interesting ways. For example, McMinn sees the use of paintings as 'offering an elaborate metaphor for an epistemological drama about authenticity and the self. Images of painting and painters are there from the beginning, their suggestive potential always evident, until they come to provide a comprehensive parable for a postmodern crisis of knowledge' (2002: 138). While this is certainly accurate, I contend that Banville's use of paintings extends beyond the metaphorical and thematic and seeks to absorb them as structurally significant aesthetic presences in the work. Alternatively, Françoise Canon-Roger recognizes the significant relation between the painting and the primary narrative in *The Book of Evidence* which 'both shows a verbal picture in the making and provides the means of a satiric interpretation for it', through the device of the painting (2002: 25). However, the relationship is more nuanced in a narratorial sense than straight satire, even if the painting holds much significance for Freddie's own artistic failings. Anja Müller, while focusing on Banville's representation of women, has argued that ekphrasis features 'a dominant technique for the representation of women' in Banville's Art trilogy although in several important ways:

> On the one hand, it is used in a traditional way in descriptions of paintings. Apart from this reproductive mode, ekphrasis is also productively employed whenever the narrator attempts to verbally represent his mental visualizations

of women by alluding to paintings or to art in general, in order to bring these women to life, as it were. (2004: 186)

Müller's focus is a valuable consideration of the ways in which women repeatedly figure in Banville's trilogy, particularly in the context of its relationships with ekphrasis, and paintings more generally, and she has an acute sense of the key strategies of representation and framing that are used in the novels. Joakim Wrethed alternatively emphasizes the link with visual and verbal narratives, especially in his analysis of *The Sea*:

> In for instance *The Sea*, the narrator often imitates the stillness and silence of a painted scene so that the manner of narration comes close to appearing as a series of word paintings or still lifes, carefully linked together in the softly flowing rhythm of the prose. This technique challenges the prevalent idea of the distinction between the temporal and spatial arts. (2014: 192–3)

Nonetheless, this tendency has been evident in Banville's work from the outset, even as early as *Birchwood* (1973), when Gabriel notices a figure in white on the grounds of the house and the whole scene approaches the quality of visual stillness: 'There was that creature in white, standing under the lilacs with a hand on the back of the seat, leaning into the sunlight, smiling, like one of Botticelli's maidens, and I can be forgiven for wondering if there were shrill trumpets in the distance, sounding the music through the earth and air' (1973: 14). In addition, as I will hereafter illustrate, Banville's more recent work is even more ambitious.

In this chapter, a rather different, if related, focus is explored: Banville's use of, and deviations from, the practice of ekphrasis is considered to demonstrate how the structure of his verbal fictions assumes some of the qualities of visual representation with a view to elevating the prose fictions closer to the status of art. It is precisely in his deviations from ekphrasis, as understood by critics like Heffernan, that Banville both transcends the limits of the form and also illustrates that such limits offer little to the creative artist who seeks to create new aesthetic forms – which is precisely what Banville aims to do.

The Art trilogy is the point at which Banville's engagement with the visual arts began to assume levels of narrative assimilation that, while previously present, were never so aesthetically significant. In *The Book of Evidence*, *Ghosts* and *Athena*, the degree of engagement deepens with each subsequent novel, although with varying degrees of success. Although the primary ekphrasis in *The Book of Evidence*, derived from Willem Drost's *Portrait of a Woman*,[5] is relatively uncomplicated, the narrative significance emerges in the surrounding context. In the preamble to Freddie's murder of Josie Bell, for example, he initially visits Whitewater House and describes the interior of the house while waiting for someone to attend to him. From the 'great Tintoretto on the stairs, swarming with angels and mad eyed martyrs', to the Fragonard painting of a 'silken lady … watching me sidelong with what seemed an expression of appalled but lively speculation', his experience is immersed in a world transformed by the presence of the visual arts (1989: 76–7). The entire scene is elevated to the level of a painting itself: 'The wallpaper was the colour of tarnished gold. The air was golden too, suffused with the heavy soft light of evening. I felt as if I had stepped straight into the eighteenth century' (1989: 77). As we shall see, the 'golden world,' or *Le monde d'or*, is the painting that radiates at the centre of Banville's *Ghosts*, and is attributed to the fictional Jean Vaublin – a near-anagram of John Banville. Crucially, the narration of the scene inside Whitewater House grows increasingly painterly in the sense that the verbal representation assumes some of the qualities more closely associated with visual representation:

> It struck me that the perspective of this scene was wrong somehow. Things seemed not to recede as they should, but to be arrayed before me – the furniture, the open window, the lawn and river and far-off mountains – as if they were not being looked at but were themselves looking, intent upon a vanishing-point here, inside the room. I turned then, and saw myself turning as I turned, as I seem to myself to be turning still, as I sometimes imagine I shall be turning always, as if this might be my punishment, my damnation, just this breathless, blurred, eternal turning towards her. (1989: 78)

Not only does Freddie become an object himself, he assumes the qualities of a visual image at the centre of its vanishing point, becoming a self-reflexive object of his own scrutiny, before becoming a self-generating image – turned, turning still, turning always, on the pivotal vanishing point. It is an extraordinary moment in which he is both visual image and verbal representation seeking to move. While not an ekphrasis in itself, it is clearly an indication of the manner in which the representation of the visual seeks to blend with momentum of the verbal, only to pivot, 'breathless, blurred' on the spot.

Furthermore, Freddie's first encounter with the Drost painting directly coincides with his first meeting with Josie:

> It was not just the woman's painted stare that watched me. Everything in the picture, that brooch, those gloves, the flocculent darkness at her back, every spot on the canvas was an eye fixed on me unblinkingly. I retreated a pace, faintly

aghast. The silence was fraying at the edges. I heard cows lowing, a car starting up. I remembered the taxi, and turned to go. A maid was standing in the open French window. She must have come in just then and seen me there and started back in alarm. Her eyes were wide, and one knee was flexed and one hand lifted, as if to ward off a blow. (1989: 79)

When Freddie next encounters the painting, on the day of the theft and murder, the scene is presented in almost identical fashion, with Josie holding precisely the same unlikely pose, 'wide-eyed, with one hand raised':

So I struggled up, moaning and sniveling, and grasped the picture in my arms and staggered with it blindly, nose to nose, in the direction of the French window. Those eyes were staring into mine, I almost blushed. And then – how shall I express it – then somehow I sensed, behind that stare, another presence, watching me. I stopped, and lowered the picture, and there she was, standing in the open window, just as she had stood the day before, wide-eyed, with one hand raised. (1989: 110)

Framed as she is on both occasions by the French windows, Josie is akin to a figure in a painting herself – in fact, Freddie forces her to carry the stolen painting to the car, practically conflating the two women. The contiguity of the two women is further invited by virtue of Freddie's descriptions in both Freddie's imagined scenario of the woman being painted and in his gruesome description of Josie as he murders, recounted in sequence in the novel. In both cases the questions of perspective and seeing are foregrounded[6] and the significance for Freddie's understanding of his own crime as a failure of imagination rests heavily on these descriptions but, in the context of the current chapter, the way that Banville sought to allow the painting (indeed all the paintings in the house) to seep into the texture of the prose is a significant departure for his work. While the problem of representation has always been at the centre of Banville's work, such overt deployment of paintings and, more importantly, the way that the sequential narrative seeks to blend aspects of the visual is significant, even if the second novel in the trilogy, *Ghosts*, offers an even more dramatic assimilation of the visual into the verbal.

The narrated landscape in which events unfold in *Ghosts* is derived from at least two paintings by Jean Antoine Watteau – *Gilles (1718-19)* and *L'Embarquement pour Cythére (1717)*, while a third, *Le pélerinage à l'île de Cythère (1718–19)*, essentially a revised version of *L'Embarquement pour Cythére*, is likely also a presence in the novel. In addition, *Le monde d'or*, the fictional Jean Vaublin's painting that dominates *Ghosts* is effectively an amalgam of the three

Watteau paintings and in many respects the sequential events that unfold on the island are intimately related to and reflect the images in these three paintings. Freddie, resurrected from *The Book of Evidence*, offers the primary first-person perspective, and frequently alerts us to the painterly context of the landscape: 'I think of them like the figures in one of Vaublin's twilit landscapes, placed here and there in isolation about the scene, each figure somehow the source of its own illumination, aglow in the midst of shadows, still and speechless, not dead and yet not alive either, waiting perhaps to be brought to some kind of life' (1993: 82). And within this reflected landscape, the characters reveal a consciousness of their own invented or borrowed status. For example, Flora dreams of the 'golden world' (echoing, of course, the Vaublin painting, *Le monde d'or*):

> Flora is dreaming of the golden world.
> Worlds within worlds. They bleed into each other. I am at once here and there, then and now, as if by magic. I think of the stillness that lives in the depths of mirrors. It is not our world that is reflected there. It is another place entirely, another universe, cunningly made to mimic ours. Anything is possible there; even the dead may come back to life. Flaws develop in the glass, patches of silvering fall away and reveal the inhabitants of that parallel, inverted world going about their lives all unawares. (1993: 55)

Later she encounters a print of *Le monde d'or* in the house and is fascinated by a figure in the painting, 'a sort of clown dressed in white standing up with his arms hanging, and people behind him walking off down a hill to where a ship was waiting, and at the left a smirking man astride a donkey' (1993: 46). Here she offers a partial ekphrasis of Watteau's *Gilles*, one of the three paintings that comprise *Le monde d'or* but also suggests that the character Felix is a version of the harlequin in the background of *Gilles*, a 'miniature in a far-off mirror, the man on the donkey in the picture grinned at her gloatingly' (1993: 49). Freddie himself is Gilles, the Pierrot figure, in the foreground of Watteau's painting, an identification that circulates about many of Banville's first-person narrators.

While *Ghosts* clearly transgresses the limits of classical modes of ekphrasis, the way that Banville develops the device reveals a desire to assimilate some of the qualities of Watteau's paintings rather than offer a strictly representational response. So, certain qualities in the Watteau paintings are absorbed and recalibrated in Banville's *Ghosts* in a number of ways: Watteau's three paintings transform into the fictional painting, *Le monde d'or*, while the deeply self-conscious novel *Ghosts* is a sequential, moving narrated version of the amalgamated Vaublin painting, and these different ontological levels repeatedly intersect and offer commentary on each other. This process of ontological fusion is evident from the outset, which is related in the present tense, slowing the sequence of movement down to almost imperceptible movement, and this is repeated throughout the novel, with Freddie's narrative focal point often hovering in the present tense, even if the novel is largely recounted in the past tense. The persistent use of the present tense suggests a sense of 'movement arrested', as Stephen Cheeke has it (2012: 23): 'Nothing happens, nothing will happen, yet everything is poised, waiting, a chair in the corner crouching with its arms braced, the coiled fronds of a fern, that copper pot with the streaming sunspot on its rim' (1993: 40). Banville's use of ekphrasis in *Ghosts* represents a quite extraordinary level of innovative development, far beyond what one encounters even in *The Book of Evidence*. While one is offered the semblance of a straight ekphrasis, it is of a painting that is fictional, and one that is also a mirror image of the verbal fiction that contains it. More significant is the way that Banville folds the static narrative of the painting into the sequential narrative of the novel, with each ramifying the other. *Le monde d'or* seeps beyond the frames of its own ontological frame while the sequential narrative, alternatively, integrates the quality of the still image especially at key moments in the novel.

While Banville retains a deep interest in paintings after *Ghosts*, very few novels attain its level of narrative assimilation, with the possible exception of *The Sea*, and in a less direct fashion, *The Blue Guitar*. Nonetheless, the presence of paintings in *Athena* is significant, if at times rather ponderous and far less innovative than *Ghosts*, and a fascination with visual images also characterizes *Eclipse*, *Shroud* and *Ancient Light*, while a painting is central to the plot of *The Untouchable*, albeit in a technically uninteresting fashion. In *Athena*, the ekphrastic mode is used as a catalogue-style framing device that summarizes the seven counterfeit paintings, each of which are related to aspects of the novel itself, or to Banville's work more generally, as detailed variously by Kenny and O'Connell.[7] An eighth painting, we are assured, is not counterfeit – presumably metaphorically connected to the novel itself. The centrally significant point here is again the way in which Banville seeks to have different ontological levels merge, albeit in less convincing ways than in *Ghosts*. The use of near-anagrams of 'John Banville' for each of the painters of the seven paintings is also perhaps a little too clever without generating any new innovative development. Ultimately, *Athena* doesn't expand the levels of innovation that one encounters in *Ghosts* in a meaningful way.

While *Eclipse*, *Shroud* and *Ancient Light* do not foreground paintings, or the process of ekphrasis in such overt ways as the Art trilogy, there are many instances throughout where echoes of the paintings from the earlier novels re-surface as when, in *Eclipse*, Quirke is described as standing 'in the doorway in the pose of Vaublin's Pierrot, trying to find something to do with his hanging hands' (1995: 200). The harlequin also features in an ekphrastic self-reflexive interlude in *Shroud*, in which the *'inexplicable being'* is attributed with the creation of *'a new form of poetry, accented by gestures, punctuated by somersaults, enriched with philosophic reflections and incongruous noises'* (2002: 380; emphasis original). More significantly, many attempts to pause the narrative flow are evident, and the insertion of cleanly defined visual images that are separate from the plot-level ontologies. For example, in *Ancient Light*, at one point Mrs Gray is witnessed by the first-person narrator in a manner that momentarily transcends the limits of straight representation, and her image splinters in a visually mesmerizing fashion:

> More confusingly still, there was another mirror, a full-length one, fixed to what would have to have been the outwards-facing side of the inwards-opening door, and it was in this mirror that I saw the room reflected, with at its centre the dressing-table, or whatever it was, with its own mirror, or I should say mirrors. What I had, therefore, was not, strictly speaking, a view of the bathroom, or bedroom, but a reflection of it, and of Mrs. Gray not a reflection but a reflection of a reflection. (2012: 28–9)

He proceeds to informs us that her body is as though disassembled in a 'jumbled arrangement' because of the positioning of the mirror panels – resembling a Picasso painting. She is doubled, and dismembered and the mirror reflections produce 'in combination a magnifying effect' (2012: 30). The narration momentarily seeks to assume the qualities of a very particular painterly quality and the prose fictional representation of the essentially visual image powerfully echoes ekphrasis as a form. So, in this instance, it is not the representation of a particular painting that interests Banville but rather the fact that ekphrasis offers him yet another mode of engagement with an aspect of being that sequential prose fiction struggles with. The supplanting of the sequential by the spatial slows or pauses time in a non-linear fashion. He thus borrows a formal attribute of the painting rather than simply effecting a straight representation.

This kind of process is also clearly evident in *The Sea* even in those moments where the overt fascination with Pierre Bonnard, Max's (formerly known as Morden) primary artistic area of interest, is not explicitly clear. In the novel

Max is writing a book on Bonnard (1867–1947), which explains the multiple references to his paintings and life, including a compelling example of ekphrasis of one of Bonnard's most famous paintings of his wife, *Nude in the Bath, with Dog* (1941–6),[8] which I offer analysis of elsewhere.[9] The way that the primary dialogic level is infused with visual imagery that is linked to Bonnard is indicative of an innovative narrative evolution in Banville's work. The links between Max's and Bonnard's wives, Anna and Marthe, are key to the nature of the aesthetic transference that is effected. Max is explicitly reminded of Anna when he looks at the painting: 'Her right hand rests on her thigh, stilled in the act of supination, and I think of Anna's hands on the table that first day when we came back from Mr Todd, her helpless hands with palms upturned' (2005: 153). Anna's hands also feature in a mirror reflection that Max sees in the window of Mr Todd's window, 'resting on her thigh' (2005: 15). Like Marthe in Bonnard's paintings, the ill Anna too spends a lot of time in her bath. But the transference of the qualities of the visual are more effective, subtle and commonplace than even such overt connections imply. While awaiting the cancer diagnosis in Anna's doctor's office Max gazes out the window and sees Anna 'palely reflected in the glass', like one of Bonnard's ghostly presences, portrait-like, 'very straight on the metal chair in three-quarters profile', with 'one knee crossed on the other and her joined hands resting on her thigh' (2005: 15). Anna, framed by the window, simultaneously occupies two ontological layers in the scene: one that contains implied movement, the other restful and silent. Later, having returned home, Anna is again transfigured via an accident of the light: 'Light from the window behind me shone on the lenses of her spectacles where they hung at her collar bone, giving the eerie effect of another, miniature she standing close in front of her under her chin with eyes cast down' (2005: 21). It is as though in this harrowing moment the spatial stillness of the visual image offers a kind of illuminated relief to the more grim existence in the narrated prose sequence.

The Sea, after *Ghosts*, is Banville's most thoroughly visual novel with echoes of Bonnard's paintings everywhere registering their presence, but it is the way that the narrative continually uses tableaux moments and the stilling of temporal sequence via a frequent use of the present tense that suggests a more integrated approach. Similarly, when ekphrastic moments are used, they are frequently blended with moments in the plot, as with the allusion to Vermeer's *The Milkmaid* (1657–8). As she washes Rose's hair, Constance stands in the 'pose of Vermeer's maid with the milk jug, her head and her left shoulder inclined, one hand cupped under the heavy fall of Rose's hair and the other pouring a dense silvery sluice of water from a chipped enamel jug' (2005: 222). Worlds continually collide in the novel, whether the paintings alluded to are real or not – and the assimilation of the visual, the stillness, with the 'noise' of the sequence, generates a form that is even more fluidly achieved than in *Ghosts*.

A similar tendency is evident in *The Blue Guitar*, the only novel of Banville's that features an actual artist as a narrator, even if many of his narrator-figures betray artistic qualities. This offers many opportunities for self-reflexive artistic commentary and, as a result the novel may be Banville's most self-conscious novel. Almost everything Oliver utters holds parallel significance for Banville's own novel, and his counterpoint as a fictionalized author is also hinted at in Oliver's surname – Orme – which surely strongly suggests 'or me'. Familiar infusions of the visual are also everywhere evident, as when Oliver and Polly momentarily meet on another ontological level, via reflected images: 'When Polly stepped out of the lavatory, the door, before she closed it, was behind her, hiding her from my view, but in the mirror, to which she had turned – which of us can resist a glance at ourselves in the glass? – she was facing me, and our eyes met, our reflected eyes, that is' (2015: 81).

But, in more explicit terms, the use of ekphrasis in *The Blue Guitar* reveals much about the essentially fluid way that Banville deploys the technique. Although Picasso's *The Old Guitarist* (1903–4) is an important presence in the novel in much the same way that it is in Stevens's poem, 'The Man with the Blue Guitar',[10] Manet's *Déjeuner sur l'herbe* is more explicitly engaged with. Manet's painting initially features in Oliver's imaginative reconstruction of a picnic that he shared with his wife Gloria, Polly and Marcus:

> Inevitably, I see the occasion in the light of old man Manet's *Déjeuner sur l'herbe*–the earlier, smaller one–with blonde Gloria in the buff and Polly off in the background bathing her feet. Polly that day seemed hardly more than a girl, pink-cheeked and creamy, instead of the married woman that she was. Marcus was wearing a straw hat with holes in it, and Gloria was her usual glorious self, a big bright beauty shedding radiance all round her. And, my God, but my wife was magnificent that day, as indeed she always is. … In fact, she is a Tiepolo rather than a Manet type, one of the Venetian master's Cleopatras, say, or his Beatrice of Burgundy. (2015: 9)

While the painting is largely a point of departure for his reverie – one that is also informed by other artists – rather than the source of a specific ekphrasis, it does reveal how effortlessly Banville fuses together shards of diverse images, and it is unlikely that Manet is of particular significance to Banville's aesthetic in the way that a painter like Bonnard is.[11] In fact, later in the novel Oliver effectively erases the significance of Manet's painting when he reconstitutes it into a work by Jean Vaublin, anagrammatic counterpoint to Banville himself:

> I spoke of it then as a version of *Le déjeuner sur l'herbe*, but time, I mean recent time, has mellowed it to something less boldly done. Instead, picture it, say, as a scene by Vaublin, *mon semblable*, nay, my twin, not in summer now but some other, more sombre, season, the crepuscular park with its auburn masses of trees under big heapings of evening cloud, dark-apricot, gold, gesso-white, and in a clearing, see, the luminous little group arranged upon the grass, one idly strumming a mandolin, another looking wistfully away with a finger pressed to a dimpled cheek. (2015: 223)

Manet is supplanted by Vaublin (or Watteau) as Oliver's imaginative recollection refocuses, while the tense also switches to accommodate the ekphrastic mode, even if the set of images that are described are ontologically indistinct, fluidly blurring between several possible paintings and the actual picnic that Oliver attended with his wife, his lover and her husband. In a Banvillean sense it matters little, because the surface texture of the prose fictional world rarely restricts itself to the material fixity of a single ontological plane.

This fluidity in many ways echoes the painterly influences that Banville frequently registers. His primary painterly presences are certainly not postmodern, or even surrealist – but as with Banville's interests in writers like Henry James, Kleist, Stevens and Rilke, the key to the pattern of influence is that they all integrate a self-consciousness about the process of writing, or painting in their work and, in almost all cases, were anti-realist.[12] Terms like 'modernism' and 'postmodernism' assume too delineated a historical sequence to be helpful with writers like Banville – the broader aesthetic sense of seeking an alternative to an unproblematic realist mode offers a clearer sense of his influences. Similarly so with his use of ekphrasis; the simple process of offering representations of representations, even with critical engagement, is essentially too limited a process and many of the objections to more expansive uses of the method are directly connected to a limited sense of what representation is or can achieve. Banville's work, while nominally related to the ekphrastic mode, extends far beyond it by virtue of a process of transference; in many respects Banville's work is a perpetual reaction against the limits of the merely representational and his use of ekphrasis conforms to this overall aesthetic characteristic. Banville's worlds themselves become elaborate aestheticized constructions, at times bearing the mark of the visual image – pausing, slowing time, offering glimpses into the deep significances of the static, or near-static image, all in an attempt to expand the limits of narration. As such he allows the texts to self-consciously become objects of their own ekphrastic perspectives, while simultaneously extending the possibilities of the narrative fictional mode. As Renate Brosch has compellingly illustrated, contemporary fiction has frequently turned to ekphrasis to enlarge its narrative range: 'Narrative ekphrasis involves the performance of seeing. By staging a visual observation, narratives are liable to reflect on particular ways of seeing and on the relation between the subject and the object of a significant act of visual scrutiny' (2018: 406). In multiple ways, within the limits of traditional ekphrasis and beyond, Banville's work has progressively deepened the possibilities for prose fiction by infusing his work with ways of seeing – and being – that previously lay beyond the remit of verbal forms.

Notes

1 In particular, Joseph McMinn, Joakim Wrethed and Anja Müller have analyzed Banville's use of ekphrasis as a literary and aesthetic device. See the list of references for details.

2 Two paintings by Jean Antoine Watteau indirectly feature in *Ghosts – Gilles (1718-19)*, and *L'Embarquement pour Cythére (1717)* – while a third, *Le pélerinage à l'île de Cythère (1718–19)*, essentially a revised version of *L'Embarquement pour Cythére* is likely also a presence in the novel.

3 Banville has disputed the very principle of representative narrative fiction as a replica of life: 'Nothing is translatable really. I don't think anything has meaning, in the sense that I define it' (Schwall 1997: 15).

4 I have previously considered the significance the presence of visual artists in Benjamin Black's works in an essay on Banville's crime-novelist persona: 'Crimes of Elegance: Benjamin Black's Impersonation of John Banville', *Moving Worlds* 13 (1) (Spring 2013): 19–32.

5 Freddie entitles the painting 'Portrait of a Woman with Gloves' at the outset of his ekphrasis, and claims it has been attributed to 'Rembrandt and Franz Hals, even to Vermeer. However, it is safest to regard it as the work of an anonymous master' (104). The actual painting to which he refers is Willem Drost's *Portrait of a Woman* (1653–5). Oil on canvas. 50.8 × 76.4 in. (129 × 195 cm). SzépművészetiMúzeum / Museum of Fine Arts, Budapest.

6 I have discussed these parallel descriptions at greater length in my monograph, *John Banville* (2018: 75–7).

7 Kenny (2009: 166), O'Connell (2013: 174).

8 The title Max uses is different to its correct title *Nude in the Bath with Small Dog* (or *Nu dans le bain au petit chien*). This variation likely represents an inclusive attempt by Banville to allude to other Bonnard paintings, several of which feature a similar dog. See, for example, *Woman with Dog*, *Dressing Table and Mirror* and *The Bathroom*, all of which include a dachshund.

9 See Murphy (2018: 105-6).

10 Wallace Stevens suggested that Picasso's painting was but loosely connected to his poem. In a letter to Professor Renato Poggioli, Stevens explained, 'I had no particular painting of Picasso's in mind and even though it might help to sell the book to have one of his paintings on the cover, I don't think we ought to reproduce anything of Picasso's' (Stevens 1966: 786).

11 Like Banville, Bonnard insisted that 'Art' was not 'nature' and repeatedly foregrounded the primacy of the act of composition (cited in Bell 2003: 17). Bonnard even felt that proximity to the object, the real, was destabilizing for the work of art: 'I am very weak,' he explained, 'it is difficult for me to keep myself under control in the presence of the object' (cited in Bell 2003: 22).

12 For example, on close examination, Banville's long-term fascination with Watteau is extremely understandable. Watteau's biographer, the Comte de Caylus, for instance, noted that 'his compositions have no subject. They express none of the conflicts of the passions and are consequentially deprived of one of the most affecting characteristics, that is, action' (cited in Weretka 2008).

References

Banville, J. (1973), *Birchwood*, London: Panther Books.
Banville, J. (1989), *The Book of Evidence*, London: Secker & Warburg.
Banvillle J. (1993), *Ghosts*, London: Secker & Warburg.
Banville, J. (1995), *Eclipse*, London, Secker & Warburg.
Banville, J. (2002a), *Shroud*, London: Picador.
Banville, J. (2002b), *The Untouchable*, London, Picador.
Banville, J. (2005), *The Sea*, London: Picador.
Banville, J. (2012), *Ancient Light*, London: Viking Penguin.
Banville, J. (2015), *The Blue Guitar*, London: Viking Penguin.
Bell, J. (2003), *Bonnard*, London: Phaidon Press Ltd.
Bergmann Loizeaux, E. (2008), *Twentieth-Century Poetry and the Visual Arts*, Cambridge: Cambridge University Press.
Brosch, R. (2018), 'Ekphrasis in Recent Popular Novels: Reaffirming the Power of Art Images,' *Poetics Today*, 39 (2) June: 403-23.
Canon-Roger, F. (2000), 'John Banville's *Imagines* in *The Book of Evidence*', *European Journal of English Studies*, 4 (1): 25-38.

Cheeke, S. (2008), *Writing for Art: The Aesthetics of Ekphrasis*, Manchester: Manchester University Press.

Heffernan, J. A. W. (2004), *Museum of Words: The Poetics of Ekphrasis from Homer to Ashbery*, Chicago, IL and London: The University of Chicago Press.

Kenny, J. (2009), *John Banville*, Dublin: Irish Academic Press.

Krieger, M. (1992), *Ekphrasis: The Illusion of the Natural Sign*, Baltimore, MD and London: The John Hopkins University Press.

Lloyd, D. (2016), *Beckett's Thing: Painting and Theatre*, Edinburgh: Edinburgh University Press.

McMinn, J. (2002), 'Ekphrasis and the Novel: The Presence of Paintings in John Banville's Fiction', *Word & Image: A Journal of Verbal/Visual Enquiry*, 18 (3): 137–45.

Müller, A. (Summer 2004), '"You have been framed": The Function of Ekphrasis for the Representation of Women in John Banville's Trilogy (The Book of Evidence, Ghosts, Athena)', *Studies in the Novel*, 36 (2): 185–205.

Murphy, N. (Spring 2013), 'Crimes of Elegance: Benjamin Black's Impersonation of John Banville', *Moving Worlds,* 13 (1): 19–32.

Murphy, N. (2018), *John Banville*, Lewisburg, PA: Bucknell University Press.

O'Connell, M. (2013), *John Banville's Narcissistic Fictions*, London: Palgrave Macmillan.

Schwall, H. (1997), 'An Interview with John Banville', *European English Messenger*, 6 (1): 13–19.

Weretka, J. (2008) 'The Guitar, the Musette and Meaning in the *fêtes galantes* of Watteau', *EMAJ: Electronic Melbourne Art Journal*, Issue 3. Available online: https://emajartjournal.files.wordpress.com/2012/08/weretka.pdf (accessed 23 July 2018).

Wrethed, J. (2014), '"A momentous nothing": The Phenomenology of Life, Ekphrasis and Temporality in John Banville's *The Sea*', in Ruben Moi, Brynhildur Boyce and Charles I. Armstrong, *The Crossings of Art in Ireland*, 192–3, Bern: Peter Lang Publishing.

Stevens, H. (ed.) (1966), *Letters of Wallace Stevens*, foreword by Richard Howard, Berkeley, CA: University of California Press.

Stevens, W. (1951), 'The Relations between Poetry and Painting', in *The Necessary Angel: Essays on Reality and the Imagination*, 159–76, New York: Vintage Books.

Index

Althusser, Louis   61
Amphitryon   1, 8, 35–9, 111–15, 121–4

Banville, John
   Ancient Light   8, 26, 31, 89, 103, 106, 111, 113, 118, 123, 134, 195, 198, 200, 204, 217, 229–30, 242–3
   Art trilogy   8, 11, 89, 94, 103–4, 111, 117, 134, 140, 229, 236–8, 243
   Athena   11, 19, 89, 95–104, 139, 236–8, 242
   Birchwood   18, 21–2, 28, 29, 106, 238
   The Blue Guitar   11, 89, 122, 149, 229, 236, 242, 245
   The Book of Evidence   10, 11, 95–8, 143, 154–9, 177–93, 197, 205, 234–42
   Doctor Copernicus   9, 28, 61, 129–42, 150–1, 155, 196
   Eclipse   6, 8, 11, 34–47, 89, 103–6, 111–23, 129, 134, 137, 154, 172, 195, 198, 204, 214–31, 242–3
   Ghosts   11, 68, 95–8, 103–4, 136, 154, 156, 199, 207, 236–45
   The Infinities   28, 68, 111–12, 123–5, 154, 198
   Kepler   28, 61, 129, 152, 155, 196
   Mefisto   32, 68, 104, 111, 121, 149, 153, 197
   Mrs Osmond   1, 7, 8, 53–84, 105, 110
   The Newton Letter   18, 20, 21, 62, 68, 104, 150, 154, 155, 220
   The Sea   9, 10, 11, 17, 26, 31, 68, 89, 111, 119–21, 132, 134, 138, 165–75, 214–31, 236–44
   Shroud   6, 8, 34–47, 54, 61–3, 89, 96, 103–7, 111–13, 122, 134, 193, 195–207, 215–16, 225, 242–3
   Todtnauberg   216–17
   The Untouchable   23, 34, 54, 60–2, 106, 221, 242

Barthes, Roland   1, 116–17
Beckett, Samuel   2, 4, 6, 7, 20, 21, 27, 34–47, 53–5, 87–8, 102, 134, 207, 211, 237
Benjamin, Walter   30–1, 138
Big House novel   19, 21, 24, 28
Black, Benjamin   1, 4, 10, 26, 29, 65, 68, 110, 200, 236
Blanchot, Maurice   9, 10, 89, 165–75
Bloom, Harold   4
Bonnard, Pierre   168–9, 236, 243–5
Borges, Jorge Luis   2, 3, 4, 5, 7, 53, 60
Bowen, Elizabeth   21–4, 43, 46

commedia dell'arte   112–14

Deleuze, Gilles   42, 106, 118, 124, 134
de Man, Paul   2, 34, 61, 204, 226
Drost, Willem   236–9

Edgeworth, Maria   6, 27, 34–7, 43, 46
ekphrasis   11, 234–47
Eliot, T. S.   41, 42, 89
existentialism   2, 8, 10, 11, 134, 195–209, 214–23

Freud, Sigmund   2, 10, 20, 64, 78, 80, 146, 197–207, 214–19, 222–3
Gaita, Raimond   11, 196, 204–10
Gans, Eric   148–60
Goethe, Johann Wolfgang von   68, 125, 146, 204
gothic (mode/fiction)   23, 63, 220, 222, 230
Gray, John   11, 196–210

Heidegger, Martin   2, 10, 11, 34, 141, 153, 195–208, 214–31
Hofmannsthal, Hugo von   9, 68, 146–61
hysteria   10, 177–93

Index

imagination 3, 4, 7, 8, 9, 19, 23–6, 31–2, 61, 84, 88–98, 105, 120, 122, 140–3, 148–9, 156–60, 186–7, 192–3, 205, 231, 240

James, Henry 2, 3, 7, 20, 53–85, 105, 110, 120, 143, 246
Joyce, James 3, 4, 7, 20, 25–9, 53–7, 83, 110, 211

Kafka, Franz 3, 4, 20, 53, 70, 121, 197
Keats, John 1, 99, 234
Kierkegaard, Søren 10, 196, 208–9
Kleist, Heinrich von 1, 6, 7, 8, 20, 35–7, 68, 110–24, 125, 246

Lacan, Jacques 10, 20, 64, 177–93
Lethem, Jonathan 4, 5

Mach, Ernst 146, 149, 152
MacNeice, Louis 34, 61
Manet, Édouard 236, 245–6
Mann, Thomas 202
marionette theatre 8, 36, 111
Maskenfreiheit 8, 110, 112
Midgley, Mary 11, 196, 204, 209
modernism 2–7, 20, 25–9, 53–5, 59, 66, 69–72, 88–90, 94, 146, 149–57, 199, 246
Moore, George 24–7, 30

Nietzsche, Friedrich 2, 10, 34, 78, 80, 118, 124, 147, 191–210, 236

Orpheus (Orphic) 8, 10, 119, 124, 165–70, 175, 234

performativity 5, 84, 88, 98, 100–13, 117, 188
Pessoa, Fernando 199–204
Picasso, Pablo 236, 243, 245
postmodernism 3, 4, 11, 20, 22, 29–30, 71–3, 90, 110, 116, 130, 151–2, 157, 160, 237, 246
post-romanticism 89, 152

Rank, Otto 63
realism 54, 56, 116–17
Rilke, Rainer Maria 1, 9, 20, 87, 90, 102, 127–42, 217, 246
romanticism 25, 88–90, 117, 234

scepticism 9, 127–9, 142, 147, 202
Stevens, Wallace 2, 8, 9, 87–106, 127–43, 230, 236, 245–6
supreme fiction 8, 87–109, 141–3, 230

the uncanny 7, 11, 30, 41, 54, 57, 62–5, 96, 98, 112, 115, 122, 214–30

Vermeer, Johannes 236, 244

Watteau, Jean-Antoine 236, 240–1, 246

Yeats, W.B. 8, 26, 29, 39, 43, 89